PROJECT CENSORED'S
STATE OF THE FREE PRESS 2026
FIFTIETH ANNIVERSARY EDITION

THE TOP CENSORED STORIES AND MEDIA ANALYSIS OF 2024–2025

EDITED BY **Shealeigh Voitl, Mickey Huff,**
AND **Andy Lee Roth,**
WITH **Project Censored**

FOREWORD BY **Mickey Huff**

ILLUSTRATED BY **Anson Stevens-Bollen**

THE CENSORED PRESS

Ithaca, New York

PROJECT CENSORED'S STATE OF THE FREE PRESS 2026: FIFTIETH ANNIVERSARY EDITION

EDITED BY Shealeigh Voitl, Mickey Huff, AND Andy Lee Roth,
WITH Project Censored
FOREWORD BY Mickey Huff

A CENSORED PRESS FIRST EDITION

Copyright © 2025 by Shealeigh Voitl, Mickey Huff, and Andy Lee Roth
Foreword © 2025 by Mickey Huff

All rights reserved. No part of this book may be reproduced, stored in a retrieval system, or transmitted in any form, by any means, including mechanical, electronic, photocopying, recording or otherwise, without the prior written permission of the publisher.

The Censored Press
PO Box 9
Ithaca, NY 14851
censoredpress.org

ISBN 979-8-9998049-0-7 (paperback)
ISBN 979-8-9998049-2-1 (electronic)
ISSN 3068-9562

College professors and high school and middle school teachers may order free examination copies of Censored Press titles. Contact shealeigh@projectcensored.org for more information.

Grateful acknowledgement is made to the University of Illinois Press for permission to use the quotation from *Rich Media, Poor Democracy*, by Robert W. McChesney, reprinted in Chapter 1. Copyright © 1999.

9 8 7 6 5 4 3 2 1

Book design by Anson Stevens-Bollen

Printed in the USA

── PRAISE FOR *STATE OF THE FREE PRESS 2026* ──

"If knowledge is power, then this book will make you strong."
—NORMAN STOCKWELL, publisher, *The Progressive*

"For fifty years, Project Censored has highlighted vital truth-telling by intrepid investigative reporters covering stories that some of the nation's most powerful special interests wish would stay hidden."
—LISA GRAVES, Executive Director of True North Research

"*State of the Free Press 2026* exposes the stories the corporate media ignored, censored, or distorted. It's more than a book. It's a public service."
—JOHN KIRIAKOU, CIA Whistleblower

"The day I was first published in Project Censored, I felt like a real journalist. In troubled times defined by a sycophantic media that's been both co-opted and complicit, Project Censored is a beacon."
—DAVE ZIRIN, author of *The People's Historian: The Outsized Life of Howard Zinn*

"Without organizations like Project Censored promoting the independent journalists still willing to speak truth to power and helping Americans distinguish news from propaganda, the free press may not survive these strange times."
—SETH STERN, Director of Advocacy, Freedom of the Press Foundation

"Fifty years of the Project's research continues to prove deliberate media bias in our nation's news system."
—PETER PHILLIPS, Director, Project Censored, 1996–2010

"Every year, I crack open the *State of the Free Press* and learn something I didn't know but won't forget. Project Censored's work is a glimpse at the media system we should have."
—CRAIG AARON, President, Free Press

── PRAISE FOR PREVIOUS CENSORED YEARBOOKS ──

"For almost fifty years, Project Censored has been a leader at calling out media doubletalk and spin, and pushing America to greater media literacy."
—JOHN FUGELSANG, author of *Separation of Church and Hate*

"Project Censored maps out the allied struggles that are crucial in making a just, equitable, and habitable planet of the only home that we have."
—DANBERT NOBACON (Chumbawamba)

"Project Censored continues to shine a spotlight on the issues that matter most."
—HAGIT LIMOR, President, Society of Professional Journalists Foundation

"Project Censored reminds us of the dangers of looking away, and ensures that we cannot."
—REBECCA VINCENT, Director of Campaigns, Reporters Without Borders

"Project Censored is on the case, showing the way where corporate media fear to tread."
—ALAN MACLEOD, senior staff writer, *MintPress News*

"Critical stories that government officials, major media companies, and assorted gatekeepers of 'respectable' journalism too often ignore."
—JUAN GONZÁLEZ, co-host, *Democracy Now!*

"In opposition to the undemocratic censorship of information, I proudly stand with Project Censored."
—SHARYL ATTKISSON, award-winning investigative journalist

"A crucial contribution to the hope for a more just and democratic society."
—NOAM CHOMSKY

"A clarion call for truth-telling."
—DANIEL ELLSBERG, *The Pentagon Papers*

"The systematic exposure of censored stories by Project Censored has been an important contribution."
—HOWARD ZINN, author of *A People's History of the United States*

"A deep and utterly engrossing exercise to unmask censorship and propaganda."
—RALPH NADER, consumer advocate, lawyer, and author

"Project Censored is one of the organizations that we should listen to, to be assured that our newspapers and our broadcasting outlets are practicing thorough and ethical journalism."
—WALTER CRONKITE, anchor, *CBS Evening News*, 1962–1981

"One of the most significant media research projects in the country."
—I.F. STONE, American muckraker

DEDICATED TO every one of the students
the Project has worked alongside these past fifty years,
Who have since turned into scholars, researchers, and reporters;
Voices raised against censorship, complicity, and silence;
Co-authors of people's history in real time;
Stewards of critical inquiry, media justice, and democratic ideals—
The heart and future of Project Censored.

CONTENTS

FOREWORD by Mickey Huff............................. IX

INTRODUCTION: Confronting the Siege on Public Knowledge With Collective Truth-Telling
by Andy Lee Roth, Shealeigh Voitl, and Mickey Huff 1

CHAPTER 1: The Top *Censored* Stories and Media Analysis of 2024–25
Compiled and edited by Jayden Lawrence, Ella Mrofka, Caitlin Suda, Amy Grim Buxbaum, Steve Macek, and Andy Lee Roth

Introduction: Democracy Under the Influence
by Steve Macek 23

Note on Research and Evaluation of
Censored News Stories..................................27

1. ICE Solicits Social Media Surveillance Contracts to Identify Critics.....................................29

2. Water Scarcity Threatens 27 Million People in the United States 32

3. Indigenous Communities in the US Underfunded and Exploited by Federal and State Governments............35

4. Meta Undertakes "Sweeping Crackdown" of Facebook and Instagram Posts at Israel's Request 39

5. Big Tech Sows Policy Chaos to Undermine Data Privacy Protections 42

6. Amazon and Walmart Use Hostile Surveillance Technology Against Warehouse Employees 46

7. Private Companies Reap More Than $100 Million to Sweep Homeless Camps in California 48

8. Underreported, Often Deadly Abuses of Police Authority 51

9. Antarctic Ice Sheets Approaching Tipping Point, Studies Find 54

10. Working Class Severely Underrepresented in
State Legislatures 57

11. UN Cybercrime Treaty Supported by Autocrats Raises
Human Rights Concerns 60

12. PFAS, Other Toxic Chemicals Found in Products
Meant to Keep Us Safe 63

Honorable Mentions 66

CHAPTER 2: Déjà Vu News: Attacks on Journalism
and Free Speech Edition
by Steve Macek and Jayden Lawrence 77

CHAPTER 3: Making America Junky Again: Poison Pills,
Peddling Hate, and the Rotting of the Public Mind
by Reagan Haynie, Shealeigh Voitl, and Sierra Kaul 97

CHAPTER 4: Stefanik, Israel, and Antisemitism:
The Long Shadow of News Abuse
by John Collins 127

CHAPTER 5: Media Democracy in Action: A Countervailing
Force Against Autocracy, with contributions by Ryan Grim (*Drop Site News*), Maya Schenwar and Lara Witt (Movement Media Alliance), Joe Lauria (*Consortium News*), Lauren Harper (Freedom of the Press Foundation), Jodi Rave Spotted Bear (Indigenous Media Freedom Alliance), compiled and introduced by Mischa Geracoulis 149

CHAPTER 6: Understanding the Digital Square:
A Critical Media Literacy Guide to Infographics
by Shealeigh Voitl and Reagan Haynie 173

ACKNOWLEDGMENTS 203

HOW TO SUPPORT PROJECT CENSORED 213

ABOUT THE EDITORS 215

INDEX 217

— FOREWORD —

FIFTY YEARS OF COVERING THE NEWS THAT DIDN'T MAKE THE NEWS[1]

MICKEY HUFF

Our country finds itself at a precipice. The United States teeters perilously due to rising economic inequality and domestic division on a host of issues, from foreign wars and immigration to civil rights and free expression, with an escalating crisis in confidence regarding the role of government, all resulting in cratering public trust in elected officials and institutions. We are perched at the verge of possible nuclear apocalypse, while our leaders avert their gaze from genocide. Fossil fuel pollution proliferates and an ensuing climate crisis rages, creating environmental devastation. The intelligence agencies and police apparatus have been exposed as the weaponized, militarized servants of the powerful, who surveil and suppress we, the people. Even as we face numerous existential threats, government corruption and lack of trustworthy information sources are—or ought to be—paramount concerns.[2]

It would be reasonable to conclude that the preceding passage describes our present circumstances. However, this characterization of the United States could just as easily refer to the nation a half-century ago, in the mid-1970s, just after its withdrawal from Vietnam, and in the wake of the Watergate scandal that led to the resignation of a president, when institutions were in crisis. The public had grown confused, restless, and agitated in the face of adversity. We went from a state of crisis to a state of civic malaise. Through it all, though, Americans held on to slivers of hope, however ephemeral. For example, press reporting on Nixon's scandals boosted the Fourth Estate's reputation, though that esteem has since flagged.[3] Senate hearings on CIA and FBI corruption gave some pause to overreaching agencies and career civil servants, even if Congressional inquiries stopped short of mass exposure and overhaul.[4]

Despite the political fallout from the early 1970s, checks and balances prevailed in some important ways, and the nation seemed to step back from a political precipice. However, the ensuing Carter presidency was hobbled by a lack of public confidence and multiple crises of the time, leading to further frustration amongst the electorate, which ultimately gave rise to the Reagan revolution and the beginning of the deconstruction of the New Deal and liberal order. Our media landscape was about to change, too, with the advent of cable television and eventually the internet. During that same period, the government removed the Fairness Doctrine in 1987 and passed the Telecommunications Act of 1996, which made deregulation and consolidation of media a bipartisan default setting. We've been drifting rightward ever since with both major political parties.[5] The circumstances described at the outset here are ever extant, and in fact, arguably worse. Project Censored was first established during the tumultuous era of the 1970s. Today, fifty years on, the Project adapts to ever-changing and challenging times in its abiding efforts to champion a free and independent press.

THE PEN IS MIGHTIER THAN THE SWORD

Project Censored's founder, media scholar Carl Jensen, was deeply influenced by the events of the 1970s. He learned from the independent muckraking journalists of the earlier twentieth century that a free press played an integral role as a check on power—so much so that he founded the Project as a research class at Sonoma State University in 1976 to teach about and promote such journalism. A former ad man and journalist himself before becoming a professor, Jensen believed in the adage that "the pen is mightier than the sword."[6] He knew that journalism, produced ethically and transparently in the public interest, could resolve conflicts and make a difference; we just needed more of it. It was in this context that he envisioned the valuable role to be played by a watchdog organization focused on exposing "the news that didn't make the news" and analyzing why the establishment press sometimes buried stories that addressed vital public issues.

Jensen's college course quickly evolved into a national effort to promote independent journalism and news literacy. The Project produced an annual list of the most important investigative news reports, which attracted attention—and praise—from some of Jensen's best-known contemporaries, including iconic broadcast journalists Walter Cronkite and Hugh Downs, reform activist and attorney Ralph Nader, and one of the great contemporary muckrakers of the time, I.F. "Izzy" Stone.

Jensen's purpose was not to tear down so-called "mainstream" media outlets but to constructively criticize their news judgment.[7] By showing what the major media missed, or even "censored," he hoped to improve what he saw as the lifeblood of democracy: a truly free press. Industry professionals didn't always take kindly to such criticism, which led Jensen to expand his critique to include a systematic study of what the "mainstream" press *did* cover. He discovered a morass of fluff, sensationalism, and pap—what used to be called "yellow journalism" in the early 1900s. In 1983, Jensen coined his own term for it, Junk Food News.[8] He saw that the public ultimately paid the price for the major media outlets' frivolous focus, tabloidized headlines, and critical omissions, in the form of accelerating civic decline. Sadly, he wasn't wrong, but those were not the only challenges ahead.

TROJAN HORSES, GATEKEEPERS, AND PUBLIC TRUST

Today, we are awash in twenty-first-century versions of Junk Food News, as produced by corporate media and propagated on social media. Worse, we are also subject to round-the-clock infotainment and propaganda masquerading as journalism, what Jensen's successor at the Project, sociologist Peter Phillips, called News Abuse in the early 2000s, now also known as "malinformation."[9] Of course, numerous media critics and scholars—including Edward Herman, Noam Chomsky, Ben Bagdikian, Neil Postman, and Robert McChesney—have long warned against rising levels of mis- and disinformation, increased consolidation of media ownership, and their combined toll on press freedom and a well-informed public. In the last decade, with the moral panic around the weaponized epithet of "fake news," these challenges have spawned a cottage industry of so-called fact-checkers—supposedly objective third parties trying to reverse declining public trust in the Fourth Estate.[10]

However, many of those efforts have been exposed as Trojan horses for re-establishing corporate media dominance in a digital era of podcasts, TikTok, Instagram Reels, and "tweets" (or "posts" as they are now called on X).[11] As *Wall Street Journal* editor-in-chief Emma Tucker bemoaned in early 2024 at the World Economic Forum (WEF) in Davos, Switzerland, news industry leaders were losing control of the narrative:

> If you go back really not that long ago, as I say, *we owned the news. We were the gatekeepers, and we very much owned the facts as well.* If it said it in the Wall Street Journal, the New York Times, then that was a fact. Nowadays, people can go to all sorts of different sources for the news, and they're much more questioning about what we're saying. So, it's no longer good enough for us just to say, this is what happened, or this is the news. We have to explain... our working. So, readers expect to understand how we source stories. They want to know how we go about getting stories. We have to sort of lift the bonnet, as it were, and in a way that newspapers aren't used to doing and explain to people what we're doing. We need to be much more transparent about how we go about collecting the news [emphases added].[12]

"Lift the bonnet." "Explain to people what we're doing." It's almost as if the public wants more fact-based, transparently sourced reporting in their news, rather than partisan propaganda. And, go figure, in a rabidly consumerist culture, they also want receipts. Tucker seems to concede the point, though the corporate media and their advertisers/investors from Big Pharma, Big Tech, the Military-Industrial Complex, and other powerful institutions whose narratives the public is questioning, likely do not. For Tucker and other gatekeepers, this public scrutiny is inconvenient, perhaps even impertinent, but also a market reality that news organizations must now pay more than lip service to address. Perhaps news executives' overdue, reluctant, and grudging acknowledgment of this changed reality contributes to the record-low levels of public approval and trust of US news media.

INDEPENDENT JOURNALISM CAN RESTORE PUBLIC TRUST

Media scholars have described the moral panic over "fake news" as an epistemic crisis, one that coincided with the development of a "post-truth" world in which "objective facts are less influential in shaping public opinion than appeals to emotion and personal belief."[13] These concerns did not originate with the presidential election of 2016, when Oxford Dictionary declared "post-truth" its Word of the Year. Concern for the degraded status of facts and evidence, in public discourse and government policy, has its roots in earlier periods of US history, including the partisanship, low morale, and cynicism that took hold in the aftermath of Watergate and Vietnam, and the hypernational propaganda promoted by the George W. Bush administration, and embraced by most US news media, in the wake of the 9/11 attacks. Project Censored observed that the media environment developing in the shadow of 9/11 contributed to a "Truth Emergency," characterized as a "rift between reality and reporting" that is the "culmination of the failures of the fourth estate to act as a truly free press."[14] Project Censored's warning of a "truth emergency" anticipated today's widespread concern with the development of a "post-truth" world, and predated it by nearly a decade.

Despite the Project's warning and best efforts to promote critical media literacy education, today's media ecosystem is rife with misinformation and disinformation that reflects the nation's ongoing "truth emergency" and "post-truth" skepticism. Establishment institutions from the World Economic Forum, to the US Congress, and the corporate press are now clutching pearls, as the American public has come to realize that lack of trustworthy information is as great a threat to our nation as terrorism or many other major social problems.[15] It is important to remember that Trump referred to the press as the "enemies of the American people," and his existential attacks on journalism and the public's right to know are growing rapidly in unprecedented ways.[16]

This book addresses new and ongoing threats to press freedom, as well as some of the numerous and noteworthy efforts by members of the independent press to restore the public's trust in journalism and to protect the profession from ideologues who would weaponize it. But we must do more in the struggle to maintain our republic. As "Izzy" Stone once noted, "If the Government makes a mistake, the newspapers will find out and the problem may then be fixed. But if freedom of the press were lost, the country would soon go to pieces."[17]

There certainly are major issues with corporate media and establishment outlets, including the omission and distortion of relevant information and perspective, which we at Project Censored have documented for half a century.[18] However, our critiques are not meant to undermine major media for partisan gain.[19] Instead, the Project's criticisms of corporate news expose systemic gaps and slant in coverage in order to pressure the nation's most prominent news outlets to use their massive budgets and influence to serve the public good, rather than private interests, by holding corporate and government abusers of power accountable. Jensen noted that the Project's criticism of the press was not driven by imagined conspiracy theories, but, instead, was based on empirical evidence that revealed how media owners often acted on the basis of their *own* best business interests, and those of their investors and allies in advertising and adjacent industries, at the expense of the public's knowledge and understanding. As Jensen himself put it at the Project's twentieth anniversary,

> There is a congruence of attitudes and interests on the part of the owners and managers of mass media organizations. That non-conspiracy conspiracy, when combined with a variety of other factors, leads to the systemic failure of the news media to fully inform the public. While it is not an overt form of censorship, such as the kind we observe in some other societies, it is nonetheless real and often equally as dangerous to the public's well being.[20]

Put another way, the predominant, for-profit model of US journalism fails to tell the American people "what is really going on," to paraphrase the investigative journalist and media critic George Seldes (1890–1995). The solution to journalism's present woes is unlikely to come from the industry's corporate leaders, biased third-party fact-checkers, or Big Tech content moderators. Instead, assuring an informed and engaged public, whose members understand "what's going on" and can act on that basis, depends on a fiercely independent free press, augmented by widespread education in critical media literacy.[21]

Since its founding, Project Censored has advocated for a healthy democracy by promoting news literacy. Jensen, for example, boldly encouraged journalism programs to help develop "more muckrakers and fewer buckrakers."[22] In the decades since, Project Censored has developed a number of original educational programs that provide hands-on training in critical media literacy for students, including our classroom teaching guides, student internships, and Campus Affiliates Program, each of which distinguishes Project Censored from other news watch organizations and press freedom groups, while promoting students' civic engagement and appreciation of journalism that serves the public interest.[23]

Further, each year, Project Censored continues to recognize some of the best independent journalism, produced by news workers ethically committed to factual, transparent reporting in the public interest.[24] These journalists and outlets are among the best advocates of news literacy, literally teaching by example. In this view, solutions to the revitalization of a floundering Fourth Estate are to be found in the work and example of its most radical independent practitioners—rather than their owners, employers, or meddling partisan outsiders. The history of muckraking journalism shows this to be so, and it behooves us to pay attention to what the past can teach us.

PAST AS PROLOGUE

Among the many books Jensen published, one of the most significant might be *Stories That Changed America: Muckrakers of the 20th Century*.[25] In it, he collected exemplary reporting by nearly two dozen legendary journalists, including excerpts from decisive reports by Ida Tarbell (*The History of the Standard Oil Company*), Lincoln Steffens (*The Shame of the Cities*), Upton Sinclair (*The Jungle* and *The Brass Check*), George Seldes (*In Fact*), Edward R. Murrow (*In Search of Light*), and I.F. Stone (*I.F. Stone's Weekly*). As Jensen wrote, "Their words led to a nationwide public revolt against social evils and a decade of reforms in antitrust legislation, the electoral process, banking regulations, and a host of other social programs."[26] The reporting Jensen collected in *Stories That Changed America* continues to inspire those of us who believe journalism can make a difference.

The iconic muckraker "Izzy" Stone once wrote, "All governments lie, but disaster lies in wait for countries whose officials smoke the same hashish they give out."[27] But Stone, like Jensen and Phillips, had great faith in the power of the press to expose and counter those lies. We need brave, independent journalists and newsrooms to tackle the most controversial and suppressed issues of our era. Stone relentlessly exposed governmental prevarications and injustices throughout his career. He also saw the shortcomings of his own profession, to the point of resigning from the National Press Club in 1941, rather than kowtowing to its racism and political sycophancy. After realizing he had limited influence in the establishment press, he started *I.F. Stone's Weekly* and dared to report the truth on his own. He took on McCarthyism at a time when his peers were being attacked, arrested, deported, and disappeared. He fought for truth and peace in the face of the unjust, murderous conflicts of the Cold War, especially in Vietnam.[28] Sound familiar?

Governments lie, but so do establishment media outlets, whether about nonexistent WMDs in Iraq or inflated threats around Russiagate. Stone's insight is timeless but seems more relevant than ever as the Project enters its fiftieth year. The second Trump administration and its craven enablers bombard us daily with lies and half-truths, which Reporters Without Borders has characterized as "a monumental assault on freedom of information."[29] At best, the *establishment* press seems capable of little more than chronicling the barrage; at worst, they capitulate to it like submissive, sycophantic lapdogs, not the vigilant watchdogs they cosplay on TV and the internet.[30]

The notion of a press "watchdog" on a governmental or corporate leash did not begin with this current administration—as Jensen and his students at Sonoma State noted in 1976, looking back on the eve of Richard Nixon's 1972 re-election, when no major news outlet even *mentioned* the Watergate scandal. Instead, the roots of a subservient press reach back to the earliest history of American journalism on the presidency.[31] But the return of Trump to power is a nadir for many of our cherished yet beleaguered freedoms, including the First Amendment, which links freedom of speech and press with the rights to assemble and petition. The public, our democracy, needs journalism that can help us awaken from what historian Timothy Snyder has described as a "self-induced intellectual coma" that is characteristic of "the politics of inevitability."[32] The combination of a truly independent press and a media-literate public, which Project Censored has promoted since its inception, is a bulwark against intellectual torpor and civic decay.

WILL PROJECT CENSORED BE NEEDED IN THE FUTURE?

Calling out counter-democratic measures is one way to resist the onslaught of authoritarianism. A free press provides the means for this, but people need to act in response. Rather than complain, as some have, that "the left" needs the media power of a mogul like Rupert Murdoch to "compete," we should open our eyes and support the amazing people and organizations *already doing* this invaluable work.[33] When Peter Phillips, the Project's second director, would routinely exclaim at public events, "Power to the People," he expressed faith in and solidarity with their work and independent journalism's mission. Each year, Project Censored's record of the most important independent news reporting marks an occasion for numerous muckraking journalists and free press organizations to strengthen existing ties, build new coalitions, and fight even harder to protect our democratic republic from anyone—whether they bat for Team Red or Team Blue—who would subvert it for their own private gain.

The Project celebrates the practice of radical muckraking journalism in the public interest, and its continuing relevance in our current Gilded Age of oligarchs and Big Tech plutocrats. The legacy of the many who have worked on Project Censored over the last half century reminds us that we cannot wait for change to simply emerge; we must create it ourselves. If the past is prologue, we also have much to learn from and pass on to the next generation, whose experiences and voices will inform and express new stories that will change America *again*, to paraphrase Jensen.

Now is not a time for cowering; it is a time to exhibit what the late political activist and whistleblower Daniel Ellsberg (of Pentagon Papers fame) called civil courage, to stand up for our Constitutional principles regardless of the risks or odds.[34] Or, as Izzy Stone noted, it is time "to defend the weak against the strong; to fight for justice; and to seek, as best I can to bring healing perspectives to bear on the terrible hates and fears of [humankind], in the hope of someday bringing about one world, in which [people] will enjoy the differences of the human garden instead of killing each other over them."³⁵

Hear, hear. Let's not get lost in the smoke of the hashish blown in our faces by divisive media, government actors, or corporate shills. Instead, let's recognize and support journalism's canaries in the coal mines, from fact-based reporting on the climate crisis (and its solutions) to the Kafkaesque raids on the most vulnerable among us, and the dismantling of education, attacks on the arts, and an ongoing genocide in Gaza. We invite you to join our efforts and act on the information that independent journalists—like those Project Censored has championed for fifty years—share at their own risk, for we ignore these bold truthtellers at our own peril. Unless or until the establishment press gets its act together, such that we would no longer need a Project Censored, here's to another fifty years of covering the News That Didn't Make The News!

MICKEY HUFF is the third director of Project Censored (serving in that role since 2010), and president (since 2016) of the nonprofit Media Freedom Foundation. This is his seventeenth yearbook with the Project. He is also Distinguished Director of the Park Center of Independent Media and Professor of Journalism at the Roy H. Park School of Communications at Ithaca College in New York.

NOTES

1. This foreword has been adapted from an article originally published in Project Censored's *Dispatches on Media and Politics* series, Mickey Huff, "All Government's Lie: Why We Need a Radical and Independent Free Press Now," Project Censored, April 3, 2025.
2. For historical perspective on public attitudes toward government, see "Public Trust in Government: 1958—2024," Pew Research Center, June 24, 2024. For more on US history of the 1970s to the present, see historian Rick Perlstein, *Nixonland: The Rise of a President and the Fracturing of America* (Scribner, 2009) and his follow up, *Invisible Bridge: The Fall of Nixon and the Rise of Reagan* (Simon and Schuster, 2014); On genocide in the 1970s, see, for example, Amy Goodman, "Jimmy Carter Championed Human Rights But Also Funded and Armed Indonesia's Genocide in East Timor," *Democracy Now!*, January 10, 2025.
3. Perlstein, *Invisible Bridge*; Mike Mather, "From High Confidence After

Watergate to Low Now, How Did Media Trust Erode?" *UVAToday*, June 15, 2022. This is an interview with author Bruce A. Williams, the University of Virginia's Ambassador Henry J. Taylor Professor of Media Studies, discussing the public erosion of trust in journalism.

4. James Risen, *The Last Honest Man: The CIA, the FBI, the Mafia, and the Kennedys—and One Senator's Fight to Save Democracy* (Little, Brown and Company, 2023).

5. Nolan Higdon and Mickey Huff, *United States of Distraction: Media Manipulation in Post-Truth America (and what we can do about it)* (City Lights Books, 2019).

6. Carl Jensen, *Stories That Changed America: Muckrakers of the Twentieth Century* (Seven Stories Press, 2000), 24. Jensen wrote, "Weapons may have won the Revolutionary War but it was words that have created the longest lasting democracy in history."

7. See Peter Phillips, "How Mainstream Media Evolved into Corporate Media," in *Censored 2018*, ed. Mickey Huff and Andy Lee Roth with Project Censored (Seven Stories Press, 2018); also online at Project Censored.

8. For more on this topic, see "Junk Food News," online at Project Censored, and Chapter 3 of this volume.

9. See "News Abuse," online at Project Censored and Chapter 4 of this volume. On "malinformation," see "Confronting Misinformation, Disinformation and Mal-information," Facing History and Ourselves, February 29, 2024.

10. Nolan Higdon, *The Anatomy of Fake News: A Critical News Literacy Education* (University of California Press, 2020); Andy Lee Roth and Steve Macek, "Corporate Fact-Checking Services Shouldn't Be Our Defense Against 'Fake News'," *Truthout*, December 18, 2020.

11. Emil Marmol and Lee Mager, "'Fake News': The Trojan Horse for Silencing Alternative News and Reestablishing Corporate News Dominance," in *Censored 2020*, ed. Andy Lee Roth and Mickey Huff with Project Censored (Seven Stories Press, 2019), also available online at Project Censored.

12. See video clip from the World Economic Forum for the quote, "Wall Street Journal Emma Tucker: 'We owned the news. We were the gatekeepers.'" YouTube, April 21, 2024. To see the event in its entirety, see World Economic Forum, "Defending Truth," January 18, 2024.

13. "Post-truth," Oxford Word of the Year 2016, Oxford Languages, 2016. Incidentally, 2016 was when Donald Trump was first electored into the White House. In 2024, when Trump was elected to a second term, Oxford's Word of the Year was brain rot, the "deterioration of a person's mental or intellectual state, especially viewed as a result of overconsumption of material (now particularly online content) considered to be trivial or unchallenging."

14. Peter Phillips and Mickey Huff, "Truth Emergency: Inside the Military Industrial Media Empire," in *Censored 2010*, ed. Peter Philips and Mickey Huff with Project Censored (Seven Stories Press, 2009), quote at 198.

15. Richard Carufel, "Majority of Americans See Misinformation and Disinformation as Greater Threats than Terrorism, Climate Change, and Border Security," Institute for Public Relations, November 11, 2023; see the latest, "Disinformation and Society Report, 5th Edition," Institute for Public Relations, April 2025.

16. " All the President's Invective," U.S. Press Freedom Tracker, January 14, 2025; Ari Paul, "Paramount Sells Out Journalism to Secure Purchase by Skydance," Fairness and Accuracy in Reporting, July 24, 2025; Liam Reilly, "Trump Baselessly Accuses News Media of 'Illegal' Behavior and Corruption in DOJ Speech," CNN, March 14, 2025; Chris Lehmann, "Trump's Attack on the Free Press is Just Getting Started," *The Nation*, December 17, 2024; Ari Paul, "Cuts to PBS, NRP, Part of Authoritarian Playbook," Fairness and Accuracy

17. in Reporting, April 25, 2025; David Bauder, "Banishing a Reporter: Trump Escalates Battle with Wall Street Journal Over Epstein Story," Associated Press, July 21, 2025; Mickey Huff and Andy Lee Roth, "The Free Press as 'Enemy of the People'," Project Censored, August 2, 2018.
17. Myra MacPherson, *All Governments Lie: The Life and Times of Rebel Journalist I.F. Stone* (Scribner, 2008).
18. Andy Lee Roth and Steve Macek, "Corporate Media Harms Not Only Through Omission, But Also by Distortion," *Truthout*, November 15, 2021; see also selected contents of the *Censored* yearbook series online at Project Censored.
19. Steve Macek and Andy Lee Roth, "It's True That Corporate Media Is Biased—But Not in the Ways Right-Wingers Say," *Truthout*, November 27, 2020.
20. Carl Jensen and Project Censored, *20 Years of Censored News* (Seven Stories Press, 1997), 14–16.
21. For an overview of educational resources developed, and provided at no charge, by Project Censored, see "Project Censored: Where Teaching Critical Media Literacy Begins," Project Censored, June 2024; for a listing of independent media resources, see the Project's Independent News Sources page.
22. Carl Jensen, *Censored: The News That Didn't Make the News and Why—The 1995 Project Censored Yearbook* (New York: Four Walls Eight Windows, 1995), 175.
23. For more Project resources on media literacy education, see "Educational Materials," online at Project Censored; "Project Censored in the Classroom," online at Project Censored; and "Internships," online at Project Censored.
24. For media ethics, see the "SPJ Code of Ethics," Society of Professional Journalists.
25. Jensen, *Stories That Changed America*.
26. Jensen, *Stories That Changed America*, 18.
27. MacPherson, *All Governments Lie*.
28. MacPherson, *All Governments Lie*.
29. "One Month of Trump: Press Freedom Under Siege," Reporters Without Borders, February 19, 2025.
30. Jeremy Herb, Fredreka Schouten, Annie Grayer, and Steve Contorno, "Trump Is Using the Power of Government to Punish Opponents. They're Struggling to Respond," CNN, March 20 2025; Paul Farhi, "Media Giants Settling With Donald Trump Are Setting a 'Dangerous' Precedent," *Vanity Fair*, February 7, 2025.
31. Higdon and Huff, *United States of Distraction*; Paul Starr, *The Creation of the Media: Political Origins of Modern Communications* (Basic Books, 2004).
32. Timothy Snyder, *On Tyranny: Twenty Lessons From the Twentieth Century* (Crown, 2017).
33. Anthony Nadler and Reece Peck, "The Left Needs Media That Competes—and Wins," *Jacobin*, March 5, 2025; for more information about news organizations doing "grassroots-aligned, social justice-driven journalism," see the Movement Media Alliance (MMA) and the article by Maya Schenwar and Lara Witt of the MMA, in Chapter 5 of this volume.
34. Daniel Ellsberg, "On Civil Courage and Its Punishments," in *Censored 2014: Fearless Speech in Fateful Times*, ed. Mickey Huff and Andy Lee Roth with Project Censored (Seven Stories Press, 2013), also online at Project Censored.
35. Quoted by Victor Navasky, "I.F. Stone," *The Nation*, July 2, 2003.

— INTRODUCTION —

CONFRONTING THE SIEGE ON PUBLIC KNOWLEDGE WITH COLLECTIVE TRUTH-TELLING

ANDY LEE ROTH, SHEALEIGH VOITL, and MICKEY HUFF

"Every crisis is in part a storytelling crisis," author and activist Rebecca Solnit observed in *No Straight Road Takes You There*, a 2025 collection of her essays.[1] Carl Jensen understood this when, in 1976, he founded Project Censored as an effort to bring wider public attention to important topics and issues that the establishment press in the United States overlooked or underreported. The absence or, more pointedly, the *omission* of relevant stories is one form of storytelling crisis.

Fifty years on, Project Censored continues to expose what Jensen characterized in the Project's first yearbook as "the systematic omission of certain issues from our national media."[2] Anticipating Solnit's observation, he recognized that a storytelling crisis in US journalism contributed to the worsening of broader societal and global crises, including economic inequality, systemic racism, militarism, corporatism, environmental degradation, and public apathy. Stated in more positive terms, by serving the public interest, journalism could make a difference in each of those domains.

While missing news stories are one type of storytelling crisis that Project Censored has addressed since its inception, recognition and concern for other, more subtle ways that the establishment press fails in its duty to inform the public developed along with the Project.

What *was* said, and *how* it was said, could be as influential—and informative or misleading—as what remained unsaid.

Thus, in 1983, Jensen introduced the term "Junk Food News" to describe reporting that entertains and distracts the public instead of informing it; in 2002, Peter Phillips, the Project's second director, coined the term "News Abuse" to highlight how the establishment press frequently covers newsworthy topics in ways that obscure or distort those stories' most important points; and, in 2023, the Project's third and current director, Mickey Huff, and his colleagues developed the concept of "censorship by proxy" to describe restrictions on freedom of information that resulted from official or covert corporate-government partnerships.[3]

Each of these developments in the Project's history stemmed from its original definition of censorship, which emphasized the consequences of censorship. Jensen defined censorship as "the suppression of information, whether purposeful or not, by any method—including bias, omission, underreporting, or self-censorship—that prevents the public from fully knowing what is happening in society."[4] Where conventional definitions emphasized *censors'* concern for controlling expressions and ideas they deemed dangerous, the Project's definition highlighted how the free flow of information was a necessary condition for the *public* to protect itself from individuals and groups that threatened democracy.

It's worth noting that, since its inception, the Project's reliance on this definition has led some would-be critics to misconstrue its charter and method. Some have questioned, *Censorship? In the United States? But we have the First Amendment.* Others have denounced the Project for reporting on stories that are not actually "underreported" or "censored."

The first of these critiques is best addressed by pointing to the fifty-year record of more than 1,200 important news stories, first and best reported by independent journalists and news outlets, which the establishment press has failed to cover, either at all or in proportion to those stories' significance.

The second criticism—that these stories were not "censored" per se—misses the point that a blockade of news coverage need not be absolute for an issue to remain all but unknown to most of the public. As Edward Herman and Noam Chomsky noted in *Manufacturing Consent*, "That a careful reader looking for a fact can sometimes find it with diligence and a skeptical eye tells us nothing about whether that fact received the attention and context it deserved, whether it was intelligible to the reader or effectively distorted or suppressed."[5]

INSIGHTS FROM TRACKING 50 YEARS OF "CENSORED" NEWS

For better or worse, American journalism frames the stories that concern or encourage the public.[6] For fifty years, the Project has worked to expose and address an enduring crisis in so-called "mainstream" US journalism by reframing the establishment press's storytelling when it marginalizes, ignores, or blocks important topics and issues addressed by independent journalists and news outlets.

In the face of ongoing and emerging societal crises—including but not limited to the second Trump administration's renewed and intensified attacks on both press freedoms and journalists themselves—it makes sense to ask: What kind of stories have we been telling for the past fifty years? And what stories will need telling during the next fifty years?

As already noted, many important stories don't get told, except by independent news outlets, which, compared to their corporate counterparts, reach relatively small audiences, and a lot of what passes for "news" in the corporate press is *junk*. These are not knee-jerk, reactionary assertions; they are conclusions based on decades of close scrutiny of patterns in coverage and omission, as presented in multiple editions of the Project's yearbook.[7]

It's also clear that, more than ever, we live in an era of "news inflation": We have access to more and more news than ever before, but "it isn't worth as much as it used to be," as Jensen presciently observed in the 2001 yearbook.[8] The internet, social media, and mobile apps have radically accelerated the 24-hour news cycle, which was pioneered by CNN and other cable networks in the 1980s. Although the hastening of the news cycle may improve the coverage of some breaking news stories, news inflation remains a concern. Change "becomes invisible when your timeframe is shorter than that change," Solnit has observed, "and the short-term view breeds defeatism and despair."[9] This is one reason why, instead of a 24/7 emphasis on breaking news, Project Censored maintains a 52/12 orientation, focused on important story themes and coverage patterns that are best tracked and analyzed over a longer 52-week, 12-month cycle. From this vantage point, we are better able to "identify and analyze systemic patterns and subsurface trends in news coverage that otherwise remain invisible or taken for granted amidst the unceasing stream of breaking news."[10]

This unceasing stream is increasingly propelled—or selectively dammed—by algorithmic gatekeepers, developed and controlled by Big Tech companies with no commitment to the journalistic ethics of reporting truth with transparency and accountability.[11] Google does not produce any news stories of its own, but, like Facebook, X, and other platforms that function as distributors and aggregators of news stories, it plays an enormous—and poorly understood—role in determining what news stories many Americans see.[12]

Prominent figures in journalism, such as billionaire Patrick Soon-Shiong, who owns the *Los Angeles Times*, not to mention countless less well-known news editors and reporters, have been tempted to use algorithm-powered tools as a means to address the crises of newsrooms' declining revenues and journalism's faltering public trust. Flawed assumptions about journalism—including, for example, the belief that "objective" news simply reflects reality—lead tech advocates such as Soon-Shiong to believe they can replace subjective human judgment, flawed as it sometimes can be, with objective algorithmic determinations.[13] But an abundance of new, critical studies of artificial intelligence clearly demonstrate how these tools reflect the biases of the existing materials on which they have been trained, if not those of their human developers.[14]

There are important, appropriate roles for AI tools in journalism, as exemplified, for instance, by CalMatters' "Digital Democracy" initiative. But continuing to chase the chimera of "objectivity" by algorithmic means is unlikely to revitalize either newsrooms' bottom lines or the public's trust in the profession. Objectivity, algorithmic or otherwise, won't protect democracy from authoritarian threats.

"THE FIRST CONDITION OF PROGRESS"

In the decades since Project Censored was founded, it has highlighted major leaps in social movements, communication technologies, and human knowledge, many of which have been championed by those devoted to exposing truths and challenging dominant narratives. However, these same years have also been marked by a parallel—and deeply troubling—rise of authoritarianism, widening inequality, global disinformation campaigns, and a seemingly relentless erosion of civil liberties and press freedom. As Solnit has observed, "We have democratized storytelling and truth to the extent that we now sometimes hear about the consequences of inequality, but not enough to end those stories."[15] After publishing last year's book, we were often asked about a vision for the future—Where do we go from here? How do we reconcile the potential for liberation with intensified forms of repression?

As George Bernard Shaw wrote in his 1902 "author's apology" for *Mrs. Warren's Profession*, "All censorships exist to prevent anyone from challenging current conceptions and existing institutions. All progress is initiated by challenging current conceptions, and executed by supplanting existing institutions. Consequently, the first condition of progress is the removal of censorship."[16]

The tools for global solidarity have never been more accessible—as we'll see repeatedly throughout this volume—but systems of censorship, both covert and overt, are more sophisticated than ever. Combine that with a lack of critical media literacy education, and we're fighting a progressively steeper uphill battle. Surveillance capitalism and the privatization of digital public spaces make it easier than ever to obscure dissent while maintaining an illusion of open discourse.[17] After taking control of Twitter in 2022 and touting himself as a "free speech absolutist," technocrat Elon Musk renamed the platform X and rapidly transformed it into a "pro-Trump echo chamber."[18] Musk made room for flawed AI-powered content moderation after sacking Twitter employees responsible for "monitoring misinformation"; temporarily suspended certain high-profile journalists, such as Donie O'Sullivan of CNN, Micah Lee of *The Intercept*, and independent reporter Aaron Rupar; and granted far-right users "new leeway to engage in homophobic and transphobic attacks."[19]

Algorithmic bias, targeted propaganda, and information overload undermine our collective capacity to engage with the truth, even when it's right in front of us. So, as climate catastrophe looms, wealth consolidates, and the government continues to dismantle the democratic institutions the public depends on, the questions we now face are not merely "How did we *get* here?" but also "How do we *move forward* from here?" It is the critical question media scholars have long wrestled with, and one we're unlikely to fully resolve in this brief introduction. But it is precisely this tension—between progress and regress—that activates Project Censored's ongoing work.

The Project has witnessed the power of journalism acting as a public service rather than a revenue generator and firmly believes that journalism remains one of the most essential checks on power, no matter who is in office. Trump 2.0 introduced compounding crises—including rampant Immigration and Customs Enforcement abuses, attacks on freedom of speech, and the crumbling of the federal government, to name a few—but the independent press took seriously its responsibility to hold these officials accountable as it had done in previous administrations. Increasingly, however, the public must broaden its understanding of press freedom to include not just the right to publish but the right to access information—that is, the right to know. This shift in perspective moves us away from the notion of "heroic, lone journalists who speak truth to power," as Mike Ananny at the University of Southern California's Annenberg School for Communication and Journalism posits in his book *Networked Press Freedom*.[20] Instead, it encourages a deeper recognition of the systemic conditions that enable (or obstruct) journalism as a democratic force.

Similarly, when Jensen founded Project Censored in 1976, he "expanded the definition of censorship": "Rather than starting with ... the obligation of an elite to protect the masses, my definition begins at the other end—with the failure of information to reach people."[21] In other words, censorship is not limited to state-imposed silence or editorial bans; it includes economic pressures, corporate filters, news deserts, and the systemic marginalization of stories and perspectives that challenge dominant power structures.

Democracy is in crisis, but it is not a crisis of apathy or disengagement. It is a crisis of distortion—of who controls and frames the narratives, and who has the power to prime public consciousness and shape culture. If censorship today is more insidious than ever, then the resistance must be more interconnected, more imaginative, and more committed to collective truth-telling.

INFORMATION CRISIS IN THE MAKING: PUBLIC KNOWLEDGE UNDER SIEGE

In the wake of the moral panic around "fake news" after the 2016 presidential election, Donald Trump and his administration sharply increased the frequency and scope of politicized attacks on the First Amendment and the rights it established and safeguards. On the premise that any kind of dissent is intolerable, Trump and his far-right allies commandeered federal agencies, emboldened state governments, and, as previously noted, facilitated proxy attacks by Big Tech and the private sector, all in Orwellian efforts to redefine "free speech" and to recast people's constitutionally protected rights to express themselves and practice their beliefs without government interference. Their targets included nonprofit organizations, public and school libraries, newsrooms, and public broadcasting. But, more broadly, these institutional attacks threatened—and continue to threaten—the public's right to be informed. Over the past decade, Project Censored has chronicled these antidemocratic developments in detail, warning that they presaged even more egregious attacks on press freedom and civil liberties.

Make no mistake: Neither Trump nor the Republicans, MAGA or otherwise, hold a monopoly on executive efforts to control information or shape official narratives about US government policy. Trump's predecessors, Democrats Barack Obama and Joe Biden, suppressed information during their administrations, including deceit about the extent of the militarized drone program under Obama, and efforts to criminalize journalism by indicting and extraditing WikiLeaks's Julian Assange under Biden (each of which Project Censored has documented). Government secrecy—with its negative consequences for the national interest, public debate, and official accountability—has a long, bipartisan history in the United States.

Nevertheless, the extent to which the second Trump administration and its enablers have ratcheted up draconian attacks on the First Amendment is unprecedented. For example, Congressional efforts to pass legislation that would gut nonprofits—by authorizing the Secretary of Treasury to unilaterally revoke, without due process, their 501(c)3 tax-exempt status if Treasury officials deem they are providing "material support" to terrorist organizations—have been like horror movie zombies that, despite being felled, rise up to continue stalking their desired victims.[22] Given that many independent news outlets and media literacy organizations are nonprofits, the repeated revival of this fateful legislation continues to threaten press and academic freedoms, not to mention nonprofits that provide vital humanitarian aid in conflict zones around the world.

White House attacks by Trump early in his second term also included specious lawsuits against corporate media outlets including ABC and CBS, cases in which Disney and Paramount, the two networks' respective parent companies, bent to Trump's will by paying millions of dollars in pre-trial settlements, rather than confronting his administration in court in battles that media and legal scholars saw as winnable. By capitulating, ABC/Disney and CBS/Paramount set dangerous precedents that normalize even more information control.[23]

In his first month back in the White House, Trump fired most of the staff of the Office of Personnel Management, which handles Freedom of Information Act (FOIA) requests, and he also forced out the leadership at the National Archives and Records Administration, prompting Lauren Harper from the Freedom of the Press Foundation to warn, "The gutting of the institutional knowledge at the National Archives is going to impact every agency across the federal government."[24]

In June 2025, Reporters Without Borders (RSF) documented a "wave of violence" against journalists covering protests in Los Angeles against Trump's immigration policies.[25] RSF verified at least thirty-five attacks on journalists—mostly by law enforcement, during protests against what the American Civil Liberties Union described as an "oppressive and vile paramilitary operation" by federal agents on multiple workplaces—in which media workers were pepper-sprayed and shot with police pepper balls, rubber bullets, and tear gas canisters.[26] RSF's report noted that the Los Angeles incidents were part of "an alarming uptick of press freedom violations" since Trump took office in January 2025. Later the same month, the Trump administration further escalated these attacks by accusing journalists of "inciting violence or lawlessness … by simply reporting the news," the Freedom of the Press Foundation reported.[27] The Trump administration claimed that CNN's straightforward reporting about

ICEBlock, an application that informs the public of ICE agents' whereabouts, was akin to inciting "further violence against our ICE officers," and threatened that the Department of Justice would consider prosecuting reporters from CNN and other outlets on the grounds that their reporting was, according to Secretary of Homeland Security Kristi Noem, "illegal."[28] Intimidation often works: Earlier, in April 2025, *Poynter* had reported that people fearful of retaliation by the Trump administration were asking news editors to remove their names from old news stories.[29]

Public media, already woefully underfunded, is also in Trump's sights as he moved to defund the Corporation for Public Broadcasting and threatened retribution against members of Congress if they did not heed his wishes.[30] In July 2025, as *State of the Free Press 2026* went to press, the Senate and the House of Representatives bowed to Trump's agenda by agreeing to cut $1.1 billion from the previously approved federal budget for the Corporation for Public Broadcasting. "With this vote, Congress has abandoned local communities, abdicated its constitutional responsibilities and dealt a devastating blow to what's left of our democracy," Craig Aaron of the Free Press and Free Press Action observed. "This is a vote to evade public accountability and hide the Trump administration's destructive actions from independent scrutiny."[31]

These attacks on the press and additional institutions that provide the public with essential information proceed in the context of an ongoing and escalating culture war, in which conservative antagonists, like Elon Musk, characterize being informed and seeking knowledge as evidence of a "woke mind virus."[32] Never mind that the term "woke" was historically a positive attribute, signaling liberating awareness of oppression, not an epithet.[33] For free speech revisionists and opponents of the right to know, ignorance is apparently strength.

Promoting exclusivity rather than inclusivity as a form of patriotism, Trump's rollback of Diversity, Equity, and Inclusion (DEI) initiatives and his threats against higher education and academic freedom have been foul hallmarks of his early second term. Even during Biden's presidency, the Democratic Party appeared ill-prepared to counter MAGA-inspired attacks on libraries and school boards by groups like Moms for Liberty that accounted for a mass uptick in book challenges and bans, which public and school librarians, supported by numerous students and parents, joined forces to resist.[34] Alongside book challenges and bans, the passage of more laws like Florida's model "anti-woke" legislation (the "Stop WOKE Act") enforce the teaching of "patriotic" and exceptionalist history, while historic sites managed by the National Park Service, such as Stonewall National Monument, are stripped of their historical significance, and inconvenient truths are cast down the memory hole.[35]

These stark results of reactionary and authoritarian actions are indicative of a post-truth society, in which beliefs and feelings too often "trump" facts, evidence, and reason. Many Americans seem locked into what historian Richard Hofstadter referred to as the "paranoid style in American politics," where political leaders and the public spend more time battling over perceived infractions and scapegoating imaginary enemies than addressing actual threats such as the climate crisis, lack of living wages and healthcare, rising homelessness, and the looming specter of nuclear winter associated with US involvement in the escalating wars of Israel, Iran, Russia, and Ukraine.[36] Hofstadter also argued that such behaviors represented a form of anti-intellectualism that made Americans prone to adopt conspiratorial beliefs, reject knowledge and expertise, and more susceptible to demagogic rule.[37] Tangible examples of how this national ignorance and incompetence have risen to the top include several appointees to the current administration. A quick sampling of some key players shows that the dystopia imagined in Mike Judge and Etan Cohen's *Idiocracy* (2006) has arrived.

Addressing Congress in May 2025, Department of Homeland Security Secretary Kristi Noem revealed her ignorance of *habeas corpus*, which is foundational to the rule of law, but which she believes authorizes the president to remove people from the country without due process.[38] Noem should study past *Censored* yearbooks to get up to speed on the significance of *habeas*, which dates back to the year 1215, as a bedrock of our legal system.[39] Defense Secretary Pete Hegseth could use a primer on his Signal app's privacy settings, as became clear after he (mistakenly?) shared top secret war intel with a prominent editor at *The Atlantic*.[40] Billionaire Secretary of Education and former professional wrestling promoter Linda McMahon might go back to school to learn why public education is a right, not a privilege, as she works, like a fox guarding the henhouse, to dismantle the Department of Education.[41] FEMA's acting director, David Richardson, who has no background in emergency management, didn't know there was an Atlantic hurricane season and was AWOL in the aftermath of catastrophic floods that wiped out entire communities in Texas.[42] And the sheer number of former Fox News personalities that have taken positions in the Trump administration, nearly two dozen as of this writing, should attract more scrutiny from the press itself.[43]

Although the practice of appointing political cronies to government positions is hardly new, the dearth of reporting by the establishment press regarding the utter lack of qualifications among these appointees is shocking and unfortunate. As Karl Marx once observed, history repeats itself, "The first time as tragedy, the second time as farce."[44]

CHALLENGING CURRENT CONCEPTIONS

Corporate news media have played a detrimental role in our civic decline. From their hyperbolic fixation on "breaking news" to their infatuation with celebrity and spectacle, the news industry has reveled in sensational distraction and helped fan the flames of partisan division. Nevertheless, there's an essential role for the media to play in addressing our fateful circumstances and reversing our shared fortunes, when reporting is conducted independently, transparently, and in the public interest. At its best, journalism spurs progress by challenging current conceptions, to adapt George Bernard Shaw's insight. Journalism that treats its audience as participants, not bystanders, can help us recognize how, as Rebecca Solnit puts it, "The future does not yet exist but is being made in the present."[45]

Pioneering figures in the US media reform movement, including Phil Donahue, Bill Moyers, Robert McChesney, each of whom recently passed on, understood this. So, too, did Hamza Al Dahdouh, Faisal Abu Al Qumsan, Wafa Al-Udaini, and the 183 additional journalists and media workers who, as of this writing, have been killed in Israel, Occupied Palestinian Territory, and Lebanon, between 2023 and 2025, many of whom were directly targeted by Israeli forces.[46] These losses are staggering, and, very reasonably, a cause for despair. But despair is not a luxury that media workers and others in violent conflict zones like Gaza can afford. And, the truth is, neither can we.[47]

When we recognize that fear-mongering, cynicism, and pessimism fuel popular support for authoritarian leaders, and continue to energize Trumpist attacks on press freedoms and the public's right to know, then it becomes absolutely clear that now is the time to renew our commitment to direct efforts at defending our civil liberties, the right to dissent, and due process under rule of law. These efforts, many of which are already underway, necessarily take many forms. For a media-focused nonprofit like Project Censored, this means now is the time to build a movement of independent journalists and newsrooms; now is the time to expand critical media literacy educational opportunities to students from K-12 through college and adulthood; and now is the time to fill the nation's news deserts with local, publicly supported news outlets that model media democracy as a human right. These aims unite the diverse contributors to this book, and each chapter of *State of the Free Press 2026* was written with this vision in mind.

INSIDE *STATE OF THE FREE PRESS 2026*

Chapter 1 presents the most important but under-reported news stories of 2024–2025. This year's highlights include reporting by independent journalists and news outlets on surveillance of social media by US Immigration and Customs Enforcement (ICE); Meta's "sweeping crackdown" on Facebook and Instagram posts related to Palestine; under-reported, often deadly abuses of police authority; and underfunding and exploitation of Indigenous communities by federal and state governments. Compiled by Jayden Lawrence, Ella Mrofka, Caitlin Suda, Amy Grim Buxbaum, Steve Macek, and Andy Lee Roth, this year's review represents the collective effort of more than 250 students from eight US college and university campuses who identified, vetted, and summarized Validated Independent News stories through the Project's Campus Affiliates Program. While the stories included in the fiftieth edition of the Project's annual survey of the "News That Didn't Make the News" stand on their own as vital dispatches on issues that deserve more extensive news coverage and broader public engagement, taken together, and added to the record of forty-nine previous years of research, they also contribute to a damning, evidence-based record of chronic failures in news judgement and systemic gaps in coverage by the nation's establishment press. Put in more affirmative terms, Chapter 1 celebrates the essential role of *independent* journalists and news outlets in alerting the public to crises—and solutions—that might otherwise go unrecognized.

This year's *Déjà Vu* News chapter revisits three previously underreported stories that involved attacks on journalism and free speech. In Chapter 2, Jayden Lawrence and Steve Macek provide updates on how a Monsanto "intelligence center" targeted journalists and activists, journalist Abby Martin's challenge to Georgia's BDS "gag law" (both from *State of the Free Press 2021*), and the impact of the Justice Department's secret Foreign Intelligence Surveillance Act (FISA) rules on journalists, the #1 story from the 2020 yearbook. These updates demonstrate that the Trump administration's current assaults on the press are only "the most recent installment in an ongoing repressive, autocratic, and often corporate-sponsored campaign that stretches back years," Macek writes. "But they also show that the assault has been consistently resisted and even occasionally turned back."

From real-life Snow White Rachel Zegler and actress Gal Gadot, to Drake versus Kendrick and the gutting of public education, not to mention Elon Musk's chain saws, Cybertrucks, and creeping techno-fascism, this year's Junk Food News chapter surveys the dubious reporting that's invading our social feeds and news sources. Just like the rest of the ghosts of Junk's past, these stories were overrepresented by the corporate media. Meanwhile, DOGE was actively compounding the United States government's technocratic problems, academic freedom and free speech were under direct attack, and the Department of Education was being splintered—as if your doomscroll wasn't terrifying enough already.

In Chapter 4, John Collins of *Weave News* examines News Abuse in the nomination of Congressmember Elise Stefanik—a staunch supporter of the far-right MAGA movement and Israel—to serve as US Ambassador to the United Nations. Although Stefanik's nomination ultimately was withdrawn, Collins analyzes how, in early 2025, the US establishment press failed to address her assertion of "biblical rights" for Israel, her attacks on UNRWA (the UN agency that has provided essential services to Palestinian refugees since they were driven from their homes in 1947–1948), and her equation of anti-Zionism with antisemitism. Comparing independent and establishment news coverage of Stefanik's positions and her Senate testimony during the nomination process, Collins demonstrates how News Abuse by corporate media outlets "reflected long-standing ideological patterns that paved the way for ongoing assaults on Palestinian lives, international students, immigrants, academic freedom, the rule of law, and democracy itself."

Media Democracy in Action highlights "the proactive, cross-sector collaborations that are reorienting journalism to its core mission to serve the public," Mischa Geracoulis writes in her introduction to Chapter 5. The chapter features contributions by Ryan Grim of *Drop Site News*, Maya Schenwar and Lara Witt of the Movement Media Alliance, Joe Lauria of *Consortium News*, Lauren Harper of the Freedom of the Press Foundation, and Jodi Rave Spotted Bear of the Indigenous Media Freedom Alliance. While the Trump administration flaunts its contempt for the separation of powers, due process, and the free press, this year's Media Democracy in Action chapter highlights alliance-building, resilience in the face of despotism, and community-centered, fact-based, investigative journalism as countervailing forces. As Schenwar and Witt write in their section of the chapter, "There is no power for the people without journalism by and for the people."

Critical media literacy has become increasingly essential as we become more reliant on online platforms. Chapter 6, this year's new zine feature, "Understanding the Digital Public Square," unpacks how online users can apply critical media literacy tools to digital infographics by evaluating calls to action, understanding performative activism, and properly vetting sources before impulsively sharing to their own followers. It also informs strategies to then become media makers, empowering users to create infographics designed to educate and mobilize their circles and communities.

Not everything good about the fiftieth anniversary yearbook is "inside" *State of the Free Press 2026*. Artist Anson Stevens-Bollen created the original art featured on the cover of this year's book, and the icons that distinguish the top "Censored" stories in Chapter 1. Stevens-Bollen ably carries forward a distinguished tradition of political art that skewers elite hypocrisies, as previous yearbook illustrators, including Tom Tomorrow and Khalil Bendib, did before him. The three-ring circus of political acrobats, truth jugglers, sideshow hypnotists, and carnival barkers imagined by Stevens-Bollen is the seventh of his rich images to grace the covers of the yearbook series.

FACING THE FUTURE:
"THINGS DON'T HAPPEN, THEY ARE BROUGHT ABOUT"

After fifty years, what if Project Censored were no longer necessary, because the establishment press stepped up and, at long last, finally began covering the challenging stories and systemic issues that their independent counterparts regularly address?

We'd welcome that as a sign of progress, and we'd claim partial credit for such a metamorphosis on behalf of the numerous intrepid independent journalists and newsrooms, past and present, whose reporting challenges the establishment press to broaden the scope of its agenda-setting influence and its otherwise narrow, exclusive definitions of who and what count as "newsworthy."

Nevertheless, for any foreseeable future, Project Censored will continue to identify, vet, and promote independent news stories that have not received public attention commensurate with their social significance. We are prepared to stay on the beat, shining spotlights on "the news that didn't make the news," because the need has never been greater.

Without inclining toward worst-case scenarios, the only meaningful threat to another fifty years of Project Censored arises not from the likelihood of the corporate press suddenly rediscovering its ethical mission to inform the public, but from crackdowns on press freedoms and civil liberties, as noted in this introduction. Media conglomeration and homogenization, wealth as protected political "speech," Big Tech censorship and surveillance, and attacks—symbolic, legal, or physical—on journalists, nonprofit organizations, LGBTQ+ folks, immigrants, and any of the nation's other, most vulnerable groups are the nightmares that wake us in the middle of the night and the real threats that motivate our work every day.

That's why, on the Project's fiftieth anniversary, we affirm its commitments to four guiding principles, first formally articulated in *State of the Free Press 2021*, but evident, one

way or another, throughout the Project's history. Based on the belief that a free press and an informed public are cornerstones of democratic government, the Project's work will continue to be guided by the following principles:
1. We champion and promote independent journalism.
2. We hold corporate media to account when they fail to provide news coverage that adequately informs the public as community members and global citizens.
3. We provide hands-on critical media literacy training to students—and we make their work public.
4. We believe that increasing public awareness of, trust in, and support for independent journalism is one essential dimension of every movement for social justice.[48]

Writing in 1945 from a federal prison in Kentucky, where he was serving time for conscientious objection to military induction, Bayard Rustin—a gay, Black civil rights strategist who went on to become an influential advisor to Martin Luther King, Jr. and the principal organizer of the 1963 March on Washington for Jobs and Freedom—told a fellow civil liberties advocate, "Things don't happen, they are brought about."[49] Democracy, civil liberties, and a truly free press depend on the choices and actions of people and human institutions; so do their counterparts: authoritarianism, deprivation of rights, propaganda, and censorship.

Mindful of Rustin's timeless insight, we at Project Censored remain committed to telling better stories. Stories that directly address crises by explaining not only how they were brought about, but also how they can be resolved. Stories that reach more people and spur them to informed engagement. The free press and its ally, critical media literacy education, provide the power to do this. We invite you to join us; our shared future is at stake.

Andy Lee Roth, Winthrop, Washington
Shealeigh Voitl, Chicago, Illinois
Mickey Huff, Ithaca, New York
July 2025

NOTES

1. Rebecca Solnit, *No Straight Road Takes You There: Essays for Uneven Terrain* (Haymarket Books, 2025), 141.
2. Carl Jensen, "Project Censored: Raising Muck, Raising Hell," in *Censored: The News That Didn't Make the News—And Why*, ed. Carl Jensen (Chapel Hill: Shelbourne Press, 1993), quote at 4.
3. For more on Junk Food News, see the online archive of past yearbooks' Junk Food News chapters, https://www.projectcensored.org/junk-food-news/; on News Abuse, see https://www.projectcensored.org/news-abuse/; and on censorship by proxy, see Andy Lee Roth, avram anderson, and Mickey Huff, "Beyond Prior Restraint: Censorship by Proxy and the New Digital Gatekeeping," Project Censored, February 9, 2023, updated August 23, 2024, and republished as "Censorship by Proxy and Moral Panics in the Digital Era," in *Censorship, Digital Media, and the Global Crackdown on Freedom of Expression*, ed. Robin Andersen, Nolan Higdon, and Steve Macek (Peter Lang, 2024), 45–64.
4. Jensen, "Raising Muck, Raising Hell," 7.
5. Edward S. Herman and Noam Chomsky, *Manufacturing Consent: The Political Economy of the Mass Media* (Pantheon Books, 1988), lxiii.
6. On the power of news frames to shape public understanding, see Shealeigh Voitl, Andy Lee Roth, and Project Censored, *Beyond Fact-Checking: A Teaching Guide to the Power of News Frames* (The Censored Press, 2025), also available, online, in PDF format, at https://www.projectcensored.org/in-the-classroom/.
7. For the archives of the Project's annual "Censored" story lists, dating back to 1976, see https://www.projectcensored.org/top-25-censored-stories-of-all-time/.
8. Carl Jensen, "Junk Food News 1877–2000," in *Censored 2001: 25th Anniversary Edition*, ed. Peter Phillips and Project Censored (Seven Stories Press, 2001), 252.
9. Solnit, *No Straight Road*, 33. Solnit goes on to note (p. 36) that short-term views are "built into the news cycle, which tends to report on events as sudden ruptures rather than the consequence of long-term forces."
10. Andy Lee Roth and Mickey Huff, "Introduction: The Pandemic and the Free Press," in Project Censored's *State of the Free Press 2021*, ed. Mickey Huff and Andy Lee Roth (Seven Stories Press, 2020), 8.
11. Andy Lee Roth, "The New Gatekeepers: How Proprietary Algorithms Increasingly Determine the News We See," *The Markaz Review*, March 14, 2021; Andy Lee Roth, "Big Tech Algorithms: The New Gatekeepers," Reynolds Journalism Institute, July 31, 2024; on transparency and accountability as cardinal principles of journalism, see "SPJ Code of Ethics," Society of Professional Journalists, September 6, 2014.
12. On Americans' poor grasp of distinctions between the producers and the sources of the news they receive, see Kirsten Worden and Michael Barthel, "Many Americans Are Unsure Whether Sources of News Do Their Own Reporting," Pew Research Center, December 8, 2020.
13. Andy Lee Roth, "System Error: Learning From a Newspaper's Plan to Deploy an AI-Powered 'Bias Meter'," Reynolds Journalism Institute, February 4, 2025.
14. See, for example, Arvind Narayanan and Sayash Kapoor, *AI Snake Oil: What Artificial Intelligence Can Do, What It Can't, and How to Tell the Difference* (Princeton University Press, 2024), and Meredith Broussard, *More Than a Glitch: Confronting Race, Gender, and Ability Bias in Tech* (MIT Press, 2024).
15. Solnit, *No Straight Road*, 120.

16. "The Author's Apology" (1902) to *Mrs. Warren's Profession* (1894) in *Plays by George Bernard Shaw* (Penguin, 1960), 41.
17. David Greene, Paige Collings, Christoph Schmon, "Online Platforms Should Stop Partnering with Government Agencies to Remove Content," Electronic Frontier Foundation, August 12, 2022.
18. Trevor Timm, "Elon Musk Has Become the World's Biggest Hypocrite on Free Speech," *The Guardian*, January 15, 2024; David Ingram, "How Elon Musk Turned X Into a Pro-Trump Echo Chamber," NBC News, October 31, 2024.
19. Ingram, "How Elon Musk"; Daniel Arkin, "Musk's Suspension of Journalists Could Embolden Authoritarians, Free Speech Experts Warn," NBC News, December 16, 2022; and Matt Lavietes, "Far-Right Figures Appear to Be Testing Twitter's Boundaries for Anti-LGBTQ Speech," NBC News, October 31, 2022.
20. Mike Ananny, *Networked Press Freedom: Creating Infrastructures for a Public Right to Hear* (MIT Press, 2018).
21. Carl Jensen, *Censored: The News That Didn't Make the News* (Shelburne Press, 1993), 6.
22. See, for example, Deborah Makari, "'Nonprofit Killer' Provision Removed from 'One Big Beautiful Bill', Concerns for Charities Remain," Charity & Security Network, May 28, 2025; for more on this issue, see Chapter 1.
23. See, for example, Jake Johnson, "'Spineless Capitulation to Extortion': Paramount Caves to Trump With $16 Million Settlement," *Common Dreams*, July 2, 2025; Tim Karr, "Why Is So Much of Corporate Media Caving to Trump?" *Common Dreams*, July 31, 2025. For more on this issue and how it relates to media ownership, see Free Press's Media Capitulation Index.
24. Angela Fu, "Firing of FOIA Officers Leaves Experts Worried About Public Records Access Under Trump," *Poynter*, February 21, 2025.
25. "USA: RSF Condemns Wave of Violence Against Journalists Covering Los Angeles Protests," Reporters Without Borders (RSF), June 11, 2025.
26. "RSF Condemns Wave of Violence"; "ACLU Statement on ICE Raids in Los Angeles," American Civil Liberties Union, June 6, 2025.
27. Caitlyn Vogus, "No, Reporting Is Not 'Incitement'," Freedom of the Press Foundation, July 16, 2025.
28. Vogus, "Reporting Is Not 'Incitement'."
29. Kelly McBride, "People Who Fear the Trump Administration Are Asking Editors to Remove Their Names from Old News Stories," *Poynter*, April 30, 2025.
30. Aaron Pellish, "Trump Threatens to Withhold Endorsements for GOP Senators Who Don't Back Rescissions Bill," *Politico*, July 10, 2025.
31. See "The House Follows the Senate and Claws Back All Federal Funding for the Corporation for Public Broadcasting," Free Press, July 18, 2025.
32. Miles Klee, "Elon Musk and Bill Maher Warn Against the 'Woke Mind Virus,' A.K.A. Historical Fact," *Rolling Stone*, April 29, 2023; "Elon Musk Warns of 'Woke Mind Virus' in AI, Says It Is an Existential Threat to Humanity," *The Economic Times*, March 7, 2025.
33. Ishena Robinson, "How Woke Went from 'Black' to 'Bad,'" NAACP Legal Defense Fund, August 26, 2022.
34. Nancy Kranich, "Free People Read Freely," Project Censored, May 15, 2024.
35. Elizabeth Gillespie McRae, "Censored, Erased, and Whitewashed: Jim Crow Education in the Twenty-First Century," Poverty and Race Research Action Council, April 24, 2024; Maria Tsvetkova, "Protesters Decry Erasure of Transgender References From Stonewall Monument Website,"

36. Reuters, February 14, 2025; Erin Reed, "After Trans People, Trump Now Erasing Bisexual People From Stonewall National Monument," *The Advocate*, July 10, 2025.
36. Richard Hofstadter, "The Paranoid Style in American Politics," *Harper's Magazine*, November 1964; Bennett Parten, "The Paranoid Style: Rereading Richard Hofstadter in the Aftermath of January 6," *Los Angeles Review of Books*, June 13, 2021.
37. Richard Hofstadter, *Anti-Intellectualism in American Life* (Knopf, 1963).
38. Meg Kinnard, "Kristi Noem Says Habeas Corpus Lets Trump 'Remove People from this Country'," Associated Press, May 21, 2025.
39. For previous Project Censored coverage of attacks on habeas corpus, see Bryce Cook, Julie Bickel, and Andrew Roth, "No Habeas Corpus for 'Any Person'," in *Censored 2008*, ed. Peter Phillips and Andrew Roth with Project Censored (Seven Stories Press, 2007), available online at projectcensored.org; and Andrew L. Roth, with Sarah Maddox and Kaitlyn Pinson, "Oiling the Dangerous Engine of Arbitrary Government: Newspaper Coverage of the Military Commissions Act," in *Censored 2009*, ed. Peter Phillips and Andrew Roth with Project Censored (Seven Stories Press, 2008), available online at projectcensored.org.
40. Joseph Gedeon, "Pentagon Launches Investigation Into Pete Hegseth's Use of Signal App After Sensitive Information Leak," *The Guardian*, April 3, 2025.
41. Collin Binkley, "How Trump Plans to Dismantle the Education Department After Supreme Court Ruling," Associated Press, July 15, 2025.
42. Leah Douglas, Ted Hesson, and Nathan Layne, "FEMA Staff Baffled After Head Said He Was Unaware of US Hurricane Season, Sources Say," Reuters, June 3, 2025; Julianne McShane, "What We Know About How FEMA Officials Are Failing Texas," *Mother Jones*, July 10, 2025.
43. Justin Baragona, "Trump Gets the Fox News Band Back Together for His Second Administration," *The Independent*, May 9, 2025.
44. Karl Marx, *The Eighteenth Brumaire of Louis Bonaparte* (International Publishers, 1963 [1852]), 15; available online at marxists.org.
45. Solnit, *No Straight Road*, 73.
46. "Journalist Casualties in the Israel-Gaza War," Committee to Protect Journalists, October 13, 2023, updated July 16, 2025.
47. See Rebecca Solnit's essay, "Despair Is a Luxury," in *No Straight Road Takes You There*.
48. Roth and Huff, "Introduction: The Pandemic and the Free Press," 6–7.
49. Bayard Rustin, letter to Kessel Johnson, March 15, 1945, in *I Must Resist: Bayard Rustin's Life in Letters*, ed. Michael G. Long (City Lights, 2012), 63.

— CHAPTER 1 —

THE TOP *CENSORED* STORIES AND MEDIA ANALYSIS OF 2024-2025

Compiled and edited by
JAYDEN LAWRENCE, ELLA MROFKA, CAITLIN SUDA,
AMY GRIM BUXBAUM, STEVE MACEK, and ANDY LEE ROTH

INTRODUCTION: DEMOCRACY UNDER THE INFLUENCE

STEVE MACEK

US democracy is in a decrepit state ... and the corporate media is an important factor ... in understanding how this sorry state came to be. The corporate media cement a system whereby the wealthy and the powerful few make the most important decisions with virtually no informed public participation. Crucial political issues are barely covered by the corporate media, or else are warped to fit the confines of elite debate, stripping ordinary citizens of the tools they need to be informed, active participants in a democracy.
—Robert W. McChesney,
Rich Media, Poor Democracy (1999)[1]

Media historian, press critic, and media reform activist Robert "Bob" McChesney—who wrote or co-authored the incisive and influential *Rich Media, Poor Democracy* (1999), *The*

Death and Life of American Journalism (2010), and *The Digital Disconnect* (2013)—died in March 2025, as work on this year's annual Project Censored book was beginning in earnest.[2]

Bob was a peerless scholar of media history and a tireless champion of the belief that, without a reliable system of public information founded on a vibrant and cantankerous press, democracy was nothing more than a "prelude to a tragedy or a farce," a phrase borrowed from founding father James Madison.[3] In one publication and media appearance after another, Bob never failed to point out all the ways that the nation's commercial, for-profit media were failing to perform the function that the authors of the US Constitution and the Bill of Rights had envisioned for them. As Bob demonstrated with relentlessness and precision, far from functioning as guardians of the public interest and protectors of our basic civil liberties, as originally intended, the media had become instead an *antidemocratic* force that most often leaves the public poorly informed, apathetic, and reconciled to an economically unjust and politically oppressive status quo.

Bob often lamented how timid, gutless, and devoid of substance corporate news had become in the twenty-first century. As he argued in the passage quoted above, by 1999, the establishment press had long since ceased to cover a whole host of "crucial political issues," or only reported on those issues in ways that "fit the confines of elite debate." In his introduction to the 2003 *Censored* yearbook, he observed, "There are no simple solutions to the problem of media. It will require study and debate and political organizing if we are to get the sort of media system befitting a self-governing people."[4] Following his own counsel, Bob helped launch a media reform organization, Free Press, that is still fighting for policies, including network neutrality, designed to create a more open, democratic, and inclusive media system in this country.

Like Bob McChesney, Project Censored believes that a democracy without adequate information about government malfeasance, political corruption, corporate misdeeds, environmental degradation, racial and gender injustice, and other pressing issues of the day is "a prelude to a tragedy or a farce." That is why we make it our mission to identify, research, and publish an annual record of the most significant news stories that corporate news organizations have either ignored or underreported.

Over the course of the past twelve months, more than 250 students from eight college and university campuses worked with faculty mentors to find, research, and synopsize news stories, covered by independent news outlets, that failed to garner the attention of the establishment press. See the following "Note on Research and Evaluation of Censored News Stories" for more on the painstaking story review process.

Among the most notable stories reported by independent news outlets and highlighted by Project Censored in its 2024–2025 inventory are an exposé about extensive Amazon and Walmart surveillance of warehouse employees, details about US Immigrations and Customs Enforcement (ICE) attempting to hire contractors to scour social media for criticism of the agency online, a report about water scarcity affecting tens of millions of Americans, an article showing that working class individuals hold only a tiny fraction of state legislative seats, and a report about potentially carcinogenic chemicals found in leading brands of condoms. These are stories that, as citizens of a democracy, we should have every opportunity to learn about. And yet they were passed over or minimized by prominent outlets like NBC News, CNN, Buzzfeed, the *Los Angeles Times,* and the *Chicago Tribune.*

Taken together, the collection of more than 1,200 stories that the Project has flagged as neglected during the past fifty years amply vindicates Bob McChesney's critique of the corporate media as one of the driving forces behind America's democratic decline. One has to believe that if these stories had gotten the attention they deserved, more citizens would be actively involved in movements aimed at addressing the injustices and problems they detail. Drawing attention, each year, to the important stories and public issues that corporate media either refuse to cover or cover only partially, can, we believe, make a small contribution to the daunting task of revitalizing our media and our democracy.

The Project's annual review of underreported stories would be impossible without the dedicated work of our expert judges, who help us assess candidate stories for their credibility, newsworthiness, and competing corporate news coverage. Their brief biographies can be found in this book's backmatter. Here, on the Project's fiftieth anniversary, we pay homage and offer special thanks to three of them, Nicholas Johnson, Jack L. Nelson, and Sheila Rabb Weidenfeld. As distinguished judges, each of them has shared their expertise every year since Project Censored's founding in 1976, a remarkable record of voluntary service.

Notes

1. Robert W. McChesney, *Rich Media, Poor Democracy: Communication Politics in Dubious Times* (University of Illinois Press, 1999), 281.
2. See, John Nichols, "Robert McChesney, the Great Champion of Journalism and Democracy, Has Died," *The Nation*, March 27, 2025. Craig Aaron, "Remembering Robert W. McChesney," Free Press, April 1, 2025.
3. Robert W. McChesney and John Nichols, *Tragedy and Farce: How the American Media Sell Wars, Spin Elections, and Destroy Democracy* (The New Press, 2006).
4. Robert W. McChesney, "The Media Crisis of Our Times," in *Censored 2003*, ed. Peter Phillips and Project Censored (Seven Stories Press, 2002), quote at 29.

NOTE ON RESEARCH AND EVALUATION OF *CENSORED* NEWS STORIES

How do we at Project Censored identify and evaluate independent news stories, and how do we know that the stories we bring forward each year are not only relevant and significant but also trustworthy? The answer is that every candidate news story undergoes rigorous review, which takes place in multiple stages during each annual cycle. Although adapted to take advantage of both the Project's expanding affiliates program and current technologies, the story vetting process remains similar to the one Project Censored founder Carl Jensen established half a century ago.

Candidate stories are initially identified by Project Censored professors and students or nominated by members of the general public, who bring them to the Project's attention. (For information on how to nominate a story, see "How to Support Project Censored" at the back of this volume.) Together, faculty and students evaluate each candidate story in terms of its importance, timeliness, quality of sources, and corporate news coverage. If it fails on any one of these criteria, the story is deemed inappropriate and excluded from further consideration.

Once Project Censored receives the candidate story, we undertake a second round of judgment, using the same criteria and updating the review to include any subsequent competing corporate coverage. We post stories that pass this round of review on the Project's website as Validated Independent News stories (VINs).

In early spring, we present all VINs in the current cycle to the faculty and students at our affiliate campuses and to our panel of expert judges, who vote to determine the year's most important but underreported independent news stories. At the same time, the judges—including media studies professors, journalists and editors, and a former commissioner of the Federal Communications Commission—offer their insights on the stories' strengths and weaknesses. (For a list of this year's judges and their brief biographies, see the acknowledgments at the back of this volume.)

Once the story list is determined, Project Censored faculty and student interns begin another, final review of each story using Nexis Uni and ProQuest databases. By the time a story appears on the pages of the *State of the Free Press* yearbook, it has undergone at least five distinct rounds of review and evaluation.

Although the stories that Project Censored highlights may be socially or politically controversial—and sometimes even psychologically challenging—we are confident that each is the result of serious journalistic effort and deserves greater public attention.

THE TOP *CENSORED* STORIES AND MEDIA ANALYSIS OF 2024–2025

ICE Solicits Social Media Surveillance Contracts to Identify Critics

Sam Biddle, "ICE Wants to Know if You're Posting Negative Things About It Online," *The Intercept,* February 11, 2025.

Brett Wilkins, "'Careful What You Post': ICE Expanding Surveillance of Social Media Critics," *Common Dreams,* February 11, 2025; republished by *Truthout,* February 12, 2025.

Ariana Baio, "ICE Plans to Monitor Social Media for Threats and Negative Comments," *The Independent,* February 12, 2025.

Student Researcher: Nicole Mendez-Villarrubia (North Central College)
Faculty Evaluator: Steve Macek (North Central College)

US Immigration and Customs Enforcement plans to hire private contractors to "monitor and locate 'negative' social media discussion" about the federal agency, according to February 2025 articles by Sam Biddle for *The Intercept* and Brett Wilkins for *Common Dreams*. Biddle and Wilkins reviewed a lengthy request for bids from contractors to monitor threats and criticism directed against ICE and its officials. The document cited increased threats to immigration and customs agents and leadership as a justification for the expanded digital surveillance.

The call for proposals specified that, for any social media content the contractors deemed hostile to ICE, the content creator's "proclivity for violence" should be assessed using "social and behavioral sciences" and "psychological profiles." Assisted by facial recognition technology, the contractors would also be expected to assemble dossiers with information about critics' offline identities, including their Social Security numbers, phone numbers, personal information, and family ties.

Immigration rights activist Cinthya Rodriguez, with the Latinx rights group Mijente, told *The Intercept*, "ICE's attempts to capture and assign a judgement to people's 'sentiment' throughout the expanse of the internet is beyond concerning… The current administration's attempt to use this technology falls within the agency's larger history of mass surveillance, which includes gathering information from personal social media accounts and retaliating against immigrant activists. ICE's attempt to have eyes and ears in as many places as we exist both online and offline should ring an alarm for all of us."

As Tim Cushing of *Techdirt* commented, the ICE bid for requests that Biddle and Wilkins obtained demonstrates the agency's intent to undermine First Amendment freedoms:

> The government shouldn't be actively monitoring social media users, much less for the stated purpose of tallying the amount of negative references caught in the dragnet. Even if all the information is 'open source' (i.e., scraped from publicly-accessible social media accounts), this is not a legitimate use of government power. It's especially questionable when the agency desiring to deploy this power can't seem to differentiate clearly between negative comments and 'threats' against ICE personnel.[1]

Biddle's article noted that ICE's procurement document was "nearly identical" to one from 2020, "which resulted in a $5.5 million contract between [ICE] and Barbaricum, a

Washington-based defense and intelligence contractor."

ICE has been scouring the internet for negative or disparaging posts about the United States by immigrants at least since the first Trump administration and this practice continued under President Biden. As detailed in a 2023 report by Joseph Cox for independent tech news site *404 Media,* ICE during this period relied on data analysis firm Giant Oak's Giant Oak Search Technology (GOST) to "scrutinize social media posts, determine if they are 'derogatory' to the U.S., and then use that information as part of immigration enforcement."[2] Information about ICE's use of GOST became available due to an ACLU Freedom of Information Act lawsuit. According to Cox, public procurement records reveal that ICE has paid Giant Oak more $10 million since 2017.

A September 5, 2023, article in the *Guardian* documents that ICE officers have also used fake social media profiles to investigate the online activities of people seeking immigration benefits or being targeted by the agency for deportation.[3] Documents secured through an open records request by the Brennan Center for Justice reveal that ICE employees are permitted to set up fake accounts to use in "masked monitoring" of social media, even though the creation of fake profiles violates the terms of service of many social media platforms, including Facebook. In 2019, the *Guardian* exposed that ICE agents had used a series of fake social media profiles linked to a fictitious university to entrap foreign students allegedly seeking to stay in the United States illegally.[4]

While independent outlets, such as *Truthout, The Independent, Techdirt,* and the *Latin Times,* have provided substantive coverage, as of February 14, 2025, corporate media have yet to report on ICE's proposed surveillance of its critics on social media.[5] *Forbes* and the *New York Times* have covered ICE's investment of millions of dollars in other digital surveillance technologies specifically targeting immigrants.[6] In March 2024, the *Wall Street Journal* reported on the broader issue of US intelligence agencies purchasing private information from data brokers.[7]

Water Scarcity Threatens 27 Million People in the United States

Carey Gillam, "Close to 30 Million Americans Face Limited Water Supplies, Government Report Finds," *The New Lede,* January 21, 2025.

Student Researcher: Ella Mrofka (North Central College)
Faculty Evaluator: Steve Macek (North Central College)

"Nearly 30 million people are living in areas of the US with limited water supplies," Carey Gillam reported for *The New Lede*, an environmental news website, in January 2025. Gillam's report was based on a US Geological Survey (USGS) study that assessed water availability in the United States from 2010 to 2020, with a special focus on water quality.

This "first-of-its-kind report," Gillam wrote, sounded the alarm on what USGS Director David Applegate characterized as "increasing challenges to this vital resource." About 27 million people live in areas where the USGS found a "high degree of local water stress." As Gillam reported, "People who are considered 'socially vulnerable' have a higher risk of experiencing limited water supplies."

Texas is a prime example of a vulnerable state because of ongoing drought, infrastructure challenges, and international water rights disputes, according to a 2025 article by *Newsweek*.[8] Other states, like Florida, are experiencing shortages of fresh water because of rising populations and overexploitation of groundwater, which accounts for 90 percent of Florida's drinking water.[9] Shortages are being exacerbated by global warming, which has led to more intense, more frequent floods and hurricanes that overwhelm wastewater systems, as well as to periods of drought. And Florida is not alone. In Virginia, large data centers use as much as five million gallons of water a day, according to a May 2024 report in *Grist*.[10] Tech companies are consuming massive amounts of groundwater in areas that are already facing water shortages due to rising temperatures. According to a January 2025 article in *Grist*, "Roughly 53 percent of the nation's aquifers are drying up as global water systems confront warming."[11]

The USGS study questioned whether there is enough clean water to sustain life in the identified shortage areas, documenting evidence of "widespread pollution" in waterways that affect human health, threaten agriculture, and reduce water availability. The report also noted the impacts of climate change—including rising water temperatures, flooding, and saltwater intrusion into freshwater supplies—on water availability and quality.[12]

The USGS found that several regions relied on water supplies that contained dangerous nitrogen and phosphorus concentrations, and about one-third of public water supplies were found to have elevated concentrations of contaminants. "Water availability is an issue everywhere in our country and beyond," Lori Sprague, then USGS national program manager for the water availability assessment, told *The New Lede*.

According to USGS data, traces of per- and polyfluoroalkyl substances (PFAS) are present in almost half of America's tap water. In a 2024 article in the *Guardian*, Tom Perkins describes PFAS as "a class of about 15,000 chemicals often used to make products resistant to water, stains and heat. They are called 'forever chemicals' because they do not naturally break down and are linked to cancer, liver problems, thyroid issues, birth defects, kidney disease, decreased immunity and other serious diseases."[13] According to a February 2025 article by Ethan Baron for the *Mercury News,* PFAS contamination of food and water is associated with multiple health risks such as developmental delays in children, low birth weight, heightened risk of certain cancers, and more.[14] Baron noted, "Almost everyone in the U.S. has PFAS in their blood, the U.S. Centers for Disease has said."

The rising number and intensity of droughts caused by climate change have left regions all over the world with ecological and economic disruptions and contributed to mass water shortages. According to Stephan Prager of *Common Dreams,* in 2024, forty-eight US states faced drought conditions.[15] This has increased food insecurity, dehydration, and disease. Dr. Mark Svoboda told *Common Dreams* that the drought affecting many parts of the country is not just a dry spell but a "slow-moving global catastrophe." A report he coauthored found that, around the world, the economic disruption caused by droughts is twice as great now as it was in 2000. One hundred percent of the state of Utah is now officially under drought conditions, while last year the state was only 25 percent dry, according to a report by the Salt Lake City Fox affiliate.[16] The dramatic increase of dry areas in Utah has forced seventeen of its twenty-nine counties to declare states of emergency.

Against this backdrop, the *Guardian* reported in May 2025 that the Trump administration had closed twenty-five scientific centers that monitor water usage and supply levels in the United States.[17] These closures undermine the USGS's ability to collect data that "plays a critical role across the economy to protect human life, protect property, maintain water supplies and help clean up chemical or oil spills." Without these crucial scientific facilities, assessments like the agency's recent study of national water availability will simply not be conducted.

Both the *New York Times* and *Washington Post* have covered the fact that large swaths of the United States are currently struggling with drought conditions.[18] But usually the corporate media's coverage discusses drought as an economic threat to agriculture and other industries rather than as a direct threat to human life. The USGS study was reported by only one national news outlet, *Newsweek*.[19] As of July 2025, no other US corporate news outlet appears to have discussed the USGS report on limited water supplies. The independent news website *Truthout* republished Carey Gillam's report for *The New Lede*.[20]

Indigenous Communities in the US Underfunded and Exploited by Federal and State Governments

Matt Krupnick, "Tribal College Campuses Are Falling Apart. The US Hasn't Fulfilled Its Promise to Fund the Schools," ProPublica, October 14, 2024.

Anna V. Smith and Maria Parazo Rose, "How States Make Money off Tribal Lands," *High Country News*, February 28, 2024; published simultaneously as "At Least 10 States Quietly Own Lands within Indian Reservations—and Profit from Them," *Grist*, February 28, 2024.

Student Researchers: Trammell Hooker, Sean Kenney, Austin Lee, Sam LoConte, and Kathleen Tonn (University of Massachusetts Amherst); Olivia Rosenberg (North Central College)

Faculty Evaluators: Allison Butler and Tyler Poisson (University of Massachusetts Amherst); Steve Macek (North Central College)

A series of articles published in 2024–25 showcases the vital role that independent investigative journalism plays in uncovering and spotlighting government mistreatment of Indigenous communities.[21] Matt Krupnick in ProPublica described the plight of tribal colleges due to longstanding federal underfunding, and a collaboration between *High Country News* and *Grist* painstakingly detailed how states profit from "trust lands" held on federal Indian reservations, generating funding for, among other things, public state universities.

In an October 14, 2024, article for ProPublica, Krupnick explained how tribal colleges across the United States face severe financial challenges due to federal underfunding, making it difficult for schools to provide adequate facilities and resources for their students. After "decades of financial neglect," tribal colleges face a "crumbling infrastructure," lacking resources to repair deteriorating foundations, roofs, electrical systems, and water pipes, not to mention the inability to invest in academic programs to meet current needs, Krupnick reported.

Congress has reneged on the commitment it made in the 1970s to fund a higher education system designed for and controlled by Indigenous communities. "These tribal colleges and universities were intended to serve students who'd been disadvantaged by the nation's history of violence and racism toward Native Americans, including efforts to eradicate their languages and cultures," explained Krupnick, who noted that these colleges often serve as the only higher education institutions in the area. They also help to preserve endangered Indigenous languages and provide access to high-speed internet, a resource that nearly 28 percent of residents of tribal lands lack, according to the US Department of Agriculture, cited in the article.

The 1970s laws authorizing the creation of the tribal colleges—now spanning thirty-seven schools across fourteen states—guaranteed funding at $8,000 annually per student affiliated with a tribe, with adjustments for inflation. But, since 2010, "per-student funding has been as low as $5,235 and sits at just under $8,700 today," according to the American Indian Higher Education Consortium, which is cited in the article. "Had Congress delivered what's required by statute, tribal colleges and universities would receive about $40,000 per student today."

Remarkably, Krupnick reported that "the federal Bureau of Indian Education, tasked with requesting funding for the institutions, has never asked lawmakers to fully fund the colleges at levels called for in the law," despite a 2003 report from the US Commission on Civil Rights calling tribal colleges the "most poorly funded institutions of higher education in the country."

Since his original reporting, things have gotten worse. In March 2025, Krupnick reported in ProPublica that the Trump administration suspended at least $7 million in federal grants to tribal colleges, affecting both student scholarships and food and agricultural research.[22]

At the same time as tribal colleges are woefully underfunded, federal policy allows state governments to profit from tribal "trust lands" which support, among other things, state land grant universities.[23]

A partnership between the independent outlets *High Country News* and *Grist* resulted in a report, jointly published on February 28, 2024, detailing how 1.6 million acres of "trust lands" managed by state agencies "generate millions of dollars for public schools, universities, penitentiaries, hospitals and other state institutions, typically through grazing, logging, mining and oil and gas production."

Trust lands originated during the late nineteenth and early twentieth centuries when the federal government seized ninety million acres of reservation land from the tribes, labeling it as "surplus," and gave it to non-Native owners and states entering the union. The program dismantled tribal power and opened tribal lands and natural resources to non-Native citizens.

Consequently, land on federal Indian reservations intended for "the use and governance of Indigenous nations and their citizens" generates state revenues that "support non-Indigenous institutions and offset state taxpayer dollars for non-Indigenous people," Smith and Rose reported.

Grist conducted a meticulous data investigation of disparate sets of records from federal, state, and tribal sources, which the Global Investigative Journalism Network (GIJN) highlighted in November 2024.[24] Until this investigation, the extent of state holdings and uses of trust land had been "almost completely unknown," according to Smith and Rose. Their analysis revealed a combined 1.6 million acres of state trust lands that fall within the borders of eighty-three federal Indian reservations in ten states. Rob Williams, a University of Arizona law professor and citizen of the Lumbee Tribe of North Carolina, told *High Country News* that the findings have wide-reaching implications for a host of issues involving tribal sovereignty, from the handling of crimes to tribal nations' ability to confront climate change.

The *High Country News* and *Grist* reports cited the case of the Confederated Salish and Kootenai Tribes in Montana, which "may have created a model for how tribes can negotiate for large-scale transfers of land back to tribal ownership." A 2020 water-rights settlement, enacted by Congress, facilitated the transfer of nearly thirty thousand acres of Montana state trust land back to the confederated tribes, Smith and Rose reported.

However, such efforts are confounded by a lack of transparency about trust lands. As explained in the GIJN report, "Many states don't make lease information publicly available, leaving reporters and researchers with an incomplete picture of the true extent of trust lands within reservations."

To overcome these limitations, *Grist* built a database of state trust land lessees, searchable by Native American reservation, and, "has been sharing the data it collects with newsrooms before publication, holding training sessions to show reporters how to use the information, and partnering with news organizations," GIJN reported.[25] *Grist*'s editor-at-large Tristan Ahtone told GIJN that its data was used by the *Flatwater Free Press* to do a local story identifying who had leased trust lands on the Nebraska reservation of the Santee Sioux, for example.[26]

Corporate news media have largely ignored these issues. One exception is a March 9, 2025, *New York Times* report about layoffs dictated by Trump's Department of Government Efficiency.[27] The *Times* reported that DOGE cuts included nearly one-fourth of the staff of the only two federally run tribal colleges in the country, but neglected to contextualize those cuts amidst the already anemic funding described in ProPublica; the *Washington Post* ran a similar story.[28]

Several independent news outlets have covered states' exploitation of Indigenous "trust lands," including *The Daily Yonder* and the *Hechinger Report*, which republished some of the *Grist/High Country News* and ProPublica reports. Oregon Public Broadcasting featured an interview with Anna V. Smith of *High Country News*.[29] Many of the related stories are catalogued on *Grist*'s comprehensive site from its investigation.[30]

Meta Undertakes "Sweeping Crackdown" of Facebook and Instagram Posts at Israel's Request

Waqas Ahmed, Nicholas Rodelo, Ryan Grim, and Murtaza Hussain, "Leaked Data Reveals Massive Israeli Campaign to Remove Pro-Palestine Posts on Facebook and Instagram," *Drop Site News*, April 11, 2025.

Student Researcher: Vivian Rose (Ithaca College)
Faculty Evaluator: Mickey Huff (Ithaca College)

Since October 7, 2023, the multinational tech company Meta, which owns Facebook and Instagram, has acted on 94 percent of the Israeli government's requests to take down posts on Facebook and Instagram that are "critical of Israel—or even vaguely supportive of Palestinians," *Drop Site News* reported in April 2025. *Drop Site News* characterized Meta's response to the Israeli government's takedown request campaign as "the largest mass censorship operation in modern history."

The *Drop Site News* report was based on internal company data compiled and provided by whistleblowers from Meta. *Drop Site News* reported that "multiple independent sources inside Meta confirmed the authenticity of the information provided by the whistleblowers." As *Drop Site News* explained, takedown requests "allow individuals, organizations, and government officials to request the removal of content that allegedly violates Meta's policies."

A significant majority of Israel's requests, *Drop Site News* reported, "fall under Meta's 'terrorism' or 'violence and incitement' categories," but *Drop Site News* also noted that every one of Israel's takedown requests since October 7, 2023, "contain the exact same complaint text, according to the leaked information, regardless of the substance of the underlying content being challenged."

Based on Meta's internal data, *Drop Site News* found that Israel's takedown requests "have overwhelmingly targeted users from Arab and Muslim-majority nations," but the Israeli government's takedown campaign is global in scope, resulting in censorship of posts from Facebook and Instagram users in more than sixty different countries. Among the top countries affected, 21 percent of targeted posts originated from Egypt, nearly 17 percent originated from Jordan, and nearly 16 percent originated from Palestine.

The leaked data show Meta acted promptly in response to the Israeli government's takedown requests. Indeed, Meta removed more than ninety thousand posts flagged by the Israeli government in an average of thirty seconds. Meta also significantly expanded the scope of automated takedowns since October 7, 2023, resulting in what *Drop Site News* reported as "an estimated 38.8 million additional posts being 'actioned upon' across Facebook and Instagram since late 2023. 'Actioned upon' in Facebook terms means that a post was either removed, banned, or suppressed."

"Israel's censorship project will echo well into the future," *Drop Site News* reported, based on insiders' comments, because "the AI program Meta is currently training how to moderate content will base future decisions on the successful takedown of content critical of Israel's genocide."

The Council on American-Islamic Relations condemned Meta's actions, stating, "Meta must stop censoring criticism of the Israeli government under the guise of combating antisemitism, and Meta must stop training artificial intelligence tools to do so."[31]

A May 2025 report by Sharon Zhang for *Truthout* exposed US government hypocrisy in criticizing other nations for "social media censorship" while actively working to silence critics of Israel.[32] As Zhang reported, in a press statement on May 28, 2025, Secretary of State Marco Rubio said, "It is unacceptable for foreign officials to issue or threaten arrest warrants on US citizens or US residents for social media posts on American platforms while physically present on US soil." Nevertheless, Zhang wrote, Rubio and the US government are colluding with Israel to "erode free speech rights of Americans who criticize Israel and its genocide in Gaza."

Beyond pressuring social media platforms to censor content critical of Israel's war in Gaza, the Israeli government has also taken steps to control the sort of information being circulated about its other wars. In June 2025, the Committee to Protect Journalists reported that a new directive from Israel's government ordered international media not to broadcast from combat zones or missile impact areas in Israel without prior approval from its military censor.[33] "Silencing the press deprives the world of a clear, unfiltered view of the reality unfolding in the region," the CPJ's regional director Sara Qudah stated.

The *Drop Site News* article on Meta's compliance with

Israeli censorship requests has been republished by independent outlets, including *ZNetwork* and Jewish Voice for Labour, but despite its alarming revelations, this story does not appear to have been picked up by any major US newspapers or broadcast news outlets as of July 2025.[34] Nor does it appear that Meta will end its obedience to Israel's wishes anytime soon. This threat to freedom of information will likely remain unaddressed as long as the United States remains allied with Israel.

Big Tech Sows Policy Chaos to Undermine Data Privacy Protections

Jake Snow, "Big Tech Is Trying to Burn Privacy to the Ground—and They're Using Big Tobacco's Strategy to Do It," *Tech Policy Press*, October 9, 2024, and ACLU of Northern California, October 9, 2024.

Student Researchers: Marcelo Lugo (Diablo Valley College) and Vivian Rose (Ithaca College)

Faculty Evaluators: Nolan Higdon (Diablo Valley College) and Mickey Huff (Ithaca College)

Big Tech companies are actively attempting to undermine legislation that protects consumer data privacy, Jake Snow reported in an article published by *Tech Policy Press* and the ACLU of Northern California in October 2024. "The biggest names in technology are trying to use their might to force Congress to override crucial state-level privacy laws that have protected people for years," Snow wrote, emphasizing that some of the most powerful corporations in the world are engaged in a coordinated campaign to shift regulatory power away from states and into the hands of federal lawmakers where corporate lobbying is more influential and effective.

Describing *preemption*—a legal doctrine in which a higher level of government overrides the powers of a lower level of government—as "the tech industry's holy grail," Snow outlined a calculated, three-step process that the tech industry is using to weaken or nullify state and local privacy protections. The aim is to create a single, weaker federal standard that blocks states from enacting or enforcing stronger protections. In doing so, Big Tech is reportedly reviving strategies originally developed by Big Tobacco thirty years ago to evade accountability and regulation. "Big Tech is pulling straight from the toxic strategy that Big Tobacco used in the 1990s," Snow reported, referring to a well-documented corporate playbook that used aggressive lobbying, deceptive legislation, and legal preemption to undermine public health efforts.

Big Tech is responding to a growing public relations crisis surrounding data privacy and surveillance capitalism with what Snow described as a multi-staged strategy. It begins with first introducing a "flood of deceptive bills" at the state level in the form of legislation that appears to offer privacy protections but is backed by industry and filled with loopholes. These bills are designed to crowd out genuine efforts to protect consumer rights. The tech industry then criticizes the resulting landscape as a confusing "patchwork" of state laws, arguing that inconsistent regulations make compliance difficult and innovation burdensome. This narrative lays the groundwork for passage of a federal preemption law, which would override these state-level regulations with a single federal standard, effectively curbing states' ability to pass any new, stronger data privacy legislation in the future.

Snow detailed each of these three steps, including how, since 2021, Big Tech companies have spent millions of dollars lobbying to "replace real privacy laws with fake industry alternatives"—bills that offer the appearance of reform while entrenching corporate interests. Although "many federal lawmakers want to do the right thing and pass long overdue protections governing privacy, artificial intelligence, and civil rights," Snow warned that federal preemption, as currently proposed, "plays right into the hands of Big Tech." Rather than strengthening protections, it risks enshrining a lower standard that serves corporate interests at the expense of consumer rights.

The One Big Beautiful Bill Act—Donald Trump's controversial 2025 omnibus tax and spending bill—was the focus of intense news coverage in May and June 2025. The version of the Big Beautiful Bill that passed the House included a provision shielding tech companies for ten years from being sued in state courts for negligence, privacy violations, or misuse of artificial intelligence. The House bill, in other words, attempted to use federal law to impede states from protecting people's data privacy. In a May 2025 *Tech Policy Press* article, David Brody, a legal expert specializing in civil rights and technology, commented that, if the House version of bill became law, "the enforcement of any state civil law regarding the use of a computer—even laws of general applicability—will be in jeopardy."[35]

Fortunately, the Senate version of the bill removed the provision protecting AI from state-level regulation, as *The Hill* reported.[36] The amendment was adopted 99–1 and the final version of the Big Beautiful Bill that President Trump signed into law on July 4, 2025, did not include the AI regulation moratorium favored by Silicon Valley.

Likely, Big Tech will now redouble its efforts in Congress to pass legislation that preempts state-level privacy laws. The pro-business think tank ALFA Institute, founded by former Republican House Speaker Kevin McCarthy, hinted in a July 1, 2025, blog post that the defeat of the AI regulation moratorium was only temporary. Congress, ALFA wrote, "continues to treat AI like something that can be safely bracketed into old models and frameworks. That instinct—to sideline, defer, delay—doesn't just waste time. It opens the door for a fragmented, 50–

state patchwork that undermines any semblance of a national strategy." To change that, ALFA pledged to work to "land the pro-AI argument" and "change the narrative."[37]

One alternative approach to regulating privacy online, the American Privacy Rights Act, is bipartisan legislation proposed by Sen. Maria Cantwell (D-WA) and Rep. Cathy McMorris Rodgers (R-WA) that would give consumers more control over their data. However, according to the *Washington Post*, House lawmakers debated this proposal, and eventually decided to scrap its civil rights protections.[38] The *Post* quoted Rep. Yvette D. Clarke (D-NY), who expressed disappointment in the removal of civil rights protections and algorithmic accountability provisions, and affirmed that "privacy rights are civil rights."

The tech industry's efforts to override state-level regulations with a single, weaker federal standard have received only partial corporate news coverage. In October 2024, for example, a *New York Times* article outlined the steps that the tech lobbying group NetChoice has undertaken to redefine the interpretation of the First Amendment in ways that could be used to stall or strike down legislation aimed at regulating the tech industry.[39] "The group, which has grown significantly in power and influence over the last decade, is the driving force behind lawsuits that have derailed several state laws regulating the tech industry, including six on child safety," the *Times* reported, underscoring NetChoice's central role in legal efforts to dismantle regulation under the guise of protecting free speech.

An April 2024 *Time* magazine report also noted that Big Tech's lobbying expenditures nearly tripled between 2022 and 2023, attributing much of that increase to efforts focused on limiting regulation of artificial intelligence and digital surveillance. Other outlets, including *Axios* and *Politico*, have covered the surge in AI-related lobbying as well.[40] However, none of this reporting has fully addressed the scale and coordinated effort detailed in Snow's report, nor has it drawn attention to the clear historical parallels between current Big Tech strategies and the precedent set by Big Tobacco in its attempts to delay and dilute public health regulations.

Amazon and Walmart Use Hostile Surveillance Technology Against Warehouse Employees

Alex N. Press, "Big Brother Is Watching Amazon and Walmart Workers," *Jacobin*, April 11, 2024.

Student Researcher: Cam Lippincott (UC Berkeley)
Faculty Evaluator: Andy Lee Roth (Project Censored)

An April 2024 report from Oxfam America, "At Work and Under Watch," detailed how Amazon and Walmart utilize workplace surveillance technology to intimidate warehouse workers and increase their productivity—at the expense of employees' physical and mental health, Alex N. Press reported for *Jacobin*.[41]

Amazon and Walmart, among the largest private employers in the United States, have pioneered the use of surveillance technology in their warehouses. While Amazon is known for its relentless focus on worker efficiency, its methods have become increasingly controversial, particularly as labor groups criticize the company's treatment of warehouse employees. Walmart has similarly extended its aggressive surveillance methods into its warehouses. The Oxfam report documents similar patterns of abuse and exploitation in both companies' warehouses.

In 2018, Walmart patented surveillance technology designed for management to eavesdrop on workers, track customer interactions, and oversee all employee movements. Amazon uses similar tracking methods, including a rating system that scores worker productivity, providing real-time feedback on individual workers' speed and efficiency.

A Walmart warehouse worker in California told Oxfam that the company uses the data it collects from surveillance to blame workers for on-site injuries: "Management would not negotiate this with you at all. You would be penalized for it because they would deem that you were working unsafe and ignore all the other possible reasons for why you got injured."

Seventy-two percent of Amazon and 67 percent of Walmart workers said that how fast they work is measured nearly all the time, compared to 58 percent of workers in other warehouse industries. Nearly half of the women employed at both companies said that they are not able to take enough breaks, and more than half of all workers at both companies said they are not given adequate time to use the bathroom. One frightening statistic: 91 percent of Walmart employees reported suffering from dehydration on the job. The scope of surveillance makes it unlikely that Amazon and Walmart managers were unaware of these issues.

One might argue that unionizing could help workers resist surveillance, but in February 2025, Amazon employees in Garner, North Carolina, voted against unionizing 2,447 to 829.[42] Amazon said in a statement that the company was "glad" workers "chose to keep a direct relationship with Amazon." However, union organizers believe the vote was the result of Amazon's nonstop intimidation of its employees.

Union organizers are not wrong: According to a March 2025 report in *The American Prospect*, Amazon has been implementing additional technologies to discipline and demobilize employees.[43] The company manipulated workplace devices to send workers anti-union messages and to ask questions that employees say were intended to assess their support for the union. Amazon also monitored the social media activity of its employees—including Facebook groups, many of which were private, and subreddits—to investigate posts that contained complaints from warehouse workers or plans for strikes and protests.

There has been some coverage of these issues by independent and specialist news outlets. *The Irish Star* published a piece that highlighted some of the more sensational findings of Oxfam's report, such as the fact that some Amazon and Walmart warehouse workers are so worried about being monitored that they skip bathroom breaks.[44] Business news site *Business Insider* also ran a story in April 2024 summarizing the main findings of the Oxfam report (in its "Retail" section).[45] But otherwise there has been zero corporate media coverage of Amazon and Walmart's surveillance and mistreatment of warehouse employees or of Oxfam's "At Work and Under Watch" report.

Private Companies Reap More Than $100 Million to Sweep Homeless Camps in California

Brian Barth, "Revealed: How Companies Made $100M Clearing California Homeless Camps," *The Guardian* and *Type Investigations*, April 16, 2024.

Student Researcher: Cam Lippincott (UC Berkeley)
Faculty Evaluator: Andy Lee Roth (Project Censored)

Cities across California, including San Jose and Los Angeles, have paid private contractors millions of dollars to sweep homeless encampments, Brian Barth reported in an article co-published in April 2024 by *The Guardian* and *Type Investigations*. Local governments have increasingly sought the services of private contractors to deal with homelessness as the state has approved more than $700 million to dismantle encampments housing its burgeoning homeless population of 123,000 people, Barth reported. Tucker, a construction company based in San Jose that pioneered the sweeping industry, has expanded massively since it first began sweeping San Jose's largest camps in 2021. As of April 2024, Barth reported, Tucker had contracts with "roughly a dozen municipalities and public agencies" across the Silicon Valley for its controversial encampment sweeping services.

The sweeping of homeless encampments has become more common since the Supreme Court ruled in *City of Grants Pass V. Johnson* that punishing homeless people for sleeping outside does not count as cruel or unusual punishment.[46]

That case addressed homelessness in Grants Pass, Oregon, where the number of unhoused people in 2018 exceeded available shelter space, but the city's municipal code denied people the right to sleep outdoors. Advocates for unhoused people argued that the city's provisions violated the Eighth Amendment's prohibition on cruel or unusual punishment. The case was eventually appealed to the Supreme Court and, in an April 24, 2024, decision of 6–3, the Court's majority ruled that the Eighth Amendment did not apply.

Before the ruling in *Grants Pass V. Johnson*, crews removing homeless encampments were required to preserve mattresses, couches, and shacks, but after it, police were allowed to confiscate any property belonging to people found sleeping on the streets. Since the Supreme Court's ruling, new bans subject unhoused residents to more severe consequences than ever before, including loss of property, fines, and even jail time.

In San Francisco, in July 2024, an unannounced sweep, assisted by police, fire, emergency management and public works staffers, "cleared out a string of homeless encampments under the central freeway in less than two hours," the *San Francisco Standard* reported.[47] Gabriella Aguirre, a homeless woman and restaurant dishwasher who had her belongings swept, told

The Guardian, which also covered the sweep, "You feel devastated, you feel in a rush, you feel like your whole world is coming to an end." Aguirre alleges that Tucker, the company conducting the sweep, violated city rules by taking the keys to her car and her daughter's car.

Companies across California, including mid-size construction companies and environmental service firms that specialize in cleaning hazardous waste, have been eyeing lucrative contracts from cities to demolish and remove homeless encampments. Tucker has received more than $10 million in contracts with the City of San Jose, during the past decade, including federal funds earmarked to address the COVID-19 pandemic. Another company, Marinship, received $3.4 million to destroy a homeless encampment with around two hundred residents. Santa Clara, a suburb of San Jose, signed a $1 million contract with Tucker to remove its encampments in 2019, despite having only 264 unhoused residents.

The cost of the sweeps does not end with cities' payments to private companies, because police and city employees must be present during them. The police presence at one sweep in Los Angeles cost around $2 million, according to Barth's reporting.

A list of cities with camping bans shows that California, with 30 percent of the homeless population in the United States, has enacted more than any other state in the country, Robbie Sequeira reported for *Stateline*.[48] These bans explicitly criminalize homelessness, despite the fact that "there doesn't seem to be much interest … from the district attorney's office or the court, in taking these cases to trial."[49]

Despite the fact that "experts agree clearing or 'sweeping' encampments alone can't end homelessness," the Supreme Court's ruling in *City of Grants Pass V. Johnson* has opened the floodgates for more sweeps in cities across the United States.[50] Since that decision, "roughly 150 cities in 32 states have passed or strengthened such ordinances," *Stateline* reported, noting that at least forty additional local bans were pending, according to data from the National Homelessness Law Center.[51] "The idea that the problem is such a small number of people …

and no matter how much we spend on it, we're not spending enough to actually fix it, is very frustrating," Harvey Ward, the mayor of Gainesville, Florida, told *Stateline*.[52]

While the national corporate media have not shied away from covering the nationwide displacement of homeless people, there has been virtually no coverage of companies profiteering from the homeless crisis in California or other states since Brian Barth's investigation for *The Guardian* and *Type Investigations* was published.

Underreported, Often Deadly Abuses of Police Authority

Sharon Zhang, "Report: US Police Killed Someone Every 6.5 Hours on Average in 2024," *Truthout*, February 27, 2025.

Pascal Sabino, "Chicago Police Made Nearly 200,000 Secret Traffic Stops Last Year," *Bolts* and *Injustice Watch*, August 21, 2024.

Student Researchers: Vivian Rose (Ithaca College) and Jaden Balonkita, Michael Diaz, River Lazzeretti, Alexis Reyes, and Jasmine Hernandez (California State University, Northridge)

Faculty Evaluators: Mickey Huff (Ithaca College) and Nolan Higdon (California State University, Northridge)

US police killed an average of nearly four people each day in 2024.[53] "According to a report by Mapping Police Violence, police killed at least 1,365 people in 2024, making it the deadliest year since the group began recording such data in 2013," Sharon Zhang wrote in a February 2025 *Truthout* article.

Black and Indigenous people were "disproportionately targeted" by police violence, Zhang reported. "In 2024, Black people in the U.S. were 2.9x more likely than White people to be killed by police," with even greater disproportions for Native Hawaiians and Pacific Islanders (7.6x) and American Indians and Alaska Natives (3.1x) compared to White people, according to the Mapping Police Violence report.[54]

Mapping Police Violence found only ten days in 2024 "when police did not kill anyone in the U.S." Nearly 65 percent of the documented killings were "in response to a 911 call," the organization found. As Zhang's *Truthout* article noted, "The majority of killings happened when police were responding to a non-violent offense."

In a previous report, Mapping Police Violence noted that out of at least 1,260 instances when police killed people in 2024, officers were only charged with crimes in nine cases.[55]

The 2024 figures contribute to a long-term pattern. Zhang quoted from a *Washington Post* database that police in the United States have shot and killed at least 10,429 people from 2015 to 2024.[56] The *Washington Post* database indicates that as of January 1, 2025, the newspaper would "no longer track police shootings." Zhang's *Truthout* report put this change of policy in context, noting that Jeff Bezos, the *Post*'s billionaire owner "has exerted an increasingly right-wing influence on the paper."

Mapping Police Violence was created by Samuel Sinyangwe, who is also the founder of Campaign Zero, an organization that advocates for a society not reliant on policing. Sinyangwe's site has gone relatively under-covered by the establishment press, with two notable exceptions. In February 2025, the *USA Today* used data from Mapping Police Violence for a report on demographic and geographic patterns in police killings in the United States.[57] And, in May 2025, the *New York Times* sourced data from Mapping Police Violence to report that "police killings keep rising, not falling," since the murder of George Floyd by a Minneapolis police officer in 2020.[58]

Routine police traffic stops often turn deadly, especially for people of color, making documentation of those stops a fundamental concern. In 2023, the Chicago Police Department (CPD) made two hundred thousand undocumented traffic stops, according to an August 2024 investigation by *Bolts* and *Injustice Watch*. Their joint investigation examined police radio dispatch data to identify two hundred thousand stops that violated a 2003 Illinois state law requiring law enforcement agencies to report specific details of every traffic stop to the state Department of Transportation.

"The significant number of undocumented traffic stops threatens to undermine any reform efforts and obscures the true impact of the police encounters from oversight groups, preventing them from fully understanding which drivers are stopped, and where in the city they are concentrated," journalist Pascal Sabino explained.

CPD traffic stops, particularly in predominantly Black neighborhoods, have "come under increased scrutiny, following the March [2024] killing of Dexter Reed, who was shot 13 times by five plainclothes officers just seconds after being pulled over for a seatbelt violation," Sabino reported.

A previous report by Sabino noted that undocumented traffic stops amounted to a new form of "stop-and-frisk," a controversial practice that allows police to search persons, places, and objects without making an arrest.[59] Since 2014, following the "botched investigation and coverup" of the murder of teenager Laquan McDonald by a Chicago police officer, CPD had officially moved away from the use of stop-and-frisk.

That reform was partly spurred by a 2015 investigation by the American Civil Liberties Union of Illinois, which found CPD's use of stop-and-frisk "regularly targeted Black Chicagoans and violated their Fourth Amendment rights," Sabino reported.[60] Now, Chicago police "fish for guns and evidence of other crimes … by stopping cars rather than pedestrians."

The findings of the investigation by *Bolts* and *Injustice Watch* recast the June 2024 assertion by Chicago Police Superintendent Larry Snelling that traffic stops were down by eighty-seven thousand, compared to the previous year. "Behind that reduction is a pattern of thousands of unreported police encounters, which accounted for one-third of all traffic stops over the first seven months of Snelling's tenure," Sabino noted.

Major national newspapers, including the *New York Times*, have covered how police stops for routine traffic violations often turn deadly for motorists but, as of November 2024, no major news outlet appear to have addressed the finding of the joint *Bolts* and *Injustice Watch* investigation on the extraordinary number of illegal, undocumented traffic stops by Chicago police.[61]

Antarctic Ice Sheets Approaching Tipping Point, Studies Find

Robert Hunziker, "Antarctic Ice Melt—Sobering New Studies," *CounterPunch*, June 28, 2024.

Matthew Rozsa, "Antarctica's Melting Ice Is Reaching a 'Tipping Point' Due to Climate Change, Study Finds," *Salon*, June 27, 2024.

Student Researcher: Elena Bantista (North Central College)
Faculty Evaluator: Steve Macek (North Central College)

Increases in ocean temperature could lead to a tipping point in the melting of Antarctic marine ice sheets, potentially triggering "runaway melting" according to a June 2024 article published in the journal *Nature Geoscience*.[62] In June 2024,

Robert Hunziker in *CounterPunch* and Matthew Rozsa in *Salon* each reported on this research and other scientific studies of potential "tipping points" in Antarctic ice melt. "Scientists have debated whether a 'tipping point' exists for this ice sheet, or a moment when the effects of this melting would be suddenly both irreversible and catastrophic," according to Rozsa.[63]

Hunziker and Rozsa each highlighted the research by Alexander T. Bradley of the British Antarctic Survey and Ian J. Hewitt, an applied mathematician at the University of Oxford, published in *Nature Geoscience* in June 2024. Drawing from recent evidence documenting that "relatively warm ocean water can intrude long distances" beneath the ice sheet and reach the grounding line—where the ice rises from the seabed and starts to float—Bradley and Hewitt warned that such "long intrusions have dramatic consequences for sea-level-rise contributions from ice sheets." They proposed a new model that accounts for these effects, which had not been previously factored into scientific modeling of ice-sheet melting.

As Rozsa explained in *Salon*,

> When warm water moves under a grounding line, the ice melts at an accelerated pace and could pass a threshold where the body's ultimate collapse is inevitable. While this process occurs, sea levels will rise at a much faster rate than currently predicted, resulting in millions of people from coastal communities being displaced over the upcoming decades and centuries.

This and other new studies show that "small increases in ocean temperature can have [a] big impact on melting," causing the ice sheet to melt much more rapidly than forecast, according to Hunziker, who noted that ocean temperatures have been setting new temperature records for over a year.[64] Yet existing scientific models have failed to adequately account for the impact of intrusion and may underestimate the pace of sea level rise. "These new facts raise very serious concerns about all projections of sea level rise," wrote Hunziker.

Evidence from the past may prove to be illustrative. In *CounterPunch*, Hunziker summarized the findings of another study published in *Nature Geoscience*.[65] In that February 2024 study, researchers examined a 2,000-foot-long ice core that is "the first paleoclimatic proof that the Antarctic ice sheet can melt very fast in a relatively short period of time," Hunziker reported. These researchers found that eight thousand years ago, part of the ice sheet melted by 450 meters in approximately two hundred years. A repeat of that sort of "cascading meltdown" would have a dramatic impact on sea levels, Hunziker reported. Sea levels would begin to rise significantly in a matter of decades, rather than centuries, posing severe challenges for coastal cities, according to experts.

In *Salon*, Rozsa pointed to current evidence that this threat may be imminent. He cited a May 2024 study published in the journal *PNAS* which predicted that "Antarctica's so-called 'Doomsday Glacier' is nearing collapse, as revealed by high-resolution satellite radar data that shows Thwaites [Glacier] is being flooded with warm sea water."[66] In a May 2024 article in *Salon*, Rozsa explained that "Antarctica's Thwaites Glacier is also known as the 'Doomsday Glacier' because it could greatly contribute to sea level rise if it collapses. And new evidence suggests that's exactly what's happening."[67]

To date, US corporate media have not covered these recent findings, especially Bradley and Hewitt's model of grounding-zone melting of ice sheets. Independent outlets, including *Salon* and *CounterPunch*, have provided more substantial coverage of this study. Jessica Corbett of *Common Dreams* reported in February 2024 on the study that found evidence of rapid ice loss in the past, which CNN, the science news magazine *Eos*, and the environmental news site Earth.com also covered.[68]

Working Class Severely Underrepresented in State Legislatures

Robbie Sequeira, "Working-Class People Rarely Have a Seat 'At the Legislative Table' in State Capitols," *Stateline*, March 15, 2024.

Student Researcher: Nicole Mendez-Villarrubia (North Central College)
Faculty Evaluator: Steve Macek (North Central College)

Only 1.6 percent of state lawmakers in the United States are considered "working class," compared to 50 percent of all participants in the American labor force, according to the 2024 results of a biennial study by Duke University and Loyola University Chicago researchers. Per a March 15, 2024, *Stateline* article by Robbie Sequeira, "Just 116 of the nearly 7,400 state legislators in the United States come from working-class backgrounds."

The authors of the study, political scientists Nicholas Carnes and Eric Hansen, defined the working class as those who have currently or last worked in manual labor, the service industry, clerical, or labor union jobs. By that definition, only about 2 percent of Democrat state legislators and 1 percent of Republican state legislators qualified as working class. The results also showed that ten states—Arkansas, Louisiana, Mississippi, North Carolina, Oregon, South Carolina, Tennessee, Texas, Utah, and Virginia—have "no working-class state lawmakers."

The *Stateline* article was republished by *Governing* and *Maryland Matters*, the latter of which added the perspective of the state's two working-class legislators.[69] According to that April 1, 2024, piece by Josh Kurtz, Maryland's state senators included a Democrat and a Republican who fit the definition of working class. *The Carolina Journal* reported on the study in February 2024, highlighting that in North Carolina, "the base salary of about $14,000 is nearly the lowest among all states."[70] Low salaries for working-class jobs are one reason why members of the working class rarely run for office. Andrew Taylor, a political science professor at North Carolina State University, told the *Carolina Journal*, "The only people who can really serve are those who can offload their working obligations to others—generally small business owners—or are retired." In a March 2024 article published by the *Utah News Dispatch*, Nicholas Carnes, one of the original study's authors, explained that the barriers to running for office are "even more burdensome when you're living paycheck to paycheck."[71]

Some members of the Utah legislature, which includes legislators who are police officers or teachers, objected to the Duke study's claim that none of its members are working class, the *Utah News Dispatch* reported. State Sen. Kathleen Riebe, for example, claimed that "working class" should be defined as someone who depends on their paycheck month to month or relies on a job to "make ends meet." Yet even with this more expansive definition, the working class is likely still severely underrepresented in state legislatures. As Dustin Guastella and Bhaskar Sunkara contended in a 2024 *Guardian* op-ed about the need for more working-class candidates for political office at all levels of government, "Even if we broaden out the category to professionals like teachers and nurses, the number is still under 6%."[72]

Of course, the problem of working-class underrepresentation in political office is hardly confined to state legislatures. In 2020, OpenSecrets, using data from lawmakers' legally-required personal financial disclosure states, found that the majority of the members of the 116th Congress were millionaires.[73] The nonprofit research group concluded that the ten richest members of Congress that year each had estimated fortunes in excess of $30 million. Meanwhile, Donald Trump has appointed so many billionaires to senior positions in his second cabinet that their estimated combined wealth, $450 billion, is greater than the gross domestic product of 175 different countries.[74]

The absence of working class elected officials means that all too often working-class perspectives on social and economic issues are missing from public policy debates. As Guastella and Sunkara put it in their *Guardian* op-ed, "To be working class, and to proudly identify as such, is not just to show voters that you 'feel their pain,' as Bill Clinton once dramatized, but that you actually understand the world from their position."

To counter the lack of working class voices in government, Dan Osborn—a pipe-fitter and union leader who in 2024 ran a surprisingly strong race for a US Senate seat in typically conservative Nebraska—recently started a political action committee called the Working Class Heroes Fund. The PAC aims to organize working-class voters, fund working-class candidates, and is "dedicated to uniting and mobilizing working people across party lines to give the working class a seat at the table."[75]

As of June 2025, there has been no national corporate news coverage of the Carnes and Hansen study on the class background of state legislators. However, its findings and the issue of working-class representation in politics have occasionally been mentioned in opinion pieces published in national newspapers. On April 24, 2024, the *Washington Post* published an op-ed by Dustin Guastella of the Center for Working-Class Politics that critiqued the dramatic lack of working-class people as candidates or holders of political office.[76] Additionally, opinion columnist Jamelle Bouie discussed the results of the biennial study in an April 30, 2024, *New York Times* column about how the dominance of upper-class legislators distorts public policy.[77]

UN Cybercrime Treaty Supported by Autocrats Raises Human Rights Concerns

Allie Funk and Yana Gorokhovskaia, "Authoritarians Are Hijacking Global Tech Cooperation to Undermine Human Rights," Freedom House, December 12, 2024.

Katitza Rodriguez, "The UN Cybercrime Convention: Analyzing the Risks to Human Rights and Global Privacy," *Just Security*, August 27, 2024.

Kate Graham-Shaw, "New U.N. Cybercrime Treaty Could Threaten Human Rights," *Scientific American*, August 9, 2024.

Jake Johnson, "Experts Warn Cybercrime Treaty Gives Governments New Powers to Crush Dissent," *Common Dreams*, December 30, 2024.

Alexa Zamora, "How the UN Cybercrime Convention 2023 Can Pose a Threat to Human Rights Defenders and Exiled Journalists," *Global Voices*, December 30, 2024.

Student Researcher: Abigail Black (North Central College)
Faculty Evaluator: Steve Macek (North Central College)

On December 24, 2024, the United Nations adopted the United Nations Convention against Cybercrime, which aims to "prevent and combat" cybercrime and "strengthen international cooperation in sharing electronic evidence for serious crimes."[78] Numerous human rights and independent news organizations noted that the international treaty raised serious human rights concerns.

On December 12, Freedom House published a preliminary analysis of the treaty, which it identified as representative of "a much larger trend to advance authoritarian norms" in international forums. Warning that "authoritarians" were "hijacking global tech cooperation to undermine human rights," Freedom House noted that the new treaty could be used to persecute dissidents and journalists and would be likely to "turbocharge transnational repression." Activists and experts expressed concern over the absence of core human rights protections, especially considering the support this treaty received from autocratic and oppressive governments.

"The U.N. cybercrime convention is a blank check for surveillance abuses," Katitza Rodriguez, the policy director for global privacy at the Electronic Frontier Foundation, told *Scientific American*. "It can and will be wielded as a tool for systemic rights violations," Rodriguez warned.

As Freedom House explained, the new understanding of cybercrime includes "any 'crime' committed using information and communications technology," a conception of cybercrime that would provide "legal cover for states to broadly criminalize the online activities of human rights defenders, journalists, researchers, and others in civil society."

Rodriguez's report for *Just Security* identified missing safeguards, including the treaty's weakening of the principle of *dual criminality*, which allows states to refuse assistance in a case if the conduct under investigation is not considered a crime under their own laws. The new UN agreement made dual criminality an optional principle, weakening the ability of states to reject cross-border data requests. Consequently, data-sharing requests regarding content-related offenses, such as political dissent or LGBTQ+ rights, would no longer be protected under dual criminality and would instead be subject to the geopolitical relationships and decision-making of the state.

The active interest that a number of autocratic, oppressive governments have taken in this treaty also raised concerns. A December 30 *Global Voices* article, by Alexa Zamora, explained how the adoption of this treaty and its lack of safeguards may threaten dissidents, activists, and exiles, stating that "exiled defenders and journalists could be accused of cybercrime in their home countries for legitimate activities carried out online from abroad" and that "these mechanisms could be used to track, identify, and persecute activists and journalists in other countries." Freedom House pointed out that Saudi Arabia, a government that engages in censorship and has regularly cracked down on domestic political dissent, hosted the Internet Government Forum (IGF), which plays a major role in policy discussions surrounding the internet.

Despite the treaty's ramifications and relatively widespread coverage by independent news organizations, none of the most prominent US newspapers appear to have covered the UN convention's passage or discussions in the preceding months of the human rights concerns it raises. Instead, the cybercrime convention has received sporadic coverage in the establishment press. For example, in April 2023, the *Washington Post*'s "Cybersecurity 202" series featured a brief article, which noted in passing that the expanded definition of cybercrime proposed by Russia "worries the United States, human rights activists and civil liberties groups."[79] Fox News amplified that theme in a November 2024 report that emphasized how Russia and China would be "welcomed into the global cybercrime governance fold," but its report made no mention of the proposed treaty's potential impacts on political dissidents, exiled journalists, or the LGBTQ+ community.[80] In January 2025, NPR's *Morning Edition* featured the cybercrime convention in a two-minute segment, during which Ilona Cohen, the chief legal and policy officer at the cybersecurity tech company HackerOne, observed, "When everybody else was waiting for Santa to come down the chimney, the U.N. was passing its five-year cybercrime convention."[81]

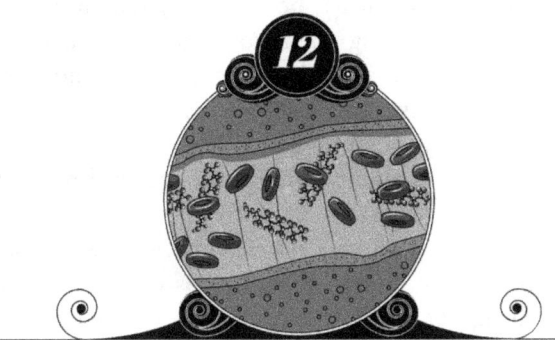

PFAS, Other Toxic Chemicals Found in Products Meant to Keep Us Safe

Rita Aksenfeld, "Thousands of Chemicals From Food Packaging Found in Humans, a Major Study Reveals," *Mongabay*, November 25, 2024.

Pien Huang, "Hazardous Chemicals in Food Packaging Can Also Be Found in People," NPR, September 21, 2024.

Tom Perkins, "Some Condoms and Lubricant Brands Contain Alarming Levels of PFAS—Study," *The Guardian*, July 28, 2024.

Tom Perkins, "Thousands of Toxins From Food Packaging Found in Humans—Research," *The Guardian*, September 27, 2024.

Student Researchers: Emily Pintar and Giselle Le Brec (North Central College)
Faculty Evaluator: Steve Macek (North Central College)

According to a study by the consumer safety advocacy group Mamavation, popular brands of condoms and lubricants contain PFAS, per- and polyfluoroalkyl substances or so-called "forever chemicals," Tom Perkins reported for the *Guardian* in July 2024. Two months later, Perkins drew attention, also in the *Guardian*, to alarming research published in the *Journal of Exposure Science & Environmental Epidemiology* that found some 3,600 chemicals present in food packaging or containers were also found in humans.[82] Among the chemicals detected in humans were eighty "food contact chemicals," or FCCs, with "hazard properties of high concern" for human health.

The per- and polyfluoroalkyl substances discovered in some brands of condoms and lubricants are known informally as "forever chemicals" because they take a long time to break down, allowing them to accumulate in humans, other animals, and the environment. The chemicals are linked to a host of human health issues, including cancers, liver problems, and birth defects. PFAS are also associated with reduced sperm counts, pregnancy-induced high blood pressure, and infertility, the *Guardian* reported. As Perkins detailed in a June 30, 2024, *Guardian* article, recent research has determined that human skin absorbs PFAS chemicals at significantly higher levels than previously documented.[83]

Mamavation commissioned a lab certified by the Environmental Protection Agency to test condoms and lubricants produced by nineteen popular brands, including Trojan condoms and K-Y Jelly. The study found that 14 percent of the tested condoms and lubricants showed "indications of PFAS 'forever chemicals.'"[84] Twelve percent of the condoms and 25 percent of the lubricants tested positive for fluorine, a marker of PFAS. Based on these findings, Mamavation recommended that consumers avoid using a number of popular condom and lubricant brands.

Although there is currently no specific evidence linking health issues to use of condoms or lubricants containing PFAS, human sex organs are particularly vulnerable to potential chemical contamination, researchers told the *Guardian*. Genitals have high densities of blood vessels, so genitalia exposed to harmful chemicals are likely to lead to the circulation of those chemicals throughout the body. Perkins's July 2024 report quoted Linda Birnbaum, one of the authors of the Mamavation study, "Because condoms are an exposure to the most sensitive areas on the human body for both men and women, I would strongly recommend the industry identify and remove these chemicals immediately."

In September 2024, Reuters reported that consumer Matthew Goodman had brought a class action lawsuit in New York against Church & Dwight, the manufacturer of Trojan condoms, on the grounds that the Trojans he bought were unsafe because they contain PFAS.[85] Goodman's suit seeks at least $5 million in damages for Trojan users nationwide.

The study about food contact chemicals published in the *Journal of Exposure Science & Environmental Epidemiology* is, if anything, even more startling. "Thousands of chemicals used in food packaging and food production are leaching into food itself," a September 2024 NPR report on the study explained, noting that chemicals used in production and packaging "can contaminate what people eat." NPR reported that eighty of the chemicals found in both food packaging and humans are of "high concern" because they are "linked to … cancers, developmental disorders, heart and metabolic diseases."

Mongabay reported that the researchers expected to find signs of several hundred FCCs already included in biomonitoring programs such as the US National Health and Nutrition Examination Survey, but their search "found thousands" of FCCs. "It surprised us that we found so many more chemicals," the study's lead author, Birgit Geueke, a senior scientist at the Food Packaging Forum Foundation in Zurich, Switzerland, told *Mongabay*.

Geueke advised people to reduce exposure by choosing foods that come with less packaging, and to transfer food from plastic containers to glass or metal ones before heating it. But, she added, "You cannot be made responsible for the chemical exposure coming from your food." Instead, she said policymakers should create regulations forcing food manufacturers to replace harmful materials that contact food with safer alternatives.

NPR's report echoed this sentiment, explaining that "regulators could do more to help by requiring better labeling for chemicals in food packaging," which could help consumers make better choices, as well as by imposing strict restrictions on the use of chemicals with known harms in food packaging.

Unfortunately, the discovery of PFAS in condoms and lubricants has received scant coverage from the establishment press. Aside from Perkins's article in the *Guardian*, Mamavation's research was mentioned only in passing in stories by Reuters and *Newsweek* about the Trojan class action lawsuit.[86] The lawsuit—but not the Mamavation study—was referenced in a single sentence of an April 2025 *New York Times* opinion piece about the fight for better regulation of PFAS.[87]

The findings of the study about widespread human exposure to food contact chemicals—reported by *Mongabay*, NPR, and the *Guardian*—received somewhat more coverage from corporate news outlets. In September 2024, the *Washington Post* covered the study in a story that featured an interview with one of its authors, but the *Post* created a false sense of balance by also quoting a spokesperson for the American Chemistry Council, who responded to the study's findings by insisting that food packaging manufacturers do extensive analysis to verify the safety of their products.[88] Both the *Chicago Tribune* and FOX 32, the Chicago Fox network affiliate, also covered the study's findings.[89]

2024-2025 HONORABLE MENTIONS

Internal Displacement Numbers on the Increase in 2023

Olivia Rosane, "Record 76 Million Internally Displaced in 2023, Largely Due to Violence," *Common Dreams*, May 14, 2024.

Student Researcher: Olivia Rosenberg (North Central College)
Faculty Evaluator: Steve Macek (North Central College)

Some 75.9 million people were displaced from their homes in 2023 due to war, conflict, or environmental disaster, according to the Internal Displacement Monitoring Center's 2024 "Global Report on Internal Displacement," as covered by Olivia Rosane for *Common Dreams*. From 2019 to 2023, the number of internally displaced people rose by 51 percent, driven by a 49 percent increase in those displaced specifically by conflict. Of the new displacements caused by conflict and war, two-thirds can be attributed to violence in Congo, Sudan, and Palestine. At the end of 2023, 83 percent of the population in Gaza was displaced. Deputy Director General Ugochi Daniels of the International Organization for Migration called the report a "stark reminder of the urgent and coordinated need to expand disaster risk reduction, support peacebuilding, ensure the protection of human rights, and, whenever possible, prevent the displacement before it happens." Jan Egeland, secretary general of the Norwegian Refugee Council, observed, "The suffering and the displacement last far beyond the news cycle."

House Passes Bill Threatening Tax-Exempt Status of Nonprofit Organizations

Seth Stern, "Criticizing Israel? Nonprofit Media Could Lose Tax-Exempt Status without Due Process," *The Intercept*, May 10, 2024.

Yves Smith, "Free Speech on the Ropes: Legislation to Revoke Not-for-Profit Status of Organizations That Support Palestine Protests Passes in House," *Naked Capitalism*, April 26, 2024.

Matthew Petti, "This Bill Would Give the Treasury Nearly Unlimited Power to Destroy Nonprofits," *Reason*, April 24, 2024.

Student Researcher: Cam Lippincott (UC Berkeley)
Faculty Evaluator: Andy Lee Roth (Project Censored)

In April 2024, the House of Representatives passed HR 6408, legislation that would grant the Secretary of Treasury authority to suspend the tax-exempt status of any nonprofit organization deemed to be a "terrorist supporting organization." The Charity & Security Network, an advocacy group for nonprofit organizations that work in conflict zones, warned that, without proper evidence, allegations targeting nonprofit groups constituted "a dangerous precedent for not only the U.S. legal system and the state of free speech but also for charitable giving and operations in crisis contexts like Gaza." The power to revoke nonprofit news organizations' tax-exempt status would allow government officials "to retaliate against journalists they don't like" and "chill reporting, not only on Israel but also on U.S. foreign policy generally," Seth Stern of the Freedom of the Press Foundation wrote in a report published by *The Intercept*. In May 2025, *The Intercept* reported that efforts to sneak a version of the "nonprofit killer" law into the Trump administration's "Big, Beautiful Bill Act" had failed.[90]

Title VI Invoked to Curb Pro-Palestinian Language in Higher Ed

Alex Kane, "The Civil Rights Law Shutting down Pro-Palestine Speech," *Jewish Currents*, November 15, 2024.

Student Researcher: Vivian Rose (Ithaca College)
Faculty Evaluator: Mickey Huff (Ithaca College)

Pro-Israel groups are increasingly using Title VI complaints to threaten the funding of colleges and universities that tolerate pro-Palestinian expression and protest on their campuses. Title VI of the Civil Rights Act of 1964 stipulates that institutions that "encourage, entrench, subsidize or result in racial [color or national origin] discrimination" are ineligible for federal funding. Alex Kane, senior reporter at *Jewish Currents* and a recipient of the 2025 Izzy Award for his reporting, writes that pro-Israel groups consistently frame anti-Zionism or pro-Palestinian sentiments as a form of antisemitism (and, hence, racial discrimination). "Title VI has been central to pro-Israel groups' attempts to silence such dissent," Kane wrote. One focus of these groups' campaign has been the Office for Civil Rights (OCR), a federal agency that enforces Title VI in academic settings. Anyone can file a complaint with the OCR, even if they are not a student or affiliated with the academic institution being targeted. The proliferation of these complaints, and the ensuing investigations, has led college and university administrators to adopt zero tolerance policies specifically targeting pro-Palestinian student activism.

UBS, the World's Largest Private Bank, Accused of Scamming Customers

Lucy Komisar, "Scam in the Caribbean," *Inside Paradeplatz*, October 8, 2024.

Student Researcher: Jayden Lawrence (North Central College)
Faculty Evaluator: Steve Macek (North Central College)

According to documents from a lawsuit, UBS Bahamas refused to send required confirmations of trades made in US markets, Lucy Komisar reported, in October 2024, for *Inside Paradeplatz*. The US Securities and Exchange Commission requires such confirmations by law. "The clients believe the trades were not executed" and that UBS "created internal trading records and stole their money," Komisar reported. According to Komisar's report, UBS officials asserted that "the allegations have no merit," but would not provide evidence to support that claim. UBS has actively sought to suppress media coverage of the case. Komisar attempted to publish her findings through thirty-three US publications and several foreign outlets, all of whom either ignored or rejected her story. Ultimately, the banking-focused outlet *Inside Paradeplatz*, based in Zurich, published the exposé.

California Students Simulate Starbucks Union Drive to Learn Workplace Rights

Nicolle Fefferman, "'Starcups Workers Unite!'—Students Learn Their Workplace Rights," *Rethinking Schools* 39, no. 2 (Winter 2024–2025).

Student Researchers: Crissy Saucier, Shawn Zhai, Tim Hagen, and Ben Hiersche (University of Massachusetts, Amherst)
Faculty Evaluator: Cecilia Zhou (University of Massachusetts, Amherst)

Students from Gardena High School in Los Angeles took part in an exercise simulating a National Labor Relations

Board union election based on Starbucks Workers United's efforts over the last few years. Writing for *Rethinking Schools*, Nicolle Fefferman reported on her facilitating a classroom activity exploring workers' rights and the power of labor organizing as part of California Assembly Bill 800, which requires public high schools to implement Workplace Readiness Week each May. During the simulation, each student took on a role as a non-union worker, union worker, community member, corporate manager, or NLRB agent. Students prepared by studying labor history, including the decline of union participation from 1955 to 2021, and key legal protections, like the National Labor Relations Act, and labor organizing campaigns such as Starbucks Workers United. The exercise helped students understand corporate power, worker rights, labor laws, and especially the impact of collective bargaining on workplace conditions.

JAYDEN LAWRENCE is a rising junior at North Central College pursuing a degree in journalism, with minors in environmental science, political science, and religious studies. He reports on politics and runs a hip-hop radio show, *Culture Shock*, for WONC FM89, North Central's student-run radio station.

ELLA MROFKA is a sophomore journalism major at North Central College. She plans to pursue her dream of becoming a travel journalist after college.

CAITLIN SUDA is a junior studying communications and media studies at North Central College. She's passionate about storytelling, digital content creation, and using media to spark meaningful conversations.

AMY GRIM BUXBAUM is a Professor of Communication at North Central College, where she teaches courses in organizational communication and rhetoric.

STEVE MACEK is a Professor in the Department of Communication and Media Studies at North Central College and serves as co-coordinator of Project Censored's Campus Affiliates Program. He writes frequently about censorship, academic freedom, and First Amendment issues for a number of independent media outlets.

ANDY LEE ROTH, PhD, is Project Censored's editor-at-large, a 2024–2025 Reynolds Journalism Institute fellow, and a sociologist. He joined the Project in 2006 and served as its associate director from 2012–2024. His research has appeared in numerous outlets, including *Index on Censorship, Truthout, The Progressive*, and the *International Journal of Press/Politics*.

NOTES

1. Tim Cushing, "ICE Wants to Set up a Social Media Dragnet So It Can Figure Out Who's Criticizing The Agency," *Techdirt*, February 19, 2025.
2. Joseph Cox, "Inside ICE's Database for Finding 'Derogatory' Online Speech," *404 Media*, October 24, 2023.
3. Johana Bhuiyan and Sam Levin, "Revealed: How US Immigration Uses Fake Social Media Profiles Across Investigations," *The Guardian*, September 5, 2023.
4. Amanda Holpuch, "US Immigration Police Broke Facebook Rules with Fake Profiles for College Sting," *The Guardian*, April 11, 2019.
5. Pedro Camacho, "ICE Plans to Monitor 'Negative' Social Media Discussion About the Agency and Its Top Officials: Report," *Latin Times*, February 16, 2025.
6. Thomas Brewster, "ICE Spent Millions on Phone Hacking Tech, Just in Time for Trump's Mass Deportation Plans," *Forbes*, November 25, 2024; Adam Satariano, Paul Mozur, Aaron Krolik, and David McCabe, "The Tech Arsenal That Could Power Trump's Immigration Crackdown," *New York Times*, January 25, 2025.
7. Byron Tau, "U.S. Spy Agencies Know Your Secrets. They Bought Them," *Wall Street Journal*, March 8, 2024.
8. Jordan King, "Texas County Refuses to Sell Excess Water: 'The New Oil,'" *Newsweek*, April 16, 2025.
9. Sachi Kitajima Mulkey and Ayurella Horn-Muller, "People Are Flocking to Florida. Will There Be Enough Water for Them?" *Grist*, January 8, 2025.
10. Sachi Kitajima Mulkey, "The Surging Demand for Data Is Guzzling Virginia's Water," *Grist*, May 8, 2024.
11. Mulkey and Horn-Muller, "People Are Flocking to Florida."
12. On saltwater intrusion, see Brianna Hickey and Andy Duncan, "Saltwater Intrusion Threatens US Freshwater Supplies," in *State of the Free Press 2025*, ed. Mickey Huff, Shealeigh Voitl, and Andy Lee Roth (The Censored Press and Seven Stories Press, 2025), 43–46; available online at projectcensored.org.
13. Tom Perkins, "PFAS May Be Contaminating Drinking Water for up to 27% of Americans—Study," *The Guardian*, November 13, 2024.
14. Ethan Baron, "Santa Clara County Accuses Companies of Causing 'Environmental and Human Health Crisis' via 'Forever Chemicals' in Drinking Water," *Mercury News*, February 4, 2025.
15. Stephen Prager, "Climate Change Fueling 'Most Widespread and Damaging' Droughts in History: UN Report," *Common Dreams*, July 3, 2025.
16. Jeff Tavss, "Utah Is the Only US State to Be 100% in Drought," FOX 13 (Salt Lake City), July 3, 2025.

17. Tom Perkins, "Trump Officials Gut 25 Centers That Monitor Flooding and Drought in the US," *The Guardian*, May 2, 2025.
18. Austyn Gaffney and Mira Rojanasakul, "In a Record, All but Two U.S. States Are in Drought," *New York Times*, November 4, 2024; Ben Noll, "Where Drought Conditions Have Plagued U.S.—And Why It's Been So Dry," *Washington Post*, April 11, 2025.
19. Tom Howarth, "Map Shows Water Supply for 30 Million Americans at Risk," *Newsweek*, January 21, 2025.
20. Carey Gillam, "Nearly 30 Million People in the US Face Limited Water Supplies, Study Finds," *Truthout*, January 26, 2025.
21. For the complete series of reports, see "Misplaced Trust: The United States Was Founded with Stolen Indigenous Land. Public Institutions Are Still Profiting from It Today," *Grist*, February 6, 2024.
22. Matt Krupnick, "She's on a Scholarship at a Tribal College in Wisconsin. The Trump Administration Suspended the USDA Grant That Funded It," ProPublica, March 10, 2025.
23. Tristan Ahtone, Robert Lee, Amanda Tachine, An Garagiola, Audrianna Goodwin, Maria Parazo Rose, and Clayton Aldern, "Misplaced Trust: Stolen Indigenous Land Is the Foundation of the Land-Grant University System. Climate Change Is Its Legacy," *Grist*, February 7, 2024.
24. Hanna Duggal, "Trust Issues: Using Data to Dig into Who Profits from US Tribal Lands," Global Investigative Journalism Network, November 13, 2024.
25. Duggal, "Trust Issues." See, for example, Maria Parazo Rose, "How to Conduct Your Own Reporting and Research on State Trust Lands. A Guide to Using Grist's Database," *Grist*, February 7, 2024.
26. Destiny Herbers, "Nebraska Tribe Pays $65K a Year to Rent Land on Its Own Reservation. It Wants It Back," *Flatwater Free Press*, September 21, 2024.
27. Rachel Nostrant, "Tribes and Students Sue Trump Administration over Firings at Native Schools," *New York Times*, March 9, 2025.
28. Annie Gowen and Dana Hedgpeth, "Across Indian Country, Mass Firings at Colleges Open Up Age-Old Wounds," *Washington Post*, March 8, 2025.
29. Sage Van Wing, "States Own and Manage Land Within Indigenous Reservations," Oregon Public Broadcasting, March 5, 2024, updated March 13, 2024.
30. "Misplaced Trust," *Grist*.
31. "CAIR Calls on Meta to Stop Blocking Anti-Genocide Posts Under Pressure From Israeli Government Censors," Council on Arab-Islamic Relations (CAIR), April 14, 2025.
32. Sharon Zhang, "Rubio Unveils Visa Restrictions to 'Protect' Americans from Foreign Censorship," *Truthout*, May 29, 2025.
33. "Israel Censors Foreign Press Coverage of Iranian Strike Sites," Committee to Protect Journalists, June 23, 2025.
34. Waqas Ahmed, Nicholas Rodelo, Ryan Grim, and Murtaza Hussain, "Leaked Data Reveals Massive Israeli Campaign to Remove Pro-Palestine Posts on Facebook and Instagram," *ZNetwork*, April 14, 2025; Waqas Ahmed, Nicholas Rodelo, Ryan Grim, and Murtaza Hussain, "Social Media Platforms Remove Pro-Palestinian Posts," Jewish Voice for Labour, April 18, 2025.
35. David Brody, "The Big Beautiful Bill Could Decimate Legal Accountability for Tech and Anything Tech Touches," *Tech Policy Press*, May 27. 2025.

36. Julia Shapero, "Senate Strips AI Provision From Megabill," *The Hill*, July 1, 2025.
37. "An Autopsy on the State AI Moratorium," ALFA Institute, July 1, 2025.
38. Cristiano Lima-Strong, "House Guts Civil Rights Protections in Privacy Bill, Sparking Outrage," *Washington Post*, June 27, 2024.
39. Cecilia Kang, "The Tech Lobbying Group Helping to Broaden the First Amendment's Reach," *New York Times*, October 7, 2024.
40. Ashley Gold, "Q2 Tech Lobbying Check In," *Axios*, July 23, 2024; Brendan Bordelon, "In DC, a New Wave of AI Lobbyists Gains the Upper Hand," *Politico*, May 12, 2024.
41. Mishal Khan, "At Work and Under Watch: Surveillance and Suffering at Amazon and Walmart Warehouses," Oxfam America, April 10, 2024.
42. Greg Bensinger, "Amazon North Carolina Workers Reject Union, Handing Retailer Win in Labor Fight," Reuters, February 15, 2025.
43. Daniel Boguslaw, "Amazon Uses Arsenal of AI Weapons Against Workers," *American Prospect*, March 13, 2025.
44. Rudi Kinsella, "Amazon and Walmart Warehouse Staff Too Worried to Go to the Bathroom During Work Hours," *Irish Star*, April 10, 2024, updated April 11, 2024.
45. Natalie Musumeci, "Amazon and Walmart Warehouse Employees Are So Surveilled That They're Worried About Breaking to Use the Bathroom: Oxfam Report," *Business Insider*, April 9, 2024.
46. *City of Grants Pass V. Johnson*, 23-175 (Supreme Court of the United States, June 28, 2024), accessed July 11, 2025.
47. David Sjostedt, "Homeless Sweeps Came Back With a Vengeance in 2024," *San Francisco Standard*, December 30, 2024.
48. Robbie Sequeira, "Many More Cities Ban Sleeping Outside Despite a Lack of Shelter Space," *Stateline*, January 27, 2025.
49. Marisa Kendall, "They Were Arrested for Sleeping Outside While Homeless. Now, These Californians Are Headed to Trial," *CalMatters*, February 25, 2025.
50. Marisa Kendall and Katie Anastas, "'Look, There's Nowhere Else to Go': Inside California's Crackdown on Homeless Camps," *CalMatters*, February 27, 2025, updated March 5, 2025.
51. Sequeira, "Many More Cities."
52. Sequeira, "Many More Cities."
53. "U.S. Police Violence in 2024: Year-End Report," Campaign Zero, February 24, 2025.
54. "U.S. Police Violence in 2024," Campaign Zero.
55. "2024 Police Violence Report," Mapping Police Violence, 2024.
56. "Fatal Force: 10,429 People Have Been Shot and Killed by Police From 2015 to 2024," *Washington Post*, December 31, 2024.
57. N'dea Yancey-Bragg, "US Sets Another Grim Record for Killings by Police in 2024," *USA Today*, February 26, 2025, updated February 27, 2025.
58. Steven Rich, Tim Arango, and Nicholas Bogel-Burroughs, "Since George Floyd's Murder, Police Killings Keep Rising, Not Falling," *New York Times*, May 24, 2025.
59. Pascal Sabino, "The New 'Stop and Frisk'? Chicago Police Make Millions of Traffic Stops While Searching for Guns," *Injustice Watch*, March 30, 2023.
60. Sabino, "Chicago Police Made Nearly 200,000 Secret Traffic Stops." See

also, "Stop and Frisk in Chicago," ACLU of Illinois, March 2015.

61. David R. Kirkpatrick, Steve Eder, Kim Barker, and Julie Tate, "Why Many Police Traffic Stops Turn Deadly," *New York Times*, October 31, 2021, updated November 30, 2021.
62. Alexander T. Bradley and Ian J. Hewitt, "Tipping Point in Ice-Sheet Grounding-Zone Melting Due to Ocean Water Intrusion," *Nature Geoscience*, June 25, 2024.
63. Matthew Rozsa, "Will Earth Hit a Climate Tipping Point? Here's Why Experts Say this Framework Is Problematic," *Salon*, March 18, 2024.
64. See also, Delger Erdenesanaa, "Ocean Heat Has Shattered Records for More than a Year. What's Happening?" *New York Times*, April 10, 2024.
65. Mackenzie M. Grieman et al., "Abrupt Holocene Ice Loss Due to Thinning and Ungrounding in the Weddell Sea Embayment," *Nature Geoscience*, February 8, 2024.
66. Eric Rignot, et al., "Widespread Seawater Intrusions Beneath the Grounded Ice of Thwaites Glacier, West Antarctica," *PNAS*, May 20, 2024.
67. Matthew Rozsa, "Scientists Worry So-called 'Doomsday Glacier' Is near Collapse, Satellite Data Reveals," *Salon*, May 23, 2024.
68. Jessica Corbett, "Antarctic Tipping Point That Occurred 8,000 Years Ago 'Could Happen Again'," *Common Dreams*, February 9, 2024; Laura Paddison, "Scientists Discover an Alarming Change in Antarctica's Past That Could Spell Devastating Future Sea Level Rise," CNN, February 8, 2024; Rebecca Owen, "Drilling into Antarctica's Past," *Eos*, April 1, 2024; Eric Ralls, "Antarctica Suffered Extremely Rapid Ice Loss After the Last Ice Age, Alarming Scientists," *Earth.com*, February 8, 2024.
69. Robbie Sequeira and Josh Kurtz, "Working-Class People Rarely Have a Seat 'At the Legislative Table' in State Capitols," *Maryland Matters*, April 1, 2024; Robbie Sequeira, "Working-Class Individuals Are Rarities as Legislators," *Governing*, March 18, 2024.
70. Brianna Kraemer, "Study: Only 2% of State Lawmakers Come From Working Class," *Carolina Journal*, February 29, 2024.
71. Katie McKellar, "No 'Working Class' in Utah Legislature? Lawmakers Beg to Differ—but Are There Enough?" *Utah News Dispatch*, March 28, 2024.
72. Dustin Guastella and Bhaskar Sunkara, "The US Needs More Working-Class Political Candidates," *The Guardian*, November 22, 2024.
73. Karl Evers-Hillstrom, "Majority of Lawmakers in 116th Congress Are Millionaires," OpenSecrets, April 23, 2020.
74. Laura Mannweiler, "All the President's Billionaires: The Extraordinary Wealth in Trump's Administration," *U.S. News & World Report*, June 4, 2025.
75. Brian Beach, "Dan Osborn Launches Political Action Committee to Help Working Class Candidates," *Nebraska Public Media*, November 19, 2024.
76. Dustin Guastella, "The Wealthy Dominate Government. Democrats Should Work to Change That," *Washington Post*, April 24, 2024.
77. Jamelle Bouie, "The Price We Pay for Having Upper-Class Legislators," *New York Times*, April 30, 2024.
78. "United Nations Convention Against Cybercrime; Strengthening International Cooperation for Combating Certain Crimes Committed by Means of Information and Communications Technology Systems and for the Sharing of Evidence in Electronic Form of Serious Crimes," United Nations Office on

79. Drugs and Crime, December 24, 2024.
79. Tim Starks and David DiMolfetta, "The Perilous Path to a New Cybercrime Treaty," *Washington Post*, April 28, 2023.
80. Alec Schemmel, "Biden Supports Bringing Adversarial Nations Into New UN Cyber Crime Alliance," Fox News, November 12, 2024.
81. Jenna McLaughlin, "U.S. And Other Countries Have Concerns Over U.N. Efforts to Fight Cybercrime," *Morning Edition* (NPR), January 16, 2025.
82. Birgit Geueke, et al., "Evidence for Widespread Human Exposure to Food Contact Chemicals," *Journal of Exposure Science & Environmental Epidemiology*, September 17, 2024.
83. Tom Perkins, "Toxic PFAS Absorbed Through Skin at Levels Higher Than Previously Thought," *The Guardian*, June 30, 2024.
84. Leah Segedie, "Condoms & Lubricants Tested For Indications of PFAS 'Forever Chemicals'—Guide," Mamavation, February 6, 2024.
85. Jonathan Stempel, "Trojan Condoms Contain 'Forever Chemicals,' Lawsuit Claims," Reuters, September 10, 2024.
86. Stempel, "Trojan Condoms"; Pandora Dewan, "Trojan Condoms Contain Cancer-Causing Chemicals: Lawsuit Claims," *Newsweek*, September 12, 2024.
87. Mariah Blake, "This Is How to Win an Environmental Fight," *New York Times*, April 27, 2025.
88. Shannon Osaka, "Scientists Just Figured Out How Many Chemicals Enter Our Bodies From Food Packaging," *Washington Post*, September 16, 2024.
89. Michael Hawthorne, "Toxic Chemicals Found in Food Packaging; FDA Under Pressure to Take Action," *Chicago Tribune*, September 26, 2024; Stephanie Weaver, "More Than 3,000 Chemicals Enter the Body Through Food Packaging, Study Finds," FOX 32 (FOX TV, Chicago), September 20, 2024.
90. Noah Hurowitz, "Nonprofit Killer Provision Quietly Disappears From Trump's 'Big, Beautiful Bill'," *The Intercept*, May 19, 2025.

— CHAPTER 2 —

Déjà Vu News
ATTACKS ON JOURNALISM AND FREE SPEECH EDITION
JAYDEN LAWRENCE and STEVE MACEK

> *To articulate the past historically does not mean to recognize it "the way it really was." It means to seize hold of a memory as it flashes up at a moment of danger.*
> —WALTER BENJAMIN, "Theses on the Philosophy of History" (1942)

INTRODUCTION
STEVE MACEK

Since the 1990s, Project Censored has regularly published yearbook chapters that review the fate of selected stories we previously identified as underreported. The annual "Déjà Vu" chapter traces significant developments involving these stories since we first spotlighted them, explores any additional media coverage they have received, and assesses the extent to which the facts they explore and the issues they raise have become part of broader public discourse.

Revisiting stories suppressed or ignored years ago is not an academic exercise. As German-Jewish cultural theorist and critic Walter Benjamin—who fled his native Germany in 1933 following the Nazi seizure of power—explained in his "Theses on the Philosophy of History," historical study offers important practical lessons for foes of present authoritarianism. It teaches us, he argued, that "the 'state of emergency' in which we live is not the exception but the rule" and that only by grasping this will we "improve our position in the struggle against Fascism."[1] Hence, he argued, to effectively reflect on the past means to "seize hold of a memory as it flashes up at a moment of danger."[2]

That we are currently living through a "moment of danger" for journalism and the right to a free press is indisputable.

In his first term as president (2017–2021), Donald Trump declared the press "truly the enemy of the people."[3] And he regularly denounced journalists as dishonest, corrupt, human scum, bad people, and "some of the worst human beings you'll ever meet."[4] His 2020 reelection campaign brought specious libel lawsuits against the *New York Times* and the *Washington Post* for reporting on possible foreign interference in the election, both of which were dismissed.[5]

Just a hundred days into his second term in office, Trump and his allies had escalated their threatening rhetoric against the news media and taken increasingly audacious steps aimed at thwarting and undermining it.

Witness, for example, Trump's unofficial right-hand man Elon Musk taking to social media to denounce the staff of CBS news show *60 Minutes* as "the biggest liars in the world" and claiming "they deserve a long prison sentence" after the show aired an unflattering interview with one of his critics.[6] Meanwhile, Trump himself, in a March 2025 speech to the Department of Justice, fumed that CNN and MSNBC "literally write 97.6 percent bad about me," insisting that "it has to stop … it has to be illegal."[7]

During the 2024 presidential contest, Trump said on the campaign trail that NBC and CNN should have their "licenses, or whatever they have, taken away" for editorial decisions he didn't like.[8] He has now installed a new Republican FCC chair, Brendan Carr, who seems determined to carry out Trump's wishes.[9] Carr has accused Comcast (owner of CNN and NBC), Disney (owner of ABC), and CBS of "news distortion," which could potentially be grounds for removing their broadcast licenses. He has opened investigations into DEI policies at Comcast and Disney. In late January, Carr also opened investigations into National Public Radio (NPR) and Public Broadcasting Service (PBS), frequent targets of Trump vitriol, on the pretext that they were running impermissible underwriting messages.[10] Of course, that was before Trump signed his May 1, 2025, executive order instructing the Corporation for Public Broadcasting to cut off all funding for NPR and PBS.[11]

As he did in his first term, Trump has been bombarding media organizations with a deluge of baseless legal actions. Trump brought a defamation suit against ABC and news anchor George Stephanopoulos over on-air comments about Trump's history of sexual abuse. Shamefully, ABC agreed to settle the case out of court in return for a $15 million donation to a "presidential foundation and museum."[12] Trump is suing the *Des Moines Register* and its parent company, Gannett, for fraud because the *Register* published a poll that (erroneously) showed him trailing Kamala Harris by 3 percentage points in the state of Iowa during the waning stages of the 2024 presidential race.[13] And he is continuing to pursue a $20 billion defamation suit against *60 Minutes* and CBS for what he claims was the program's misleading editing of an interview the show did with his opponent, Kamala Harris.[14]

In addition, the President has banned Associated Press reporters from covering the White House because the news agency refuses to use his preferred term, the "Gulf of America," for what the rest of the world knows as the "Gulf of Mexico."[15] He has also pardoned over a dozen individuals charged and, in some cases, convicted of violent crimes against journalists committed during the January 6 storming of the US Capitol.[16]

Attacks on journalism in the United States (and around the world) are not new. The censorship, mistreatment, smears, and legal harassment that journalists and news organizations have been subjected to in the past year are different in degree, but not in kind, from earlier periods. In the past, as now, those with political and economic power have worked to silence, intimidate, or demean journalists who dig up inconvenient facts, expose authoritarian lies, and amplify the voices of the oppressed. As Walter Benjamin correctly pointed out, the state of emergency is not the exception but the rule.

This is why, at this juncture, we have chosen to focus this chapter on three stories Project Censored highlighted not long ago that concern attacks on journalism and freedom of speech. From *Censored 2020*, we look back on and update story #1 about the Justice Department's use of Foreign Intelligence Surveillance Act (FISA) authority to spy on reporters. From *State of the Free Press 2021*, we update story #2, about agrochemical giant Monsanto's efforts to monitor and discredit journalists reporting on the dangers of its Roundup pesticide, and story #24, about journalist Abby Martin's battle against the state of Georgia's anti-BDS laws.

What these three updates demonstrate is that the current assault on the press is just the most recent installment in an ongoing repressive, autocratic, and often corporate-sponsored campaign that stretches back years. But they also show that the assault has been consistently resisted and even occasionally turned back. In that way, reflecting on them can perhaps, as Benjamin contended, "improve our position in the struggle against Fascism."

Censored 2020 #1
Justice Department's Secret FISA Rules for Targeting Journalists

Trevor Timm, "Revealed: The Justice Dept's Secret Rules for Targeting Journalists with FISA Court Orders," *Freedom of the Press Foundation*, September 17, 2018; republished by *Common Dreams*, September 17, 2018.

Ramya Krishnan, "Targeting Journalists under FISA: New Documents Reveal DOJ's Secret Rules," Knight First Amendment Institute, September 17, 2018.

Cora Currier, "Government Can Spy on Journalists in the U.S. Using Invasive Foreign Intelligence Process," *The Intercept*, September 17, 2018.

Jessica Corbett, "The US Government's Secret Rules for Spying on Journalists Are 'Terrifying,'" *MintPress News*, September 18, 2018.

"US Can Spy on Journalists Domestically Using FISA Warrants, Declassified Guidelines Show," RT, September 19, 2018, updated September 20, 2018.

Student Researcher: Andrea Blado (Sonoma State University)
Faculty Evaluators: Brent Mortensen (Healdsburg High School) and Peter Phillips (Sonoma State University)

As Project Censored highlighted in its 2020 yearbook, a pair of 2015 memos, from former Attorney General Eric Holder to the Department of Justice's National Security Division, showed how the government could use court orders under the Foreign Intelligence Surveillance Act (FISA) to monitor the communications of journalists and news organizations. The Knight First Amendment Institute at Columbia University and the Freedom of the Press Foundation had obtained the documents through a Freedom of Information Act (FOIA) request and a lawsuit challenging the lack of disclosure that request yielded.[17]

Since 1978, the Foreign Intelligence Surveillance Court has processed electronic surveillance and physical search requests by federal law enforcement and intelligence agencies for foreign intelligence purposes. Holder's memos spelled out the guidelines for processing FISA applications that target "known media entities" or "known members of the media." As Cora Currier reported for *The Intercept*, the secret rules "apply to media entities or journalists who are thought to be agents of a foreign government, or, in some cases, are of interest under the broader standard that they possess foreign intelligence information." Ramya Krishnan, a staff attorney with the Knight Institute, told *The Intercept*, "There's a lack of clarity on the circumstances when the government might consider a journalist an agent of a foreign power."

Because of government pressure to register Russian state-controlled news outlet RT as a "foreign agent" with the Department of Justice in November 2017, their reporters—and even their sources—were even more likely to be subject to FISA court-ordered surveillance.[18] For its part, RT argued that details contained in the memos made it "highly likely" that both the Trump and Obama administrations had surveilled journalists they considered to be "foreign agents."[19]

The revealed memos raised three "concerning" questions about the government's surveillance of news organizations and journalists, Trevor Timm, director of the Freedom of the Press Foundation, noted at the time. First, how many times have FISA court orders been used to target journalists, and are any journalists currently under investigation? Second, why did the Justice Department keep these rules secret when it updated its "media guidelines" in 2015? And, third, is the Justice Department using FISA court orders—along with the FBI's similar rules for targeting journalists with national security letters (NSLs)—to "get around the stricter 'media guidelines'"?[20]

In January 2015, after the Obama administration secretly seized phone records from the Associated Press, Attorney General Eric Holder revised the set of procedures, known as the "media guidelines," that determine when government officials can surveil journalists. Though the secret 2015 memos specified that FISA applications must be presented to the attorney general for approval before they are submitted to the Foreign Intelligence Surveillance Court, the memos allowed for exceptions and, as Trevor Timm and others noted, FISA rules were "much less stringent" than the Justice Department's media guidelines for obtaining subpoenas, court orders, and warrants against journalists. These rules enable government officials to circumvent the media guidelines' requirements that the information sought is "essential" to a successful investigation, that "reasonable alternative attempts" have been made to obtain the information, and that the government should inform the affected journalists.

As Project Censored noted in its original report, although most reporters are probably aware that they may be subject to surveillance, their sources may not be. The unredacted portions of the Holder memos did not specify how to mitigate risks posed by exposing journalists' sources.

Corporate news outlets failed to cover the revelations about the two secret memos on targeting journalists and news organizations when they were first made public in September 2018. In 2019, establishment outlets carried a flurry of news stories and editorials about Carter Page, a foreign policy adviser to Donald Trump during the 2016 presidential election campaign, whom the FBI wiretapped under the authority of FISA.[21] Page had been suspected of being a Russian foreign agent. However, the controversy over the use of FISA to surveil a presidential campaign adviser did nothing to raise awareness about the threat posed by FISA warrants targeting reporters and news organizations.

Update

Sadly, the alarms raised by the Freedom of the Press Foundation and the Knight First Amendment Institute have since been vindicated.

On May 7, 2021, the *Washington Post* reported that during Trump's first term as president, the Department of Justice (DOJ) had secretly obtained phone records—and attempted to obtain email records—for three of its journalists who had investigated Russian interference in the 2016 US elections.[22] Around the same time, CNN revealed that the Trump DOJ had accessed two months' worth of 2017 phone and email records for its main Pentagon correspondent, Barbara Starr.[23] And, in a June 4, 2021, article, the *New York Times* disclosed that the Trump DOJ had initiated a covert legal effort to obtain the email records of four of its reporters.[24] That effort continued under the Biden administration and, in fact, the Biden DOJ imposed a gag order on *Times* executives preventing them from informing their employees or the public about the legal fight. Google, which operates the *Times'* email system, ultimately refused to turn over the records.

The news about the Trump and Biden administrations spying, or attempting to spy, on journalists immediately sparked an outcry from news organizations and civil libertarians. On June 5, 2021, the Biden DOJ announced that it would "no longer secretly obtain reporters' records during leak investigations."[25] Nevertheless, as Anna Diakun of the Knight Institute and Trevor Timm of the Freedom of the

Press Foundation pointed out in a June 9, 2021, blog post, the new policy left ambiguous who exactly counts as a member of the news media, creating uncertainty about whether it applied "to those engaged in less traditional newsgathering, like bloggers, newsletter authors, or other independent journalists who don't fit neatly within the traditional mainstream news-style rubric."[26]

Donald Trump's new attorney general, Pam Bondi, on April 25, 2025, completely rescinded the (somewhat flawed) Biden-era policy preventing subpoenas of reporters' phone records in criminal and leak investigations.[27] As the *Guardian* and other news organizations reported, Bondi claimed in a memo that the policy change was necessary to stop "disclosures that undermine President Trump's policies, victimize government agencies, and cause harm to the American people." However, Bondi insisted that the DOJ would attempt to minimize "the use of compulsory legal process" to force the release of journalists' records.

Potentially even more alarming is that in April 2024, Biden signed a bill reauthorizing for two additional years Section 702 of FISA, a statute that permits warrantless searches of phone calls, text messages, and emails intercepted by US intelligence agencies that monitor foreign communications in order to obtain information about US citizens.[28] According to the Brennan Center for Justice, the FBI "conducted 200,000 of these 'backdoor searches' in 2022 alone and has engaged in what the FISA Court called 'widespread violations' of the rules governing such searches."[29] Civil libertarians and press freedom advocates opposed reauthorization of the statute in part because the authority provided by Section 702 can be, and has been, abused to seek information about US journalists and their sources.[30]

Given President Donald Trump's well-known hostility to the press, these developments, which open the door to more frequent and more aggressive spying on journalists, are foreboding indeed.

State of the Free Press 2021 #2
Monsanto "Intelligence Center" Targeted Journalists and Activists

Sam Levin, "Revealed: How Monsanto's 'Intelligence Center' Targeted Journalists and Activists," *The Guardian*, August 8, 2019.

Student Researcher: Sarah Ghiorso (Sonoma State University)
Faculty Evaluator: Kyla Walters (Sonoma State University)

As featured in the Project's 2021 yearbook, based on reporting by Sam Levin for *The Guardian*, the agricultural giant Monsanto created an "intelligence fusion center" in order to "monitor and discredit" journalists and activists.

Levin's article detailed Monsanto's "multi-pronged strategy" to target Carey Gillam, a Reuters reporter who had covered the likelihood of Monsanto's Roundup weed killer (glyphosate) causing cancer. Monsanto also monitored a nonprofit organization focused on the food industry, US Right to Know, and the Twitter account of musician Neil Young, a prominent critic of Monsanto.

A lawsuit over the dangers of Monsanto's Roundup weed killer led to the disclosure of the internal documents. As Levin reported, company communications "add fuel to the ongoing claims that Monsanto has 'bullied' critics and scientists and worked to conceal the dangers of glyphosate, the world's most widely used herbicide."

Internal company communications documented how Monsanto planned a series of "actions" to attack the credibility of Gillam's 2017 book, *Whitewash: The Story of a Weed Killer, Cancer, and the Corruption of Science*, by providing "talking points" for "third parties" and explaining to "industry and farmer customers" how to post negative book reviews; how the company paid Google to promote search results for "Monsanto Glyphosate Carey Gillam" that criticized her work; and how it considered pressuring Reuters, where Gillam had worked for seventeen years, to reassign her to another beat.

After musician Neil Young released a 2015 album titled *The Monsanto Years*, Monsanto's fusion center also produced reports on Young's public criticism of the company, and the center evaluated the album's lyrics "to develop a list of 20+ potential topics he may target." According to documents Levin reviewed, Monsanto at one point considered legal action against Young.

According to the LinkedIn page of one person identified as a manager of Monsanto's "global intelligence and investigations," the fusion center included a team "responsible for the collection and analysis of criminal, activist/extremist, geo-political and terrorist activities affecting company operations across 160 countries," the *Guardian* reported.

A spokesperson for Bayer, which acquired Monsanto in 2018, told the *Guardian* that Monsanto's activities were "intended to ensure there was a fair, accurate and science-based dialogue about the company and its products in response to significant misinformation."

As the *Guardian* reported, Bayer "has continued to assert that glyphosate is safe," but three US court cases, in 2018 and 2019, resulted in verdicts against Monsanto, holding the company liable for plaintiffs' non-Hodgkin lymphoma, a blood cancer.[31]

In August 2019, *The Hill* reported that, in response to more than 18,000 people having filed suit against Monsanto alleging cases of non-Hodgkin lymphoma caused by Roundup, Bayer was offering $8 billion to settle all outstanding claims.[32]

When Project Censored first spotlighted the story, Monsanto's campaign to monitor and discredit journalists and other critics had received almost no corporate news coverage. A June 2019 report by ABC News was a rare exception, but this report consistently emphasized the perspective of Monsanto and Bayer.[33] ABC quoted a statement made by the PR firm FleishmanHillard that sought to normalize Monsanto's actions and its own business relationship with Monsanto: "Corporations, NGOs and other clients rightfully expect our firm to help them understand diverse perspectives before they engage. To do so, we ... gather relevant information from publicly available sources." Other than the PR firm FleishmanHillard, the ABC News report quoted only Bayer officials, including soundbites from the company's head of corporate communications and the chair of its board.

Update

Since Project Censored included Levin's report among its top stories from 2019–2020, Bayer has continued to face mounting financial challenges due to litigation over Roundup. In 2020, the company agreed to pay upwards of $10.9 billion to settle some 100,000 Roundup lawsuits.[34] Yet, as Reuters reported in October 2024, Bayer is still facing 58,000 lawsuits by individuals claiming its weedkiller had harmed their health.[35] Although the company has won most of the cases that have gone to trial, on two recent occasions, juries have found them liable for damages, ordering awards of $1.56 billion in November 2023 and $2.25 billion in January 2024. However, it should be noted that these awards were subsequently reduced to $611 million and $400 million, respectively.

Bayer's strategy of appealing adverse verdicts to the Supreme Court on the theory that state laws mandating warnings on potentially toxic chemicals are preempted by "federal labeling laws regulating crop protection products" has, so far, failed miserably.[36] In 2022, for example, the Supreme Court refused to hear an appeal of a lower court ruling that upheld a $25 million award to a California Roundup user.[37]

Reuters earlier this year reported that Bayer has told US lawmakers it may be forced to stop selling Roundup to US consumers if legislators do not "strengthen legal protection against product liability litigation."[38]

In order to burnish its public image, Bayer in May 2019 retained the global law firm Sidley Austin to investigate the lists of European journalists, politicians, and others that

FleishmanHillard had previously assembled for Monsanto. As the *Irish Independent* reported in September 2019, Sidley Austin's independent review concluded that the PR agency "did not act illegally and that no 'sensitive' information was tracked."[39] The law firm also found "no support for allegations that the stakeholder lists tracked stakeholders' personal hobbies, leisure activities, or other personal interests."

Despite Sidley Austin's apparently exculpatory findings, the French Data Protection Authority (CNIL) fined Monsanto approximately $450,000 in July 2021 for failing to alert some two hundred journalists, activists, and politicians that it had collected information about them in violation of European Union and French privacy regulations. As *Politico* reported, Monsanto "infringed European privacy rules by not informing people that it had recorded their information in a lobbying file."[40]

Investigative journalists have continued to dig into the agrochemical industry's systematic campaign to discredit its critics and opponents of dangerous pesticides, particularly Roundup. Nonprofit public health watchdog and research organization US Right to Know in 2022 released a report, *Merchants of Poison: How Monsanto Sold the World on a Toxic Pesticide,* which mapped Monsanto's network of front organizations, websites, social media accounts, and PR consultants dedicated to "trolling" journalists, academics, and activists who raise awareness about the hazards of glyphosate, or who expose the company's secretive efforts to influence scientific research that could support regulation of the chemical's use.[41]

A joint 2024 investigation by *The Guardian*, *Le Monde*, and other international media outlets revealed that a boutique PR firm employed by Monsanto, v-Fluence, was gathering "intelligence" about influential critics of pesticides—such as food journalist Michael Pollan—and making it available to pesticide industry insiders via an "online private portal."[42] The firm had received some of its funding from the US Department of Agriculture and USAID grants. v-Fluence ceased operations shortly after its activities were exposed by *The Guardian*, *Le Monde*, and their partners.[43]

Although the establishment press occasionally cite experts from US Right to Know in their reporting on other topics, they failed to so much as mention *Merchants of Poison* and its findings about pesticide disinformation.[44] Meanwhile, revelations about US government support for v-Fluence and the PR company's profiling of pesticide critics were completely ignored by corporate news media in the United States.

State of The Free Press 2021 #24
Silenced in Savannah: Journalist Abby Martin Challenges Georgia's BDS "Gag Law"

"Abby Martin Banned from Speaking at US University for Refusing to Sign Pro-Israel Pledge," *teleSUR English*, January 17, 2020.

"Abby Martin Sues Georgia State over Law Forcing Loyalty to Israel," *teleSUR English*, February 10, 2020.

Sheldon Richman, "Anti-BDS Laws Violate Our Freedom," *CounterPunch*, February 17, 2020.

Alan MacLeod, "Journalist Abby Martin Sues State of Georgia over Law Requiring Pledge of Allegiance to Israel," *MintPress News*, February 10, 2020.

Student Researcher: Kathleen Doyle (University of Vermont) and Troy Patton (Diablo Valley College)

Faculty Evaluators: Rob Williams (University of Vermont) and Mickey Huff (Diablo Valley College)

On the weekend of February 28 and 29, 2020, journalist and documentary filmmaker Abby Martin was scheduled to give a keynote speech to the International Critical Media Literacy Conference at Georgia Southern University (GSU). Martin is a well-known supporter of the Boycott, Divestment and Sanctions (BDS) movement, dedicated to using economic boycotts and divestment to end support for Israel's oppression of Palestinians. However, the conference organizers told Martin she must comply with Georgia's anti-BDS law or they'd be forced to cancel her talk. Martin refused, and the university abruptly called off her speech.

As Project Censored noted, in 2020, Georgia was one of twenty-eight states that had adopted anti-BDS laws prohibiting state agencies from doing business with boycotters of Israel. Georgia's Republican-led legislature passed legislation in 2016 requiring anybody contracting with the state and being paid more than $1,000 to sign an oath swearing they would not urge a boycott of Israel.

In defiance of the Georgia law, Martin steadfastly refused to sign a contractual pledge not to boycott Israel. According to a February 17, 2020, article in *CounterPunch*, the conference sponsors supported her stance. Eventually, the state of Georgia canceled the entire conference, according to *MintPress News*. On February 10, 2020, Martin, with assistance from lawyers from the Council on American-Islamic Relations (CAIR), filed a federal lawsuit claiming her right to free speech had been violated.

"We must stand firmly opposed to these efforts and not cower in fear to these blatant violations of free speech," Martin posted via Twitter (now X) following the cancellation, according to *MintPress News*.

Not long before Georgia sought to muzzle Abby Martin, President Donald Trump issued an executive order designed to stifle BDS activism. In December 2019, he signed an order defining Judaism as both a religion and a nationality under federal law. The stated aim of the order was to combat "antisemitism on college campuses." However, the terms of the order effectively meant colleges and universities could lose funding for allowing BDS activism on their campuses.

Project Censored spotlighted this case in 2021 before Abby Martin's suit reached the courts. At the time, the story received little corporate coverage. Outside of a single report in the Associated Press, reporting was limited to independent outlets or news sources that specialized in Israeli/American affairs.[45]

Update

On May 21, 2021, US District Court Judge Mark H. Cohen ruled in favor of Martin, finding that Georgia's anti-BDS law violated her free speech rights guaranteed by the First Amendment. According to the Associated Press, Cohen held that forcing people seeking to do business with the state "to pledge that they are not engaged in a boycott of Israel is 'unconstitutional compelled speech.'"[46]

In a press release hailing the decision, CAIR acknowledged that, although "the judge's opinion clearly indicates his view that the law is unconstitutional, the decision does not yet strike down the law. The next stage of the case will regard what steps the court will take to address ... the constitutional violation identified."[47]

However, Cohen in his ruling dismissed the claims Martin had brought against specific GSU officials who enforced the unconstitutional contract oath, citing qualified immunity (which protects government employees from legal liability for doing their jobs).[48] Martin and CAIR appealed this decision, and, in June 2023, the Eleventh Circuit Court of Appeals ruled that the GSU officials were indeed protected by qualified immunity.[49]

In 2022, the Georgia legislature amended the state's anti-BDS law to raise the threshold for the anti-boycott pledge to contracts worth more than $100,000 and specified that the requirement only applies to contracts involving contractees with five or more employees.[50]

Free speech advocates criticized the revisions to Georgia's anti-BDS statute as a gambit to protect the law from judicial review by excluding individual plaintiffs like Martin. As CAIR attorney Justin Sadowsky told the *Atlanta Journal-Constitution*, "This is one of many cases in which governments who have anti-BDS laws have modified those laws to exclude people who bring lawsuits, showing that even they believe these laws are constitutionally problematic."[51]

BDS gag laws elsewhere across the country have faced a rising number of court challenges. According to *Al Jazeera,* in 2018, the *Arkansas Times,* a newspaper based in Little Rock, defied the state's anti-BDS law by refusing to sign a pledge so that it could secure advertising from a public university.

The Arkansas Times sued and, after losing in district court, appealed to the Eighth Circuit Court of Appeals, where a three-judge panel ruled that the state's anti-BDS law violated Constitutional free speech rights. However, in June 2022, the full Eighth Circuit reversed the panel's ruling, concluding that boycotts are a form of "commercial activity" and not "expressive activity" protected by the First Amendment.[52] In February 2023, the Supreme Court declined to hear an appeal of that decision, leaving Arkansas's anti-BDS law in force.[53]

As of April 2025, thirty-eight states have adopted some version of the anti-BDS policies on the books in Georgia and Arkansas, either by statute or through executive order.[54] Further legal challenges against these blatant forms of government censorship seem inevitable.

While local and independent media have dutifully covered the legislative and courtroom battles surrounding anti-BDS laws, the most prominent national news outlets' coverage of this story has been haphazard and intermittent at best. *The New York Times*, for instance, ran an in-depth cover story about political struggles over BDS in the March 28, 2019, issue of its Sunday magazine.[55] In 2021, the newspaper carried an op-ed written by the publisher of the *Arkansas Times*, Alan Leveritt, about why he refused to sign an anti-BDS oath.[56] Amazingly, though, the *Times* failed to cover Abby Martin's successful lawsuit challenging Georgia's anti-BDS law, or the subsequent legislative changes to that law, even though they had covered Martin and her career as a TV journalist in the past.[57]

JAYDEN LAWRENCE is a sophomore journalism major, minoring in political science and environmental studies, at North Central College in Naperville, Illinois.

STEVE MACEK is a Professor of Communication at North Central College and co-coordinator of Project Censored's Campus Affiliates Program.

NOTES

1. Walter Benjamin, "Theses on the Philosophy of History" in *Illuminations: Essays and Reflections*, ed. Hannah Arendt (Schocken Books, 1968), 257.
2. Benjamin, "Theses," 255.
3. Brett Samuels, "Trump Ramps Up Rhetoric on Media, Calls Press 'The Enemy of the People'," *The Hill,* April 5, 2019.
4. Leonard Downie Jr., "The Trump Administration and the Media," Committee to Protect Journalists, April 16, 2020.
5. Soraya Ferdman, "Trump Campaign Sues Washington Post for Defamation, One Week After New York Times Lawsuit," First Amendment Watch, March 4, 2020.
6. Alex Griffing, "Elon Musk Says '60 Minutes' Staffers 'Deserve a Long Prison Sentence'—In Response to Show's Interview with a GOP DOGE Critic," *Mediaite,* February 17, 2025.
7. "Trump Blasts Foes and Media in Speech at 'Department of Injustice'," France 24, March 14, 2025.
8. Steve Benen, "Trump Renews Focus on Targeting Networks' Broadcast Licenses," MSNBC, January 18, 2024.
9. Meg James, "How Trump's FCC Chair is Stoking the Culture War," *Los Angeles Times*, April 28, 2025.
10. David Folkenflik, "Trump's FCC Chief Opens Investigation Into NPR and PBS," NPR, January 30, 2025.
11. Scott Nover, Herb Scribner, and Frances Vinall, "Public Media Ready to Fight 'Unlawful' Trump Order Defunding PBS, NPR," *Washington Post*, May 2, 2025.
12. Paula Reid and Katelyn Polantz, "ABC News Settles Defamation Suit with Trump for $15 Million," CNN, December 14, 2024.
13. Robin Opsahl, "Trump Sues Des Moines Register, Pollster over Preelection Iowa Poll," *Iowa Capital Dispatch*, December 17, 2024.
14. Todd Spangler, "Paramount, Trump Agree on Mediator for President's $20 Billion '60 Minutes' Lawsuit," *Variety,* April 7, 2025.
15. Maya Yang, "White House Bans AP Journalists from Oval Office amid Continued Gulf Dispute," *The Guardian*, February 14, 2025.
16. "One Month of Trump: Press Freedom Under Siege," Reporters Without Borders, February 19, 2025.
17. "As Leak Investigations Surge, Our New Lawsuit Seeks the Trump Admin's Guideline on Surveillance of Journalists," Freedom of the Press Foundation, November 29, 2017.
18. Jack Stubbs and Ginger Gibson, "Russia's RT America Registers as 'Foreign Agent' in US," Reuters, November 13, 2017.
19. "US Can Spy on Journalists Domestically Using FISA Warrants, Declassified Guidelines Show," RT, September 19, 2018.
20. Cora Currier, "Secret Rules Make It Pretty Easy for the FBI to Spy on Journalists," *The Intercept*, January 31, 2017.
21. Matthew Rosenberg and Matt Apuzzo, "Court Approved Wiretap on Trump Campaign Aide over Russia Ties," *New York Times,* April 12, 2017. See also, John Fritze, "Trump Calls for Release of Classified Documents Tied to Russia Probe in Fox Interview," *USA Today*, March 27, 2019, updated March 28, 2019, and Liam Brennan, "The Truth about 'Spying' on the Trump Campaign," *New York Times,* May 3, 2019.
22. Devlin Barrett, "Trump Justice Department Secretly Obtained Post Reporters' Phone Records," *Washington Post,* May 7, 2021.

23. Jeremy Herb and Jessica Schneider, "Trump Administration Secretly Obtained CNN Reporter's Phone and Email Records," *CNN*, May 20, 2021.
24. Charlie Savage and Katie Benner, "U.S. Waged Secret Legal Battle to Obtain Emails of 4 Times Reporters," *New York Times*, June 4, 2021, updated June 9, 2021.
25. Eric Tucker, "Justice Dept. Says It'll No Longer Seize Reporters' Records," *Associated Press*, June 5, 2021.
26. Anna Diakun and Trevor Timm, "For the Biden Administration, Who Counts as News Media?" Knight First Amendment Institute (blog), June 9, 2021.
27. Léonie Chao-Fong, "Pam Bondi Rescinds Biden-Era Protections for Journalists," *The Guardian*, April 25, 2025.
28. Dell Cameron, "The Next US President Will Have Troubling New Surveillance Powers," *Wired*, April 22, 2024.
29. "FISA Section 702 Backdoor Searches: Myths and Facts," Brennan Center for Justice, November 28, 2023, updated November 30, 2023.
30. Gabe Rottman, "House Passes 2-year Extension of Section 702," Reporters Committee for Freedom of the Press, April 15, 2024.
31. See, for example, Sam Levin and Patrick Greenfield, "Monsanto Ordered to Pay $289 M as Jury Rules Weedkiller Caused Man's Cancer," *The Guardian*, August 11, 2018. A federal jury in 2019 found Monsanto liable in a third case, ruling that Roundup was to blame for another California man's cancer and ordering the company to pay $80 million in damages. See Sam Levin, "Monsanto Found Liable for California Man's Cancer and Ordered to Pay $80m in Damages," *The Guardian*, March 27, 2019.
32. Nathaniel Weixel, "Monsanto Sought to Discredit Journalists, Critics: Report," *The Hill*, August 9, 2019.
33. Soo Youn, "Monsanto Is Contacting the Journalists, Activists It Tracked on 'Watch Lists' in 7 Countries," ABC News, June 18, 2019.
34. Ludwig Burger and Tina Bellon, "Bayer to Pay Up to $10.9 billion to Settle Bulk of Roundup Weedkiller Cancer Lawsuits," Reuters, June 24, 2020.
35. Brendan Pierson, "Bayer Must Pay $78 Million in Latest Roundup Cancer Trial, Jury Finds," *Reuters*, October 10, 2024.
36. "Managing Roundup Litigation," Bayer Global, April 5, 2024.
37. "Bayer: Supreme Court Rejects Chemical Maker's Weedkiller Appeal," BBC, June 21, 2022.
38. Patricia Weiss and Ludwig Burger, "Bayer Tells US It Could Halt Roundup Weedkiller Sales over Legal Risks," Reuters, March 7, 2025.
39. Donal O'Donovan, "PR Firm Cleared After Probe into Monsanto 'Lists'," *Irish Independent*, September 5, 2019.
40. Vincent Manancourt, "French Privacy Regulator Fines Monsanto for Privacy Breach," *Politico*, July 28, 2021.
41. Stacy Malkan, Kendra Klein, and Anna Lappé, *Merchants of Poison: How Monsanto Sold the World on a Toxic Pesticide* (US Right to Know, 2022).
42. Carey Gillam, Margot Gibbs and Elena DeBre, "Revealed: The US Government Funded 'Private Social Network' Attacking Pesticide Critics," *The Guardian*, September 27, 2024; Stéphane Foucart, Elena DeBre and Margot Gibbs, "Diving into the Black Box of Global Pesticide Propaganda," *Le Monde*, September 28, 2024.
43. Carey Gillam, Margot Gibbs and Elena DeBre, "US-funded 'Social Network' Attacking Pesticide Critics Shuts Down After Guardian

44 See, for instance, Alice Callahan, "Food Industry Influence Could Cloud US Dietary Guidelines, a New Report Says," *New York Times*, October 4, 2023.
45 Jeff Martin, "Filmmaker Who Wouldn't Sign Georgia's Israel Oath Sues State," Associated Press, February 12, 2020.
46 "Judge Rules Against Georgia in Legal Fight over Israel Oath," Associated Press, May 25, 2021.
47 "CAIR & PCJF Win 'Major Victory' in Federal Lawsuit Against Georgia's Anti-Israel Boycott Law; Court Rules Anti-BDS Law Violates the First Amendment," CAIR, May 24, 2021.
48 "CAIR Files Federal Appeal Against Officials Who Implemented Georgia's Anti-BDS Law," CAIR, Nov 7, 2022.
49 Abby Martin v. Chancellor for The Board of Regents of The University System Georgia, et al., no. 22-12827 (11th Cir. 2023); see Davis Giangiulio, "Appeals Court Sides with State over Law Targeting Boycotts Against Israel," *Atlanta Journal-Constitution*, June 29, 2023.
50 Greg Bluestein, "New Georgia Law Revives Israel Oath for Large State Contracts," *Atlanta Journal–Constitution*, February 21, 2022.
51 Giangiulio, "Appeals Court Sides with State."
52 Ali Harb, "'Frightening': US Appeals Court Upholds Arkansas Anti-BDS Law," *Al Jazeera*, June 22, 2022.
53 Ali Harb, "Top US Court Refuses to Review Anti-BDS Law. Here's What It Means," *Al Jazeera*, February 21, 2023.
54 Alexandra Martinez, "Midwest Organizers Lead Push to Repeal Anti-Boycott Laws as Free Speech Battle Intensifies," *Prism*, April 30, 2025.
55 Nathan Thrall, "How the Battle over Israel and Anti-Semitism Is Fracturing American Politics," *New York Times Magazine*, March 28, 2019.
56 Alan Leveritt, "We're a Small Arkansas Newspaper. Why is the State Making Us Sign a Pledge About Israel?" *New York Times*, November 22, 2021.
57 See, for example, Ellen Barry and Ravi Somaiya, "For Russian TV Channels, Influence and Criticism," *New York Times*, March 5, 2014; and Russell Goldman, "Russia's RT: The Network Implicated in U.S. Election Meddling," *New York Times*, January 8, 2017.

CHAPTER 3

Making America Junky Again:
POISON PILLS, PEDDLING HATE, AND THE ROTTING OF THE PUBLIC MIND

REAGAN HAYNIE, SHEALEIGH VOITL, and SIERRA KAUL

INTRODUCTION

Donald Trump's second term in office rapidly descended into full-tilt fascism, all with the help of his former plucky sidekick, Elon Musk.[1] (True love didn't last this time.) But the writing was always on the wall, wasn't it? The Heritage Foundation rolled out Project 2025 (we were as disappointed with that name as you are) back in April 2023, laying out a menacing agenda for the next conservative administration way ahead of Trump's reelection, although the corporate media waited much too long to pay attention.[2] And remember when General Mark Milley said Trump demanded that he direct forces to "crack [the] skulls" of protestors in 2020?[3] Or, of course, in 2017 when he referred to the news media as the "enemy of the American people"?[4] Did we really think he wasn't practicing for the *real* thing? That we weren't being forced to sit through an excruciating dress rehearsal for bona fide far-right authoritarianism? Weren't your spidey senses *tingling* for that infamous Musk Nazi ("Roman," eyeroll) salute?[5] Or as the Anti-Defamation League would have you believe, a sort of whoopsie-daisies "awkward gesture in a moment of enthusiasm."[6]

This year was filled with accused deathcare CEO assassin Luigi Mangione fancams and thirst traps (we kinda liked those), self-proclaimed Nazi Kanye West peddling cheap swastika t-shirts and releasing songs called "Heil Hitler" (definitely didn't like those, although Joe Rogan thought the song was "kinda catchy"), and Mark Zuckerberg claiming we can all replace the gift of friendship with a little help from AI.[7] We also bore witness to the misogynistic ways in which corporate media reported on workplace harassment, i.e., Blake Lively and Justin Baldoni, and made light of sex trafficking, i.e., Sean "Diddy" Combs.[8] But who's surprised? Never us!

These stories, and particularly the way the establishment press *frames* them, are what we at Project Censored call Junk Food News—a term originally coined in the early 1980s by Project Censored's founder, Carl Jensen. Junk Food News refers to the often trivial and inconsequential stories—think celebrity gossip, political theater, and other entertainment-related hoopla—that get considerable coverage from corporate *news* media outlets and detract from important news stories, like the ones highlighted in each year's Top *Censored* Stories list.[9] These sensationalized stories feed something in us, including our fixation on fame. Each year, Junk Food News examines the cultural values and frames perpetuating the sloppy news coverage that steers us off course. In *The Image: A Guide to Pseudo-Events in America*, published in 1962, American historian Daniel Boorstin presciently predicted the blurring of media and reality in the twenty-first century, anticipating how junky stories, or "illusions," would come to flourish, ultimately distracting us from news affecting our everyday lives.[10] Moreover, Boorstin noted, "We have become so accustomed to our illusions that we mistake them for reality. We demand them. And we demand that there always be more of them, bigger and better and more vivid."[11]

But, juicy as these stories may be, you can't base a balanced news diet on them. Don't fret, reader; we know a little reality enhancement can be delicious! But these distractions ultimately leave you malnourished in your understanding of the forces that shape the world and the systemic inequalities that affect our daily lives.

While the establishment press enticed us with the latest about Kanye, Lively, and Diddy, among others, these outlets effectively invited us to ignore reporting about the intricacies of the dismantling of the United States government, its technocratic makeover, and the Trump administration's deportation of international students for speaking up in support of Palestinian people and a permanent ceasefire in Gaza.[12] But when actress Rachel Zegler called for a free Palestine on X, corporate news outlets' ears perked up, spinning it like a scandal that derailed the premiere of the live-action *Snow White*.[13]

In January 2025, Musk and Trump launched the Department of Government Efficiency (DOGE), which, among other sweeping initiatives, systematically dismantled, gutted, or sought to defund numerous essential government agencies; rolled back Diversity, Equity, and Inclusion (DEI) programs; and cut funding for cutting-edge medical research. *Bad dog(e)!* Musk and Trump assaulted the federal government, and JD Vance might have killed Pope Francis?[14] We're still looking into it.

Among the government agencies on the chopping block is the Department of Education. And while news outlets, including the *New York Times* and CNN, covered pop culture stories like the Drake and Kendrick Lamar feud beat by beat, coverage was considerably sparser for how federal cuts to education, particularly special education, could hit low-income families.[15]

Trump's war on the press escalated in his second term, restricting Associated Press journalists from White House media events for failing to refer to the Gulf of Mexico as "Gulf of America" in its reporting, enabling the interim US attorney for the District of Columbia to threaten "criminal investigations of members of Congress and the media who have criticized Elon Musk and his team of DOGE budget-cutters," and vindictively suing any broadcast networks that dare to paint him in an unfavorable light.[16] We're not sure; he makes up new rules all the time. Once Trump realized his influence on the corporate media, he set his sights on international student activists and journalists, threatening their visa status for any criticism of Israel's ongoing attacks on Gaza.

Although he denied knowledge of its existence during his 2025 presidential run, Donald Trump made the proposals from the conservative Heritage Foundation's Project 2025 into a promise kept.[17] Suffice it to say, we're nervous that what's left of our rights by the end of this Trump presidency could be listed in full on a Mar-a-Lago cocktail napkin.

If you're unfamiliar with it, Project 2025, a nine-hundred-page blueprint for reshaping the federal government, is almost entirely fueled by its disdain for "wokeness." The document proposes, among other terrifying ideas, mass deportations, rolling back reproductive and LGBTQ rights, limiting voting access, and censoring classroom discussions about race, gender, or systemic oppression. In the administration's first one hundred days, Trump fulfilled "policies that mirror about a third of the more than 300 policy objectives outlined in the blueprint," *Grist* reported.[18] At this rate, the only place to speak freely might be a Signal group chat labeled "Definitely NOT Woke Stuff." We'll have to check in with Secretary of Defense Pete Hegseth about that, since he's so adept at using Signal.[19]

Musk's interest is purely to expand the technocratic empire—a world in which his technologies, including Neuralink and SpaceX's Mars colonization, are rolled out free of any democratic guardrails.[20] In a January 2025 article for the *New Yorker*, Anna Wiener wrote of Musk's government influence: "Tech executives see an opportunity to shape the world in their image." Unsurprisingly, Trump looked out for his precious billionaires, packing his cabinet with the wealthiest of the wealthy—or gaudiest of the gaudy.[21]

Let's review this year's bountiful range of Junk Food News and what you may have missed during your endless doom scrolling.

FROM FEUD TO FEUDAL: DRAKE V. KENDRICK AND THE DEPARTMENT OF THE UNEDUCATED

In last year's Junk chapter, we had the honor and distinction of relaying the rap feud between Pink Barbie herself, Nicki Minaj, and the Queen of Hot Girl Summer, Megan Thee Stallion. We briefly mentioned how their beef transitioned to include Drake and Kendrick Lamar, but we finished writing our chapter before we got to see the big picture, namely, Kendrick Lamar's worldwide hit, "Not Like Us," in which Lamar called Drake a "certified pedophile." Yikes!

Now, a year later, we've seen: Drake sue streaming services and his own (and Lamar's) record label, Universal Music Group, for "boosting" Lamar's numbers, and for defamation and harassment; Lamar divide the nation at the Super Bowl halftime show with a single smile; and a glimpse of a future in which legendary rap artists like Lamar never develop because of the impending destruction of the nation's public education system.[22] Don't worry, we'll break everything down just like Lamar broke down Drake's cred.

Drake and Lamar crossed paths multiple times before their 2024 beef, slyly dissing each other during the last decade since their first collaboration in 2011. But it wasn't until Drake released two songs, "Push Ups" and "Taylor Made Freestyle," in April 2024, that the war really began. As Drake and Lamar exchanged diss tracks over a two-week span, corporate media reacted in real time. True to its slogan, "Go There," CNN sidelined its other reporting to cover the release of Lamar's songs.[23]

Since the release of "Not Like Us" on May 4, 2024, to the time of this writing, Lamar's song has been streamed nearly 1.6 billion times on Spotify alone, not including views of the music video on YouTube or plays on other music streaming services.[24] Since the "end" of Drake and Lamar's rapid-fire battle, some fans have continued to argue over who "won," because this was a fight between men, so someone has to be the alpha. Kanye West, as always, had his own opinion: appearing for an interview in a black KKK outfit, he claimed Drake was a million times better than Kendrick. Hey Drake, in case it was unclear, it's never a good thing when Nazis side with you.[25] As far as we are concerned, Lamar was the clear winner since he hasn't had to sue streaming services, claiming they're falsifying streaming numbers (and because— unlike his rival— he's never needed to defend a relationship with a thirteen-year-old).[26]

But beyond the numbers, headlines, and internet chaos, Lamar's superpower developed in his early education. He has credited his high school English teacher, Regis Inge, who works for the Compton Unified School District, for recognizing his potential early on.[27] Inge gave Lamar a thesaurus when he was a student to help him expand his vocabulary, and his mentoring fostered Lamar's poetic sensibilities. As Lamar received accolades for his artistry, he has also invested time and money in supporting a next generation of young scholars—despite Drake accusing Lamar of "not even (going) back to (his) hood and plant(ing) no money trees" in "The Heart Part 6."

In 2015, Lamar donated $50,000 to his high school's music program, according to Global Citizen, which noted that he has "donated hundreds of thousands of dollars to the Compton Unified School District's music, sports, and after-school programs."[28] Thirteen years after graduating from high school, Kendrick Lamar was honored with a 2018 Pulitzer Prize for his album *DAMN.*, "a virtuosic song collection unified by its vernacular authenticity and rhythmic dynamism that offers affecting vignettes capturing the complexity of modern African-American life."[29]

The current White House administration wants to defund the Department of Education, claiming that doing so would empower parents and free schools around the country from federal oversight.[30] However, as the Center for American Progress, a progressive think tank, has noted, the Trump administration's March 2025 decision to reduce the Department of Education's workforce by nearly half was "a direct blow" to an estimated fifty million pre-K-12 students in public schools across the country and nineteen million students enrolled in higher education.[31] Increasingly, we'll be turning to millionaires, like Lamar, and billionaires to keep our public schools alive, as the federal government turns its back on children. In fact, the Trump administration has enacted $2 billion worth of federal education cuts to varying states; among the hardest hit are states Trump won in the 2024 election.[32] The people who voted for the man in the Oval Office are among the many who rely on federal tax funds for access to quality education. Perhaps gutting federally funded and mandated education makes those working in this administration feel smarter. As Trump himself once put it, "I love the poorly educated."[33]

There seems to be some semblance of sense in the state of Colorado, where, in March 2025, more than a thousand teachers, dressed in red, went to the state capital to demand that lawmakers create a long-term plan to enhance the state's education budget. Teachers marched because the state was staring down a 1.2 billion dollar budget deficit, and legislators seemed likely to target funding for public education.[34] Unfortunately, the rest of us, with IQs higher than the ages of the girls Drake seems to favor, are likely to witness the consequences of the Department of Education becoming the Department of the Uneducated. The Secretary of Education, former CEO of World Wrestling Entertainment, Linda McMahon, is launching a total SmackDown of American schools.

Let's be real: If the kids are not going to be attending school, they may as well be doing something useful. Thankfully, the trend-setting state of Florida is providing a wonderful example of exactly what children should be doing, now that school seems to be a waste of time. With ICE agents raiding the state like there's no tomorrow (or Bill of Rights), Florida needs new members of its workforce on the double. With an overabundance of job openings that no red-blooded American adults seem to be willing to fill, Florida's new age solution is relaxing its child labor laws![35] Maybe *this* is the source of Musk's hand-wringing over low birthrates and why he is trying to single-handedly repopulate the workplace (more on that later)![36]

The Florida state legislature is considering a bill that, if passed, would allow children as young as fourteen to work overnight on school nights. Currently, state law prohibits them from working later than 11 p.m. or earlier than 6:30 a.m. In fact, last year the state already passed a law that allowed homeschooled 16- and 17-year-olds to work at any time of the day.[37] Florida has seen an ever-increasing number of homeschooled children over the years, roughly 154,000 children out of its 4.3 million children.[38] Since that isn't a noticeable contribution to Florida's workforce, they have to squeeze kids out of the public schools to make a difference.

For symmetry, the government had to make teachers' working conditions as hostile as possible. Brevard County, Florida, has become the first to follow a state law that allows teachers to use students' preferred names in the classroom only after a parent gives express permission. One such teacher, Melissa Calhoun, used a student's preferred name and has since been told that the school would not renew her contract for the following school year. The state of Florida considered revoking her teaching credential, effectively blacklisting Calhoun from teaching jobs in Florida, despite the fact that the state ranks among the top five suffering from significant shortages of qualified classroom teachers.[39]

The parent of the student whose preferred name was used found out that their child was not being called the name on their birth certificate and complained directly to the school board, a genuine Karen move straight out of a 2020-

era meme. Outrageously, teachers in Florida must obtain parental approval even before using a student's *nickname* in the classroom.[40] Ah, so this is what so-called parental rights groups like Moms for Liberty mean by liberty—the freedom to relax child labor laws and fire teachers for respecting their students? What's next, Florida, fraudulently diverting funds from a charity straight to the GOP?[41] Good kids, mad state—classic Lamar for these twisted times.

DEMOCRACY DIES IN THE REPLIES: ELON, TECHNOCRACY, AND DICK-TATORSHIP

In Trump's first hundred days, Elon Musk's growing presence in the Trump White House drew nonstop coverage from corporate media. Much of that attention was centered not on the unprecedented political power Musk now wielded, but on the sensational and the superficial. A viral video of Musk's son, X Æ A-Xii (yes, that is his name, don't blame the child—blame his parents), allegedly telling Donald Trump to "go away" captivated the news cycle. Corporate media debated the child's words, his antics in the Oval Office, and what it all meant for the President and Musk's public relationship. *Newsweek*, ABC News, and the *New York Post* all devoted ample coverage to the moment—yet few questioned why a billionaire was parading his child through a presidential press conference and other public places perched around Musk's neck like a "prop," or as other commenters online remarked, the child looked like a "human shield."[42]

Corporate media also focused on Musk's efforts to build what he calls a "legion" of high-intelligence children. Reports from the *New York Post*, *Wall Street Journal*, and *Forbes* revealed Musk's messages to women on X, asking them to bear his children in order to preserve "civilization."[43] As the modern-day Caligula, Musk has taken it upon himself to repopulate Earth and Occupy Mars.[44] What can we say— the gadfly, ketamine-fueled CEO is apparently a busy guy: spreading his seed while tanking his company's stock and gutting what's left of FDR's New Deal. And he still averages a hundred Tweets per day![45] The makings of a legend. Boorstin said heroes are no longer—clearly, the historian never met Elon Musk (manufactured by myth).

In another media spectacle, Trump turned the South Lawn of the White House into a Tesla showroom to help improve Elon's public image, because the Dark MAGA hat and hair plugs haven't improved ratings or sales. Turns out people don't like it when unelected billionaires LARP (live action roleplay) as politicians. NBC News, *Politico*, and CNN reported on the situation, highlighting the optics of Trump praising Musk as a "patriot" while Tesla's stock plummeted amid backlash over Musk's role at DOGE and the federal job cuts.[46] Corporate media mentioned the ethical concerns of a sitting president endorsing commercial products and staging a press event to boost the billionaire's ratings, but they failed to interrogate the deeper issues. On the surface, corporate media's coverage of the event appears critical and thorough. NBC took the extra step to connect Elon's actions with his broader plan of weaponizing American politics to suit his *long-term* interests.[47] But, for the most part, establishment press coverage looked a bit like a used car lot ad, airing at 2 a.m. on a cable access channel. With his eyes glazing over, Trump called the car "beautiful," saying, "everything's computer!" Propelled by its awkward formulation, the president's enthusiastic assessment quickly went viral.[48] Meanwhile, Senator Chris Murphy (D-CT) took to X to offer a PSA on the spectacle: "Just because corruption plays out in public doesn't mean it's not corruption."[49]

At this year's Conservative Political Action Conference (CPAC), Musk wielded a red chainsaw gifted to him by Argentinian President Javier Milei with his libertarian slogan, "Long Live Freedom, Damn It!" Musk vowed to slash even more while shouting from the stage, "This is the chainsaw for bureaucracy."[50] Musk looked like he was taking a page out of Mike Judge's satirical 2006 film *Idiocracy*, where President Dwayne Elizondo Mountain Dew Herbert Camacho (a former pro wrestler and porn star) unloaded the clip of an automatic rifle into the air at his State of the Union Address to command attention. Musk also accused Democrats of "treason" and voiced support for auditing the Federal Reserve. His performance, covered by major media outlets including the *New York Times* and AP, captivated attention, but the corporate media again failed to ask more pressing questions: Why is an unelected, South African billionaire shaping so much of American politics?[51] *And* what is he doing, wielding a chainsaw at a conference and harassing young women online to have his babies?

These moments might seem random or absurd, but they follow a recognizable pattern. As Boorstin wrote in *The Image: A Guide to Pseudo-Events in America*, modern media thrives on pseudo-events, which are staged or strategically planned happenings, designed to attract media attention and shape public discourse.[52] Rather than occurring naturally, these stories are purposely framed to distract, fill air time, manipulate public perception, and promote broader establishment agendas. Musk, who rose to power as a businessman and technocrat, now functions as a producer of pseudo-events—generating a steady stream of spectacles and controversy to keep his name in the headlines.

Nowhere is this dynamic more visible than in the media circus surrounding Musk. While corporate outlets dedicate seemingly endless airtime with ample coverage to his antics—his children, eugenics-motivated romantic entanglements, exploding rockets, drug-addled behaviors, and headline-grabbing publicity stunts—the real story goes largely ignored: the shift toward technocratic rule in which billionaires shape public policy to promote private interests. Musk is not just a megalomaniac; he is the wealthiest person in the world and an *unelected* political actor who is attempting to restructure American democracy to serve his interests. These scandals aren't irrelevant—it is newsworthy that the world's richest man is using the White House as a personal playground and boardroom. But when corporate media focus solely on spectacle, without context, critique, or continuity, these stories become fodder for more junk food news. Additionally, when corporate media get caught in the spectacle instead of holding Musk (or Trump, who appointed him) accountable, they further enable Musk's broader ambitions of establishing a technocratic overhaul of American democracy.

A technocracy is a system where power is held not by elected representatives but by unelected tech experts—engineers, billionaires, and data scientists—who justify their dictatorship through technical skill rather than public support.[53] Technocrats like Musk believe in conquering the world through technological dominance, stripping away human agency in favor of technological optimization of government. In a technocracy championed by Musk, and primarily led by Curtis Yarvin and Peter Thiel, his business ventures and interests, such as Neuralink, Mars colonization, autonomous cars, and AI governance, would be implemented because they can be, not because the public voted for them. Technocracy is fundamentally anti-democratic. It sidesteps public debate, suppresses dissent, and treats people as data points rather than human beings. In a technocracy, technological "progress" becomes the goal, even if it comes at humanity's expense.

Luckily, our so-called democratic process hasn't been totally overhauled *yet*, but we are inching closer to this reality. In early 2025, Elon (did we mention he's the richest man in the world?) leveraged his reputation as a "tech expert" (and his extraordinary wealth) to secure a front-row seat in the Trump White House, sidestepping the democratic process. His newly found position as "special government employee" of the DOGE granted him the not-so-altruistic ability to restructure government spending, under the guise of "eliminating waste and redundancy."[54]

So far, Musk's role in reshaping the government spending has been about as popular as his Cybertruck (which seems to resemble Musk's torso lying down), also one of the worst dumpster fires in automotive history—we mean that literally, given Tesla's unique ability to lock passengers inside as they combust into flames. Earlier this year, the Cybertruck deathmobile was awarded with a fatality rate of 14.5 per hundred thousand units, which is seventeen times greater than the fatality rate of the infamous Ford Pinto—but we digress.[55] What were we talking about, again? Oh yeah, the Death of Government Efficiency (DOGE).

DOGE, manned by AI, Musk allies, and a squad of six fail sons seemingly grown in Peter Thiel's cryo-pod chamber. Chief among them is 19-year-old cybercriminal Edward Coristine, the final boss of the Broccoli-haired Hitlerjugend, also known as "Big Balls" in online circles. In 2021, Offizier Balls ran a privacy-focused image sharing website, where URLs that linked users to his site referenced "the sale of child sexual abuse material, racial slurs, and rape," according to *Musk Watch*.[56] He was also a member of the cybercriminal Telegram channel "The Com" and ran a company called DiamondCDN that provided network services to a group of cybercriminals known as "EGodly."[57]

Another DOGE henchman, Marko Elez, is a 25-year-old graduate from Rutgers, who was axed from DOGE for committing the only fireable offense within the federal agency—being more racist than Elon.[58] In a series of now-deleted tweets, Elez made statements like, "Normalize Indian Hate" and "You could not pay me to marry outside of my ethnicity." JD Vance, whose wife, Usha Vance, is the daughter of Indian immigrants, advocated for Elez's reinstatement, saying, "I obviously disagree with some of Elez's posts, but I don't think stupid social media activity should ruin a kid's life."[59] Again, Elez is 25.

He also tweeted, "Just for the record, I was racist before it was cool" and "I just want a eugenic immigration policy, is that too much to ask."[60] In response to Elez's resignation, the Führer of X took to his platform to poll his audience on whether or not he should rehire the "@DOGE staffer who made inappropriate statements."[61] Consequently, Musk rehired Elez in February. According to *Politico*, the lapdog rejoined DOGE and currently works in the Department of Health and Human Services, as well as four other agencies overseeing child support dealings (convenient for Elon, considering he has public child support disputes with two of his four baby mamas), Medicare and Medicaid payments, and HHS contracts.[62,63]

Since the inception of DOGE, and at the time of this writing, our Big-Tech–overlords–in–training have eliminated more than 260,000 federal jobs and closed several fundamental federal agencies, including the U.S. Agency for International Development and the Consumer Financial Protection Bureau. They have terminated hundreds of diversity, equity, and inclusion grants and canceled billions in federal contracts.[64] These moves are branded as "efficiency" measures, but in practice, they concentrate power at the top and limit public oversight. It should be headline-dominating material (but it isn't) that Musk has "a direct business interest in over 70 percent of the agencies and departments targeted by DOGE since its inception," according to Public Citizen.[65] That is certainly an efficiency measure if the goal is for Musk to enrich himself and his companies.

Neuralink, Musk's brain chip technology that could turn the human brain into a computer interface, is benefiting greatly from these conflicts of interest. In their investigation into DOGE, Public Citizen found that Neuralink was under federal investigation for disturbing animal testing practices—killing over 1,500 animals—before the USDA inspector overseeing the probe was abruptly fired in January 2025, part of a broader purge carried out by the Trump administration and Musk's DOGE initiative.[66] At the same time, DOGE gutted the FDA's Office of Neurological and Physical Medicine Devices, terminating at least twenty employees, several of whom worked directly on Neuralink.[67] It's a textbook conflict of interest: Musk is using his position in DOGE to dismantle the very agencies meant to hold his companies accountable, conveniently, just as Neuralink moves closer to human implantation.

Currently, Neuralink is being tested and marketed as a mobility solution for disabled people, but Musk hasn't been shy about his hopes to bridge the gap between humans and machines by bringing Neuralink to mass markets, further advancing his technocratic "utopia." However, not all dreams live up to the fantasy. If implemented into the consumer market, the chip poses a huge surveillance threat and has the potential to create new forms of inequality.[68] Just imagine: a world where you can pay $50,000 (if you can afford it, of course) to transform yourself into a real human-robot hybrid! Whether it's *Blade Runner, 2001: A Space Odyssey*, or *WestWorld*, sci-fi fans can rejoice in their favorite cautionary tales about technological advancements and artificial intelligence becoming a reality. Surely nothing could go wrong...

Predictably, corporate media failed to cover these stories effectively. *The New York Times* published one article referencing the FDA firings, but only within a broader three-thousand-word report documenting Elon's conflicts of interest as head of DOGE.[69] Similar to Public Citizen's DOGE report, the *New York Times*'s piece calls out the many conflicts of interest surrounding Elon's position as the head of DOGE. However, the *Times*'s report frames the Elon-led firings and budget cuts as isolated incidents, failing to connect them with Musk's broader technocratic ambitions. The Public Citizen report, on the other hand, directly connects Musk's business interests to deregulation, technocratic overreach, and corporate capture of federal agencies. It also offers a real call to action for Congress to "tighten conflict of interest rules on special government employees" that stop them from holding government contracts. Additionally, they ask Congress to "hold hearings" and "request documents" that hold those in power accountable.[70]

There's no question the *Times* coverage offers a thorough catalog of facts and figures.[71] But the article bombards readers with disconnected data and lacks a clear call to action. There's a difference between informing an audience and providing them with meaningful, substantive information they can act on. This is what media scholar Neil Postman referred to as the "information-action ratio." In a 1990 speech to the German Informatics Society, Postman said,

> The tie between information and action has been severed. Information is now a commodity that can be bought and sold, or used as a form of entertainment, or worn like a garment to enhance one's status. It comes indiscriminately, directed at no one in particular, disconnected from usefulness; we are glutted with information, drowning in information, have no control over it, don't know what to do with it.[72]

The New York Times coverage of Musk's conflicts of interest may inform, but in the Postman sense, it fails to empower and apply context. Without context, consequences, or confrontation of Musk's abuse of power, information is as good as noise.

The corporate media, for the most part, has failed to connect the dots. Outlets continue to frame Musk's actions as bizarre, isolated spectacles rather than distractions from Elon's broader goal of reshaping American democracy to serve his technocratic interests. As *Common Dreams* noted, there is a knowledge gap within mainstream political and media institutions.[73] They remain stuck in a 1990s worldview—unprepared or unwilling to grapple with the implications of technocratic rule or Big Tech's blind demand for continuous technological advancement. Elon's newfound, short-lived position in government wasn't motivated by his desire to serve the public interest. The reality is that Elon, the richest person in the world, seized an opportunity to reshape the US government in his favor. Corporate media's focus on the legality and ethical concerns of Elon's government "takeover" is not enough. The deeper issue is structural: Musk is not just influencing government policy; he is restructuring governance itself. From Neuralink and SpaceX to Tesla and X, his companies form a digital empire capable of surveilling, shaping, and monetizing human behavior at an unprecedented scale. His previous role as head of DOGE and close proximity to the Trump administration only accelerated this trajectory. And even after Trump kicked Musk to the curb, later saying Musk had gone "crazy," regular people were left to wonder why billionaires were so fickle with everything besides making the world a better place.[74]

The press must shift its focus, or more accurately, its framing. It is no longer sufficient to treat Musk's antics as entertainment or scandal. They are evidence of a larger plan to merge state and tech power. If we fail to recognize the rise of technocratic governance now, we may soon find ourselves governed not by elected officials, but by unaccountable billionaires cloaked in the language of efficiency and innovation.

GAL GADOT AND THE POISONED APPLE OF ZIONISM?

In March 2025, actress Gal Gadot was honored with a star on the Hollywood Walk of Fame. Not long before, *Variety* published an interview with Gadot, ahead of the premiere of her new live-action *Snow White* film, focusing primarily on her moral duty to advocate for Israeli hostages after October 7.[75] Gadot, who served as a combat trainer in the Israel Defense Forces (IDF) for two years and hosted screenings for *Bearing Witness*—a 2023 documentary produced by the IDF—told *Variety* she was "all about humanity" (Note: That humanity does not extend to Palestinians) and referred to herself as an "eighth-generation Israeli." Although that implies two hundred years of ancestry in a country less than a century old, but, hey, a legacy of settler-colonialism makes math a little tricky.[76]

"After October 7th [2023] ... I was shocked by the amount of hate, by the amount of how much people think they know when they actually have no idea," Gadot said. "And also by how the media is not fair many times. So I had to speak up."

Which media, Gal? Certainly not CNN, which has received massive backlash for its pro-Israel bias.[77] And indeed, not the *New York Times*, whose article about systemic sexual violence perpetrated by Hamas against Israeli women had been repeatedly and comprehensively discredited and debunked by numerous investigative journalists, as covered in Robin Andersen's News Abuse chapter in *State of the Free Press 2025*.[78] The paper even directed its journalists to avoid using the terms "genocide," "ethnic cleansing," and "refugee camps" when reporting on Palestine, according to an internal memo obtained by *The Intercept*.[79] *NYT* editors were motivated to avoid use of words that were "too incendiary on both sides." However, *The Intercept*'s analysis revealed that the *Times* described Israeli deaths as a "massacre" on fifty-three occasions and "those of Palestinians just once," as of November 24, 2024.[80] This, despite the death count of Palestinians being far greater.

"The majority of news since the war began, regardless of how accurate the initial reporting, has been skewed by a systemic and institutional bias within the network toward Israel," one CNN staffer told the *Guardian*.[81] "Ultimately, CNN's coverage of the Israel-Gaza war amounts to journalistic malpractice."

Later that month, a sour narrative emerged about the production of *Snow White*, even more bitter than the Evil Queen's poison apple.[82] Gadot's co-star Rachel Zegler's vocal support for Palestine via X ahead of the film's release had Disney executives reeling.[83] Apparently, they hadn't accounted for the part of the story where the "fairest of them all" has her own politics. *Variety* even reported that death threats against Gadot spiked after Zegler's post, prompting Disney to hire additional security for the "mother of four." Yes, *Variety* actually wrote it that way.

Snow White producer Marc Platt flew to New York to speak with Zegler about removing the post, allegedly convincing her to work with a "social media guru paid for by Disney to vet any posts before the film's March 21 bow." "Vet," of course, is Hollywood-speak for censor.

Embarrassingly, Platt's son Jonah responded on Instagram to news of his father's meeting with Zegler in a now-deleted comment, saying, his daddy had to "reprimand his 20 year old employee for dragging her personal politics into the middle of promoting the movie for which she signed a multi-million dollar contract to get paid and do publicity for."[84] Jonah insisted Zegler's actions "hurt the film's box office," calling the actress "narcissistic." Jonah, dear, we advise you not to pursue a future in PR!

Nevertheless, Zegler refused to remove the original post in which she advocated for a free Palestine.

Variety's article implicitly attributes the film's failure to Zegler's cowboy-like behavior online, framing her support of Palestine as highly controversial and Gadot's advocacy for Israeli hostages as unproblematic. This messaging reinforces a dangerous double standard, wherein corporate media valorizes pro-Israel sentiments and casts pro-Palestinian support as disruptive, career-jeopardizing, and inherently antisemitic.

In 2023, Spyglass, the studio that produces the horror film series *Scream*, fired actress Melissa Barrera for posting and sharing content they deemed "antisemitic."[85] Barrera had been posting support for Palestine amidst Israel's bombardment of Gaza and criticism of Israel's government.

However, *Snow White*'s epic flop—earning $87 million globally in its opening weekend, when it cost roughly $350 million to make and market—was almost certainly not the result of its lead actress's support for Palestine, but rather a fundamental issue with the retelling of the classic Disney story. Disney conveniently made Zegler into the perfect "scapegoat," according to *Vanity Fair*.[86]

The reviews were scathing, with *Guardian* film critic Wendy Ide calling *Snow White* "a film made by people with cartoon dollar signs for eyes and not even the tiniest glimmer of art in their souls."[87] The *Rolling Stone*'s David Fear said the film "may not be the worst live-action adaptation of an animated touchstone, though it's a strong contender for the blandest."[88]

Not to mention, there have been plenty of other highly successful film releases in the past year in which members of the main cast were vocal supporters of Palestine. *Poor Things* earned north of $115 million at the box office—a film that starred both Mark Ruffalo and Ramy Youssef, who have each been steadfast in their support of Palestine, signing an open letter to the Screen Actors Guild-American Federation of Television and Radio Artists (SAG-AFTRA) labor union, asking leaders to protect pro-Palestine union members from being blacklisted.[89] In his SNL monologue, Youssef said he was praying for God to "free the people of Palestine."[90]

The New York Times and other national papers reduced Zegler's support of Palestine to just one of the film's *many* controversies, lumping it in with *Snow White*'s use of CGI to create the seven dwarfs.[91] Framing Zegler's position this way, as frivolous and misguided, or even worse, something that puts Gadot's safety at risk, legitimizes and normalizes the Trump administration's actions against pro-Palestinian activists and weaponizes antisemitism, which, as Raz Segal reported for *Time* in May 2024, puts all Jewish people at risk.[92]

The Trump administration's attack on international students who participated in pro-Palestinian advocacy primarily targeted those from Muslim-majority countries or other countries in Asia and Africa.[93] On March 8, 2025, Palestinian Columbia University graduate student Mahmoud Khalil was taken by federal agents to a detention center in Louisiana for the prominent role he played in the protests demanding that the university cut ties with Israel.[94] Immigration and Customs Enforcement (ICE) revealed later that they didn't even have a warrant when they arrested Khalil.[95]

A year after publishing an op-ed critical of Tufts University's ties to Israel, Turkish Tufts grad student Rümeysa

Öztürk was ambushed by ICE agents on her way to meet friends for dinner and swiftly transported to a detention center in Louisiana.[96] The government accused Öztürk of publicly supporting terrorist organizations and being involved in anti-Israel activism. Once again, agents failed to produce a warrant, making ICE's detention of Öztürk more of an abduction than an arrest.[97] Öztürk returned home in May 2025 after spending six weeks in a Louisiana ICE detention center.[98]

By mid-April 2025, the Trump administration had systematically terminated more than 4,700 student visas "in the government's Student and Exchange Visitor Information System (SEVIS), an online system used by the Department of Homeland Security to track international students who come to the U.S. to attend school."[99] The mass upheaval triggered upwards of a hundred lawsuits, pressuring the administration to "temporarily undo its actions."[100] But the chilling effect, particularly on international student activists like Khalil and journalists like Öztürk, could not be undone.

"Since we're a journalism department, we don't tell them that there are things that they can't do or can't write," Charles Seife, journalism department director at New York University, told *Poynter*.[101] "But we do tell them that it's a very tricky political environment right now, and we're particularly worried about retaliation against students who are on visas for exercising their rights to report and to speak and to peaceably assemble." In other words, don't eat the poison apple of ethical, truth-telling journalism.

University newspapers, such as the *Harvard Crimson*, have received several requests to remove quotations or identifying information, including "dorms, majors, and class years," from previously published reports for fear of retaliation.[102] The University of Florida's independent paper, the *Independent Florida Alligator*, broke a story in April 2025 about the university collaborating with ICE to enforce immigration policies on campus.[103] The University of South Florida and the University of Central Florida have also signed similar agreements, effectively selling out their students by allowing federal immigration authorities to access campus resources and student data.[104]

Although celebrity news is junk-y by nature, the case of Rachel Zegler underscores how Hollywood, which epitomizes corporate mass media, functions as an extension of broader political and ideological battles—a major studio trying to silence someone who is unyielding in their support for Palestinian liberation. Moreover, the way the corporate media cover these issues, even concerning celebrities, shapes cultural values and often undermines systemic progress. However, Zegler is more protected than many others who align with her advocacy, as evidenced by the countless international students in the United States currently in limbo, left to pick up the pieces after facing visa cancellations, deportation threats, and academic discipline for exercising their constitutionally protected right to free speech and assembly by speaking out against Israel's genocide.

FIFTY YEARS OF NONSTOP JUNK

In a year when dystopian satire blurred uncomfortably with reality, Junk Food News wasn't just a sideshow—it was the main event, distracting us while real power was seized, rights were rolled back, and fascist policies found bureaucratic footing. As Trump and Musk played tag-team autocrats, the corporate press focused on clickbait scandals and celebrity sideshows, failing spectacularly to confront the magnitude of democratic backsliding.

After fifty years of Project Censored calling out blatant media incompetence, you'd think they'd hear us by now.

But it's not just incompetence, it's complicity. When newsrooms prioritize spectacle over substance, they help normalize authoritarianism by keeping the public fixated on the absurd instead of the alarming. While the establishment press devoted a disproportionate amount of space and time to Junk, it was neglecting consequential stories about public policy, the distribution of power and wealth, and attacks on freedom of expression.

As always, we encourage deftly recalibrating rather than completely unplugging. A little Junk never hurt anyone, but the corporate media and Big Tech's "socials" would have us supping on a steady diet of manipulation, distraction, and complacency all the time, if they had their way. A media reset, balancing a little delicious Junk, now and then, with consistent, substantial servings of independent journalism is how each of us can resist the spectacle machine and nurture the collective vigilance, shared curiosity, and critical thinking necessary to make a better, more inclusive future.

REAGAN HAYNIE is Project Censored's social media manager. This is her third time coauthoring *State of the Free Press's* Junk Food News chapter. Reagan also co-authored this year's graphic chapter and co-hosts Project Censored's YouTube series, "Frame-Check."

SHEALEIGH VOITL is Project Censored's associate director. This is her second time co-editing *State of the Free Press*. In addition to her involvement with the Project's Campus Affiliates Program and yearbook series, Shealeigh also helped develop and write Project Censored's *Beyond Fact-Checking: A Teaching Guide to the Power of News Frames*, alongside Andy Lee Roth, and co-hosts Project Censored's YouTube series, "Frame-Check."

SIERRA KAUL recently completed her Master's in Library and Information Science. She currently watches the censorship of media and the defunding of education with a deep form of anger mixed with apathy that verges on rage. This is her fifth time writing for the Junk Food News chapter and her five millionth time wondering exactly what the F is going on in the world. Otherwise, she enjoys crinkle-cut fries and strong alcoholic beverages.

NOTES

1. Stephen Fowler and Shannon Bond, "What Has DOGE Done in Trump's First 100 Days?" NPR, April 28, 2025.
2. Mischa Geracoulis, "The Corporate Press (Finally) Sounds The Alarm On Project 2025," Project Censored, August 8, 2024, updated October 17, 2024.
3. Martin Pengelly, "Trump Told Top US General to 'Just Shoot' Racism Protesters, Book Claims," *The Guardian*, June 25, 2021.
4. Mickey Huff and Andy Lee Roth, "The Free Press As 'Enemy Of The People'," Project Censored, August 2, 2017, updated May 22, 2023.
5. Katrin Bennhold, "What Elon Musk's Salute Was All About," *New York Times*, January 24, 2024, updated January 25, 2025.
6. ADL (@ADL), "This is a delicate moment. It's a new day and yet so many are on edge," X, January 20, 2025.
7. Ivana Saric, "How the Internet Cheered the UnitedHealth Shooting Suspect as a Folk Hero," *Axios*, December 10, 2024; Jordan Valinsky and Hadas Gold, "Kanye West Is Selling $20 T-Shirts with Swastikas," CNN, February 10, 2025; Justin Baragona, "Joe Rogan Claims Banning Kanye's 'Kinda Catchy' Hitler Song 'Kind of Supports' What He Says About Jews," *The Independent*, May 16, 2025; Gili Malinsky, "Mark Zuckerberg Says People Can Fill the Need for Friends with AI, but 'There Is No Replacement' for Human Relationships, Psychologist Says," CNBC, May 9, 2025.
8. Peter Kiefer, "Justin Baldoni's Leap of Faith," *The Hollywood Reporter*, February 21, 2025; and Marco della Cava and Anika Reed, "Diddy's Star-Studded Parties Were Cultural Extravaganzas: Inside the White Party," *USA Today*, April 20, 2025.
9. "Junk Food News," Project Censored, accessed May 21, 2025.
10. Daniel J. Boorstin, *The Image: A Guide to Pseudo-Events in America* (Atheneum, 1962). On the relevance of Boorstin's work to the analysis of Junk Food News, see Mickey Huff, Andy Lee Roth, Nolan Higdon, Michael Kolbe, and Andrew O'Connor-Watts, "American Idle: Junk Food News, News Abuse, and the Voice of Freedumb," in *Censored 2013: Dispatches from the Media Revolution*, ed. Mickey Huff and Andy Lee Roth with Project Censored (Seven Stories Press, 2012), 152–3.
11. Boorstin, *The Image*, 5–6.
12. Moira Donegan, "We Are Witnessing Slow Constitutional Collapse in the US," *The Guardian*, April 30, 2025.
13. Brooks Barnes, "Snow White and the Seven Kajillion Controversies," *New York Times*, March 20, 2025.
14. Edith Olmsted, "Did JD Vance Kill the Pope? An Investigation," *The New Republic*, April 21, 2025.
15. Jessie Gómez, "Changes to Federal Education Department Could Harm NJ Students with Disabilities, Advocates Warn," *Chalkbeat*, April 28, 2025.
16. David Folkenflik, "Judge Orders White House to Allow AP Access to News Events," NPR, April 9, 2025; Steven Greenhut, "Trump Is Targeting Media and Chilling Free Speech," *Reason*, March 7, 2025; and "USA: Trump's Vengeful Lawsuits Against Media Lack Legal Basis, but Harm American Press Freedom," Reporters without Borders, December 23, 2024.
17. Zoya Teirstein, "Project 2025 Was Extreme. Trump's First 100 Days Have

Been Even More Radical," *Grist*, April 30, 2025.
18. Teirstein, "Project 2025."
19. Quil Lawrence and Tom Bowman, "Hegseth Is in Hot Water Again over Sharing Attack Plans. But This Time It May Be Worse," NPR, April 22, 2025.
20. Tom Valovic, "What Is the Mainstream Media Missing About Elon Musk? He Is Instituting Technocracy," *Common Dreams*, February 10, 2025.
21. Bill Barrow, "After Running on a Working-Class Message, Trump Fills His Government with Billionaires," PBS, January 28, 2025.
22. Shannon Power, "Drake Withdraws Spotify, UMG Lawsuit over Diss Track," *Newsweek*, January 15, 2025.
23. Lisa Respers France, "Kendrick Lamar and Drake Gave Us an Epic Hip-Hop Beef Weekend. Here's What to Know," CNN, May 6, 2024.
24. "Not Like Us by Kendrick Lamar," My Stream Count, accessed September 26, 2025.
25. Trace William Cowen, "Ye Wears KKK-Style Hood While Admitting to Kendrick Jealousy: 'Drake is a Million Times Better,'" *Complex*, March 31, 2025.
26. Power, "Drake Withdraws."
27. Karma Dickerson and Carla Rendon, "LA Teacher Who Once Taught Kendrick Lamar Reflects on Rapper's Early Start," NBC Dallas-Fort Worth. February 5, 2025.
28. Daniele Selby, "Activism & Charity: The Many Ways Kendrick Lamar Gives Back," Global Citizen, September 20, 2016.
29. "*DAMN.*, by Kendrick Lamar," The Pulitzer Prizes, 2018.
30. "Improving Education Outcomes by Empowering Parents, States, and Communities," The White House, March 20, 2025.
31. Weadé James and Veronica Goodman, "Department of Education Staff Cuts Will Harm America's Children and Schools," Center for American Progress, March 14, 2025.
32. Robbie Sequeira, "Federal Education Cuts and Trump DEI Demands Leave States, Teachers in Limbo," *Stateline*, April 16, 2025.
33. Julianne Malveaux, "Trump Loves the Poorly Educated," *Chicago Crusader*, March 28, 2025.
34. Erica Breunlin, "Hundreds of Teachers Rally to Protect Schools at the Colorado Capitol as Lawmakers Look for Cuts," *Colorado Sun*, March 20, 2025.
35. Dara Kam, "Florida Sheriffs Agree to Work with ICE on Mass Deportation Efforts," WLRN, February 24, 2025.
36. Lisa Hagen, "They Say They Want Americans to Have More Babies. What's Beneath the Surface?" NPR, April 25, 2025.
37. Jordan Valinsky, "Florida Debates Lifting Some Child Labor Laws to Fill Jobs Vacated by Undocumented Immigrants," CNN Business, March 25, 2025.
38. C.A. Bridges, "Is Florida's Population Getting Younger? Land of Retirees Has More Company, and Here's Why," *Daytona Beach News-Journal*, January 19, 2024; Nancy Guan, "Homeschooling Is Growing in Florida, Especially in the Tampa Bay Area," WFSU *News*, November 7, 2023.
39. Devlin Peck, "The Ultimate List of Teacher Shortages by State in 2025," *Devlin Peck*, January 3, 2025.

40. Danielle Prieur, "Parents in Florida Must OK a Teacher Calling Their Child by a Nickname," NPR, August 11, 2023.
41. Lawrence Mower and Alexandra Glorioso, "Here's Where $10 Million Donation to DeSantis' Hope Florida Effort Went," *Tampa Bay Times*, April 11, 2025.
42. James Bickerton, "What Did Elon Musk's Son Say to Trump? White House Video Goes Viral," *Newsweek*, February 22, 2025; Cherisse Halsall and Emily Chang, "Musk's Son 'Lil X' Steals Spotlight in the Oval Office," ABC News, February 11, 2025; Chris Nesi, "Trump Swaps Out Resolute Desk in the Oval Office Days After Elon Musk's Son X Appeared to Wipe a Booger on It," *New York Post*, February 20, 2025.
43. Emily Crane and Nicholas McEntyre, "Ashley St. Clair Reveals How Her Son With Elon Musk Was Conceived—and the Jaw-Dropping Amount He Offered Her to Keep Quiet About Him," *New York Post*, April 16, 2025; Dana Mattioli, "The Tactics Elon Musk Uses to Manage His 'Legion' of Babies—and Their Mothers," *Wall Street Journal*, April 15, 2025; Conor Murray, "Elon Musk Still Hasn't Commented as Right-Wing Influencer Claims She Had His 13th Child," *Forbes*, February 15, 2025.
44. On Musk, see, for example, Zara Zimbardo, "Marketing Mars," Project Censored, June 5, 2025, updated July 9, 2025.
45. Sasa, "Elon Musk Definitely Tweets Too Much," *Stats with Sasa*, undated, accessed July 30, 2025.
46. David Ingram, "Trump Turns the White House Lawn Into a Tesla Showroom," NBC News, March 11, 2025; Adam Cancryn, "White House Prepares High-Profile Purchase of Tesla Auto," *Politico*, March 11, 2025; Zachary B. Wolf, "Pitchman President Drives Americans to Their Corners," CNN, March 12, 2025.
47. Ingram, "Trump Turns the White House Lawn Into a Tesla Showroom."
48. Matt Stopera, "People Can't Stop Saying 'Everything's Computer' Because of Donald Trump," *Buzzfeed*, March 12, 2025.
49. Chris Murphy (@ChrisMurphyCT), "Just because the corruption plays out in public doesn't mean it's not corruption," X, March 11, 2025.
50. Adriana Gomez Licon, "Musk Waves a Chainsaw and Charms Conservatives Talking up Trump's Cost-Cutting Efforts," AP News, February 21, 2025.
51. Jess Bidgood, "What That Chain Saw Was Really About," *New York Times*, February 21, 2025.
52. Boorstin, *The Image*, 39–40.
53. Jack Lasky, "Knowledge Advantage," EBSCO, 2022.
54. Allison Stranger, "Efficiency – or Empire? How Elon Musk's Hostile Takeover Could End Government as We Know It," Ash Center for Democratic Governance and Innovation (Harvard Kennedy School), February 7, 2025.
55. Kay Leadfoot, "It's Official: The Cybertruck Is More Explosive Than the Ford Pinto," *FuelArc News*, February 6, 2025.
56. Caleb Ecarma, "DOGE Teen Ran Image-Sharing Site Linked to URLs Referencing Pedophilia and the KKK," *Musk Watch*, February 11, 2025. The original *Musk Watch* article has since been purged, but the quoted

57 material remains accessible (at the time of this book's publication) online. See Travis Gettys, "DOGE Worker's Image Hosting Service Referenced Child Sex Abuse and KKK: Report," *Raw Story*, February 11, 2025.

57 Brian Krebs, "Teen on Musk's DOGE Team Graduated From 'The Com'," *Krebs on Security*, July 3, 2025; Raphael Satter, "Exclusive: DOGE Staffer 'Big Balls' Provided Tech Support to Cybercrime Ring, Records Show," *Reuters*, March 26, 2025.

58 Miles Klee, "What We Know So Far About the Young Techies Working for DOGE," *Rolling Stone*, February 6, 2025.

59 Michelle L. Price, "Vance Says DOGE Staffer Who Resigned After a Report of Racist Postings Should Be Brought Back," PBS, February 7, 2025.

60 Bobby Allyn and Shannon Bond, "Member of Elon Musk's DOGE Team Resigns After Racist Posts Resurface," NPR, February 7, 2025.

61 Elon Musk (@elonmusk), "Bring back @DOGE staffer who made inappropriate statements via a now deleted pseudonym?" X, February 7, 2025.

62 Kyle Cheney and Josh Gerstein, "DOGE's Marko Elez Is Back on U.S. Payroll," *Politico*, March 29, 2025.

63 Taylor Alexis Heady, "How Much Does Elon Musk Pay in Child Support? He's Got 14 Kids," *PopCrush*, February 17, 2025.

64 Ivan Pereira and Emily Chang, "Here Are All the Agencies That Elon Musk and DOGE Have Been Trying to Dismantle So Far," ABC News, February 27, 2025.

65 "New Report: Elon Musk Has Conflict of Interest at Over 70% of Doge's Targets," Public Citizen, May 8, 2025.

66 Elizabeth Beavers and Mike Tanglis, "Duplicitous Oligarch Grifting Endlessly: Elon Musk Has a Conflict of Interest at More Than 70 Percent of Agencies Targeted by DOGE," Public Citizen, May 8, 2025.

67 Beavers and Tanglis, "Duplicitous Oligarch Grifting Endlessly."

68 "Elon Musk's Neuralink Dilemma: Decoding Minds, Challenging Ethics," *TRT Global*, October 3, 2023.

69 Eric Lipton and Kirsten Grind, "Elon Musk's Business Empire Scores Benefits Under Trump Shake-Up," *New York Times*, February 11, 2025.

70 "Musk Has Conflict of Interest," Public Citizen.

71 Lipton and Kirsten Grind, "Elon Musk's Business Empire Scores."

72 Neil Postman, "Informing Ourselves to Death" (speech, German Informatics Society, Stuttgart, Germany, October 11, 1990).

73 Tom Valovic, "What Is the Mainstream Media Missing About Elon Musk? He Is Instituting Technocracy," *Common Dreams*, February 10, 2025.

74 Brandon Drenon, "Trump Says Relationship with Musk Is Over," BBC, June 7, 2025.

75 Todd Gilchrist, "'Snow White' Star Gal Gadot on Playing Wonder Woman and Speaking Out About Israel: 'I Had to Advocate for the Hostages'," *Variety*, March 18, 2025.

76 "About the Nakba," United Nations, accessed May 22, 2025.

77 Chris McGreal, "CNN Staff Say Network's Pro-Israel Slant Amounts to 'Journalistic Malpractice'," *The Guardian*, February 4, 2024.

78 Randa Abdel-Fattah, "A Critical Look at the New York Times' Weaponization of Rape in Service of Israeli Propaganda," Institute for Palestine Studies, January 14, 2024.

79. Jeremy Scahill and Ryan Grim, "Leaked NYT Gaza Memo Tells Journalists to Avoid Words 'Genocide,' 'Ethnic Cleansing,' and 'Occupied Territory'," *The Intercept*, April 15, 2024.
80. Scahill and Grim, "Leaked NYT Gaza Memo."
81. McGreal, "CNN Staff."
82. Tatiana Siegel, "Inside Disney's 'Snow White' Fiasco: Death Threats, Beefed-up Security and a Social Media Guru for Rachel Zegler," *Variety*, March 25, 2025.
83. Rachel Zegler (@rachelzegler), "and always remember, free palestine," X, August 12, 2024.
84. Jack Smart, "Snow White Producer's Son Says Rachel Zegler 'Hurt the Film's Box Office' with Her 'Actions' in Since-Deleted Comment," *People*, March 26, 2025.
85. Alex Abad-Santos, "Did the Scream Franchise Just Fall Apart?" *Vox*, November 28, 2023.
86. Chris Murphy, "Snow White's Failure Has Turned Rachel Zegler Into a Scapegoat—and an Icon," *Vanity Fair*, March 28, 2025.
87. Wendy Ide, "Snow White Review – Toe-Curlingly Terrible Live-Action Remake," *The Guardian*, March 23, 2025.
88. David Fear, "'Snow White' Is Like Being Stuck in the Most Controversial Disney-Adult Nightmare Ever," *Rolling Stone*, March 19, 2025.
89. Pamela McClintock, "How 11-Time Oscar Nominee 'Poor Things' Got Rich at the Global Box Office," *The Hollywood Reporter*, March 9, 2024; Christy Piña, "Mark Ruffalo, Ramy Youssef and More Call On Sag-AFTRA Leaders to Protect Pro-Palestine Members from Being Blacklisted (Exclusive)," *The Hollywood Reporter*, September 11, 2024; Wesley Stenzel, "Ramy Youssef Says Palestine Remarks in SNL Monologue Were 'Completely Inoffensive': 'Nothing Controversial'," *Entertainment Weekly*, April 12, 2025; and "Mark Ruffalo Supports Pro-Palestine Protest at Oscars," *Middle East Monitor*, March 12, 2024.
90. Ethan Shanfeld, "Ramy Youssef Asks God to 'Free the People of Palestine' and 'Free the Hostages' in Heartfelt 'SNL' Monologue," *Variety*, March 30, 2024.
91. Barnes, "Snow White and The Seven"; Tom Smyth, "A Timeline of Snow White and Its Many Controversies," *Vulture*, March 28, 2025.
92. Sean Mandell, "Disney Forced to Beef Up Gal Gadot's Security After 'Snow White' Star Got Death Threats over Pro-Israeli Comments: Report," *New York Post*, March 25, 2025; Raz Segal, "How Weaponizing Antisemitism Puts Jews at Risk," *Time*, May 14, 2024.
93. Jonah Valdez, "Trump Appears to Be Targeting Muslim and "Non-white" Students for Deportation," *The Intercept*, April 8, 2025.
94. Jake Offenhartz, "Immigration Agents Arrest Palestinian Activist Who Helped Lead Columbia University Protests," Associated Press, March 9, 2025; and Gwynne Hogan, "The Protests Shook Columbia to Its Core. Now Trump Is Trying to Upend the University Altogether," *The City*, April 28, 2025.
95. Eloise Goldsmith, "ICE Admits They Didn't Have a Warrant When They Abducted Mahmoud Khalil," *Common Dreams*, April 25, 2025.
96. Anemona Hartocollis, "Targeting of Tufts Student for Deportation Stuns Friends and Teachers," *New York Times*, March 29, 2025.

97. Lauren Watson, "Student Journalists Wrestle with Censoring Their Own Work," *Columbia Journalism Review*, April 17, 2025.
98. Gloria Pazmino, Rebekah Riess, and Dalia Faheid, "Tufts University Student Rümeysa Öztürk Arrives Back Home After Spending Six Weeks at a Louisiana Detention Center," CNN, May 10, 2025.
99. Alexa Robles-Gil, "International Students in the U.S. Are Reeling amid Revoked Visas and Terminated Records," *Science*, April 15, 2025.
100. Jessica Corbett, "After Uproar, Trump Reverses on Mass Suspension of Student Visas," *Common Dreams*, April 25, 2025.
101. Angela Fu, "The Trump Administration's Crackdowns on the Press and Universities Fuel Fear Among International Student Journalists," Poynter, April 29, 2025.
102. Watson, "Student Journalists."
103. Vivienne Serret, "UF Partners with ICE for On-Campus Immigration Enforcement," *Independent Florida Alligator*, April 10, 2025.
104. Kathleen Magramo, "Florida Universities Join Statewide Push to Partner with ICE on Immigration Enforcement," CNN, April 12, 2025.

CHAPTER 4

STEFANIK, ISRAEL, AND ANTISEMITISM:
THE LONG SHADOW OF NEWS ABUSE

JOHN COLLINS

> *The capitalist papers are so far ahead of the news that they know tonight what happened tomorrow, but they never do go to the trouble of informin' their readers about what they really knew yesterday.*
>
> —Woody Guthrie[1]

When Donald Trump nominated Congressmember Elise Stefanik (R-NY) to serve as US Ambassador to the United Nations during his second administration, it was a reminder of how hard Stefanik had worked to build and burnish her political credentials in two closely related areas: uncompromising support for Trump's far-right MAGA movement and uncompromising support for Israel. Those two positions were on full display during her confirmation process in the Senate beginning in January 2025.

Trump eventually withdrew Stefanik's nomination in March 2025, reportedly out of concern for maintaining the GOP's razor-thin majority in the House of Representatives. The withdrawal came as the Trump administration was engaging in a wave of extra-judicial detainments, deportations, and other shocking actions against international students in retaliation for their public speech in favor of Palestinian rights and against Israel's genocidal assault on Gaza. Often framed by administration officials and defenders as a campaign against antisemitism, these actions drew directly on an earlier effort by the GOP to tar major universities such as Columbia with the brush of antisemitism—an effort in which Stefanik, in her role on the House Education and the Workforce Committee, had played a prominent role.[2]

While Stefanik never became UN ambassador, there is still a great deal to learn from an examination of how US establishment media covered her initial nomination. This coverage revealed establishment media's failure to interrogate how spurious accusations of antisemitism serve not only to drive US support for Israel's settler colonial project, but also to fuel a MAGA movement that is itself deeply antisemitic.

Had these outlets done a more critical job of interrogating Stefanik's claims at the time, they might have been better positioned to explain the ideological forces driving the wave of authoritarian repression that followed. As such, their coverage represented a clear case of "news abuse"—coverage that presents major public issues in a way that "minimizes their deeper importance, distorts what is happening, or otherwise encourages the public to interpret the story in a way that falls into line with the interests of the power elite"—and a missed opportunity whose damaging consequences continue to surround us.[3]

NCPR AND STEFANIK

To dig into this dynamic, it is useful to take a close look at the reporting provided by a news outlet that has covered Stefanik extensively throughout her career in Congress: North Country Public Radio (NCPR), which serves a wide region including parts of northern New York, Vermont, Ontario, and Quebec. In recent years, NCPR's detailed reporting on her MAGA makeover and emergence as a top Trump lieutenant has sometimes made the station a lightning rod for public criticism in a region where Stefanik (like Trump himself) has enjoyed considerable electoral support.[4]

NCPR reporter Emily Russell covered Stefanik's January 21 confirmation hearing, framing it primarily in terms of what the Congress member had to say in support of Trump's "peace through strength" agenda and his well-documented calls to reform the UN in line with his ideological demands.[5] Russell also highlighted how Stefanik, faithfully parroting a MAGA talking point that emerged during the coronavirus pandemic, accused the World Health Organization (WHO) of having "too strong ties to the Chinese Community Party."

All news articles employ framing, and all frames (by definition) include and exclude. Shealeigh Voitl, Andy Lee Roth, and Project Censored define a news frame as "the central idea or primary storyline that organizes the information included in a news story and gives meaning to it."[6] As critical news analysts have been arguing for decades, what is absent from coverage matters at least as much as what is present. In this case, as we'll see below, NCPR's story was shaped by a striking and consequential absence regarding an issue that also came up during the hearing: Stefanik's explicit support for Israel's supposed "biblical right" to control Palestinian territory. In addition, the story featured other missed opportunities to address clear and obvious mischaracterizations in Stefanik's testimony, particularly concerning the relationship between the issue of antisemitism and the issue of support for Israeli violence and expansionism.

BURYING THE LEDE: "BIBLICAL RIGHTS" VS. INTERNATIONAL LAW

A core element of news abuse is the failure to recognize and convey clearly what is most important about the events being reported. In this case, NCPR and most establishment media outlets glossed over what was arguably the most shocking aspect of Rep. Stefanik's testimony: her explicit support for the idea of "biblical rights"—at least in the case of Israel.

A key moment in the confirmation hearing was an exchange between the nominee and Sen. Chris Van Hollen (D-MD). The Senator referenced an earlier, one-on-one meeting at which he and Stefanik had discussed the claims made by some Israeli officials (such as Bezalel Smotrich and Itamar Ben-Gvir, both far-right members of Benjamin Netanyahu's cabinet) that Israel possesses a "biblical right" to control all the territory of historic Palestine. "[I]n that conversation, you told me that yes, you shared that view," Van Hollen noted at the hearing while questioning Stefanik. "Is that your view today?" Stefanik responded, "Yes."

While it is hardly unusual for members of Congress to express unqualified public support for Israel, or even to endorse the idea that Israeli domination of the Palestinians has biblical justification, Stefanik was speaking not as an elected official but rather as the nominee for the position of UN ambassador. As such, her views on anything related to international law were of particular interest, and any views running directly counter to international law ideally would have provoked significant media and public scrutiny. Indeed, it should have raised the question of whether the person initially tapped to be Trump's UN ambassador believes in international law at all.

In this case, however, Stefanik's "biblical law" statement was omitted from NCPR's report on the confirmation hearing. The significance of this absence becomes clear when we compare NCPR's frame with the frame used by the *Guardian*, the UK-based outlet that provides substantial coverage of US politics. In its story on the hearing, the *Guardian* led with the fact that Stefanik "endorsed Israeli claims of biblical rights to the entire West Bank" in her testimony.

Guardian reporter Joseph Gedeon correctly noted that Stefanik was explicitly endorsing a view that aligned her with the position of the Israeli far right. (Notably, it also put her in direct opposition to the UN Secretary General's warnings about Israel's annexationist agenda.)[7] Obviously this would have implications for any potential US diplomacy in the region, not to mention the ongoing US-Israeli strategic relationship that includes billions of dollars in military aid each year (including, as of Trump's first day in office, the reported resumption of transfers of 2,000-pound bombs that Israel has used to level Palestinian communities in Gaza).[8]

Unlike NCPR, Gedeon provided essential contextual information, noting clearly that the endorsement of the idea of "biblical law"—which, to state the obvious, is not a recognized concept in any credible international legal framework—"puts Stefanik at odds with longstanding international consensus and multiple UN security council resolutions regarding Israeli settlements in occupied territories." Gedeon further told readers that the US had a history of protecting Israel by vetoing dozens of UN Security Council resolutions over the years.

Several influential US-based establishment outlets such as National Public Radio (NPR), the Associated Press (AP), the *New York Times*, and *USA Today*, also covered the Stefanik hearing, providing varying degrees of detail.[9] While none led with the "biblical rights" issue, all at least briefly noted her statement in response to Van Hollen's question. None, however, made any significant effort to foreground the obvious contradiction between supporting the idea of "biblical rights" for one country and serving as an ambassador to a body grounded in international law that is supposed to apply to all.

Many critical scholars, of course, would argue that this "contradiction" only reveals that international law itself is a colonial construction that reflects and protects the interests of colonial powers.[10] A full reckoning with the illegal and colonial nature of Israel's occupation of Palestine would require not only consistency in how the idea of international law is applied, but also a willingness to name the ongoing impact of colonialism as a fundamental aspect of contemporary global power dynamics. Unfortunately, establishment media have shown little if any inclination to acknowledge this reality, much less integrate it into their coverage.

By failing to identify colonial realities for what they are, the US establishment media coverage of Stefanik's hearing effectively provided Zionism with two layers of protection, hiding the colonial nature of the Zionist project while simultaneously normalizing a troubling, fringe position on the question of Palestine and on international politics as a whole: the position that a state (Israel, in this case) can possess "biblical rights" over a piece of territory it controls or seeks to control. Admitting "biblical rights" into the conversation at all has far-reaching implications. The fact that most establishment news outlets are essentially acting as stenographers, instead of exploring those implications, suggests that either they don't see it as important or else that they are willing to go along with treating Israel as an exception.

THE ATTACK ON UNRWA AND PALESTINIAN REFUGEES

As noted above, news abuse often involves elements of distortion that can leave the public either confused or thoroughly mistaken about important issues. Such is the case with Stefanik's harsh accusations against the United Nations in general, and UNRWA (the UN agency that has been providing essential services to Palestinian refugees ever since they were driven from their homes in 1947–1948) in particular.

NCPR reported that "one of the things that drew [Stefanik] to the UN Ambassador role" was the opportunity to address what she condemned as an "antisemitism rot" at UNRWA. In the full transcript of the hearing, we learn that Stefanik went further, alleging that antisemitism is "pervasive within the UN system."[11] Both the nominee and the news story zeroed in on specific information regarding UNRWA. On this point, NCPR's reporter did provide partial context, noting that a UN investigation had found that a small number of UNRWA employees "may have been involved in the Oct 7th terrorist attack on Israel."

There are two problems with this section of the NCPR story. First, UNRWA itself has strongly pushed back against the leap in logic made by people like Stefanik and others who have used the investigation's findings as justification for broad-brush characterizations of the agency (and even the entire UN). In March 2024, for example, UNRWA issued a statement condemning the campaigns of "misinformation and disinformation" against it that it said had "intensified" after the October 7 attacks.[12] It noted that the agency has a staff of over thirty thousand employees (a figure that underlines the sheer scope of the 75-year Palestinian refugee crisis) and that it has made a good faith effort to investigate claims of neutrality breaches:

> Since 2022, 66 investigations, out of 30,000 staff across UNRWA and not just in Gaza, looked at a range of allegations related to neutrality breaches, including alleged support for Hamas and other groups. Some of these investigations are still ongoing. *Sixty-six cases out of 30,000 staff—not all of which have been substantiated—is just 0.22 per cent. There is absolutely no ground for a blanket description of "the institution as a whole" being "totally infiltrated."* Rather, the small percentage underscores that the absolutely overwhelming majority of UNRWA's highly dedicated staff adhere to the principles to which they commit when they join the Agency. [Emphasis in the original.]

Given the inflammatory nature of Stefanik's allegation, not to mention the fact that Stefanik herself was clearly taking Israel's own allegations at face value, providing information about the size of UNRWA's workforce would have helped contextualize the issue. NCPR's reporter knew enough to mention UNRWA's internal investigation but failed to acknowledge what UNRWA itself has said about the polemical accusations against it. This incomplete contextualization effectively left the narrative in Stefanik's control and followed a broader establishment media pattern in which official Israeli talking points are regularly taken at face value rather than being seen as claims to be weighed against all available evidence (including the perspectives of Palestinians themselves).

The second problem concerns the clear political motivation behind the accusations against UNRWA. Even if NCPR had included UNRWA's own statements, that would not have provided the contextualization necessary for audiences to understand why Israel and its supporters might be seeking to discredit UNRWA during a severe humanitarian crisis caused by Israel's ongoing bombing and blockade of Gaza.

In fact, there is considerable evidence to suggest that the Israeli government saw the October 7 attacks as an opportunity to advance the goal of pushing as many Palestinians as possible out of Gaza by rendering the territory unlivable. Finance Minister Smotrich, one of the Israeli government's most aggressive and unapologetic proponents of killing and displacing Palestinians, drew widespread condemnation for suggesting in August 2024 that it might be "justified and moral" to starve Gaza's entire population in order to secure the release of Israeli hostages.[13] He later called for forcing most of Gaza's population out of the territory and replacing them with Israeli settlers who, he said, could "make the desert bloom."[14] The effort to dismantle the agency that has provided basic support to refugees in Gaza for decades was a key step in the direction Smotrich was advocating.

Just a day before the Stefanik hearing, Trump had announced a freeze on US foreign aid, including funding for UNRWA. As Reuters noted in a "fact check" report, however, Trump's executive order only extended what the Biden administration had begun when it suspended US aid to UNRWA a year earlier.[15] While a number of US allies also suspended their support for UNRWA, other countries such as Spain, Norway, and Ireland did not. UN officials condemned the aid freeze as a form of "collective punishment."[16]

Barely a week after Stefanik testified before the Senate committee, Israeli legislation banning UNRWA from operating in the West Bank and Gaza took effect. UNRWA spokesman Jonathan Fowler described the move as a "very, very nightmarish scenario" for the agency and the people it serves.[17] The AP reported that one Israeli settler activist spray painted a Star of David over the UNRWA headquarters in Jerusalem, while deputy mayor Arieh King "popped a champagne cork" to celebrate "a happy and special and historic day."[18]

As political commentators such as Peter Beinart have pointed out, all of this suggests a coordinated campaign against UNRWA designed to generate support for starving the agency of funding to provide essential services to Palestinians who continue to be denied their right of return.[19] NCPR's report on the hearing essentially allowed Stefanik to propagate a questionable narrative without reference to countervailing evidence or relevant context that might have helped the story's readers understand who had an interest in undermining UNRWA's reputation and why.

DEFAULTING TO DOMINANT IDEOLOGIES

At this point, some might argue that such a detailed critique of a single public radio news report is unwarranted. Staunch defenders of NPR and its local affiliates, for example, might insist that it is their job simply to present information and let the listener or reader engage in its interpretation. Yet, as critical scholars have long maintained, it is never that simple. Edward Said, for example, famously wrote that facts "do not at all speak for themselves, but require a socially acceptable narrative to absorb, sustain and circulate them."[20] The concept of news frames is a common way to explain how this process of narrative and ideological shaping works.

Even if we acknowledge that all news outlets frame stories in ways that go beyond an uncomplicated presentation of "the facts," some might see this inevitability as unproblematic—essentially a natural part of the work of communicating events to an audience. Don't news outlets, their defenders might argue, have the right to frame things as they see fit?

But while news frames are inevitable, they are hardly innocent. For example, as I have argued elsewhere, US establishment media outlets consistently provide coverage that naturalizes settler colonial projects around the world from Palestine to Australia to North America.[21] They do this by failing to name settler colonialism as such, failing to identify settler populations as such, failing to treat settler projects as ongoing in the present, failing to identify settler wealth as a product of land and resource theft, and failing to connect Indigenous resistance with the actual structures it is resisting.

The result of such coverage is a kind of chronic decontextualization that generates explanatory vacuums: Things are happening in the world, but the real reasons behind those events are hidden from view. When such absences become endemic in the routines and coverage patterns of entire news organizations, reporters and audiences alike end up filling the vacuum with misleading explanations that reflect and reinforce dominant ideologies. In the case of settler colonial societies, the failures listed above have their corresponding ideological substitutions: not settler societies but multicultural democracies; not settlers but immigrants and citizens; not present colonization requiring material transformation but "complex histories" requiring, at most, acknowledgment and perhaps liberal forms of reconciliation; not ill-gotten wealth but a naturalized capitalist economy; not resistance but violence and "terrorism."

What this kind of analysis shows us is that news frames are ideological choices with profound material consequences. For example, the establishment media coverage of the Stefanik hearing reproduces a pattern that we see through the wider coverage of Israel's domination of the Palestinians. It is extremely rare for news outlets to note that most of the Palestinians in Gaza have the right, under international law, to return to their homes in what is now Israel.[22] Is this not a relevant (indeed, essential) piece of contextual information? Its omission is all the more shocking given that Palestinians in Gaza literally launched a mass movement in 2018 called The Great March of Return, revealing the ongoing nature of Israel's settler project and demanding that they be allowed to return home.[23]

We have already seen some of the ways in which NCPR's coverage of the Stefanik hearing lacked important contextual information, thereby paving the way for dominant ideologies to do their work. What remains is to explore what is arguably the most dangerous and far-reaching shortcoming of most establishment media coverage of this story: the failure to understand and explain how spurious accusations of antisemitism play a fundamental role in naturalizing Israeli domination, promoting state repression of those who oppose this domination, and hiding the blatant antisemitism of the global far-right movement.

DISTORTING ANTI-ZIONISM, EXCUSING ANTISEMITISM

A deeper look at the NCPR report reveals how thoroughly dominant ideologies about Zionism and antisemitism have become embedded in the "common sense" of journalistic discourse. This has profound implications not only for Palestinians facing the full force of Israeli violence and dispossession, but also for anyone seeking to speak up for human rights, Palestinian rights in particular, and global justice more generally.

To make sense of this issue in the context of the Stefanik hearing, it is important to recall that the hearing took place just a day after Elon Musk, the world's richest man and Trump's top campaign donor, made two fascist salutes at a Trump inauguration rally. As the public debate about his gesture reverberated, Sen. Chris Murphy (D-CT) asked Stefanik whether she was bothered by the fact that many in the far-right movement had clearly understood it as a neo-Nazi salute and were celebrating it as such.

The NCPR report notes Murphy's pointed question, then pivots immediately in a way that mirrors how Stefanik herself pivoted in response to the question.[24] Insisting that Musk had not, in fact, done a Nazi salute, Stefanik suggested that Murphy's question was impertinent. Why? "I have a very strong record when it comes to combatting antisemitism," she said. NCPR's report quotes this sentence, followed directly by a statement from the reporter that "Both Democrats and Republicans at Stefanik's hearing praised that record."

Readers who are familiar with the ideological function of US establishment media will recognize the significance of this passage. Within a system dominated by two major political parties, establishment media coverage tends to allow these parties—whether they agree or disagree on a given issue—to define the limits of acceptable and relevant discourse. When they disagree, reports present both positions, rarely stopping to identify whether either one is actually more accurate than the other. When they agree, their shared discourse is simply presented as if it were unproblematically true, as opposed to recognizing it as a shared project of the social construction of reality.

In this case, the report fails to challenge two interlocking assumptions that lie behind Stefanik's response to Murphy's question. First is the assumption that "Nazi" equals antisemitism and nothing more. Implicitly accused of siding with neo-Nazis, she assumes that when the news media and the public hear "Nazi," they will think only of antisemitism and the Holocaust and not of the wide range of other horrifying things that Nazism represents (eugenics, radical homophobia, territorial expansionism, extreme nationalism, a fetishization of corporate power, attacks on disabled people and other minorities, etc.). Consequently, she knows that all she needs to do to bat away the accusation is to insist that she has fought against antisemitism.

But has she? This takes us to the second assumption behind her response, which is that anti-Zionism is inherently antisemitic. This assumption is based on the idea that Israel and the Zionist movement represent all Jewish people—a demonstrably false claim that nonetheless goes unchallenged in far too many establishment media reports.

Any examination of Stefanik's history of public statements—including, perhaps most famously, her interrogation of university presidents during student protests against the genocide in Gaza—would show that she regularly categorizes criticism of Israel's actions as *ipso facto* antisemitic. Stefanik is arguably aware that this claim is completely disingenuous, yet she is also arguably aware that few, if any, news outlets will challenge it. By noting that her record on antisemitism received bipartisan praise, NCPR implicitly validates a framing that represents one of Zionism's greatest ideological successes.

Some may interpret this analysis as suggesting that it is NCPR's job to "take down" Stefanik in the way one might expect from an openly partisan news outlet. Not so. Yet NCPR itself has shown in the past that it is entirely possible to do critical reporting on Stefanik without being partisan. Why not in this case?

Similarly, some might argue that we shouldn't expect all reporters to be experts in the minutiae of debates over Palestine and Israel. Yet journalists from public radio and other establishment outlets regularly make the effort to seek out multiple viewpoints (albeit within a limited ideological spectrum). In the case of perspectives about Israel, critical viewpoints are widely available, including those that would challenge the "anti-Zionism equals antisemitism" frame; indeed, groups such as Jewish Voice for Peace make regular efforts to get establishment media to pay attention.[25] Any news outlet that goes along (passively or actively) with the idea that Jewish opinion is monolithic, or that criticism of Israel is inherently antisemitic, is choosing to exclude valid critical perspectives from the conversation.

In short, just as we saw with the material on Stefanik's claims of a supposed "antisemitism rot" at the UN, the report's narration of her efforts to deflect the Musk/Nazi issue reveals a willingness to take the nominee's understanding of antisemitism at face value, allowing her worldview to frame the story. Aside from the inclusion of Murphy's question—which did not address the issue of Zionism in any way—NCPR provides no contextual information that might challenge Stefanik's narrative.

The lack of such context suggests two possible explanations: either the reporter and/or the NCPR don't think it is important to hold a public official such as Stefanik accountable for her words, or they don't think there is anything problematic about equating criticism of Israel with antisemitism. The first option seems unlikely given NCPR's lengthy record of detailed investigative reporting on Stefanik's career trajectory. This leaves us with the second option: the reporting is framed by an acceptance of explanations provided by the dominant ideology.

Equally important, such coverage ignores what is right in front of journalists (and indeed, all of us) in the form of a far-right movement that claims to be pro-Israel yet trades openly in anti-Jewish rhetoric such as theories about the so-called "Great Replacement" or the influence of individuals like George Soros. The fact that such attitudes can co-exist in the same movement gives the lie to Stefanik's claim that those critical of Israel are the real antisemites. In short, paying attention to the rise of the far right—as NCPR has done, to its credit—should cause journalists to be skeptical of both the dominant ideology about Israel and testimony like Stefanik's.[26]

The failure to ask these critical questions of Stefanik ultimately lets her off the hook for her political and ideological links with the far right. It also perpetuates the incorrect, dangerous, and ultimately antisemitic assumption that all Jews are supporters of Israeli violence. In other words, Stefanik used her grandstanding against the UN and anti-genocide activists to whitewash her own links with real antisemitism. Unfortunately, few if any establishment media outlets have chosen to foreground that issue in the way they have foregrounded her role in the broader MAGA movement.

SEARCHING FOR THE MISSING CONTEXT

As is often the case, a look at independent media coverage can help reveal the nature of establishment media's news abuse. In the case of the Stefanik nomination and hearing, there were marked differences between establishment and independent reports. Specifically, the independent media coverage did a more rigorous job of providing relevant context and subjecting the misleading and contradictory aspects of Stefanik's position to critical scrutiny.

Whereas NCPR and other establishment outlets avoided any direct acknowledgment of the contradiction between international law and the idea of "biblical rights" that Stefanik endorsed in her testimony, independent media foregrounded this contradiction.[27] In *Truthout*'s January 21 article on the hearing, for example, Sharon Zhang didn't simply report Stefanik's statement about "biblical rights." Instead, Zhang included a brief but fundamental piece of context:

> The belief in a supposed "biblical right" to Palestine is central to Zionism, an ideology effectively calling for Israelis to drive Palestinians out of Palestine and colonize the territory. It is an ideology held widely by Trump's team.

Further, *Truthout*'s headline ("Trump's UN Pick Says Israel Has 'Biblical Right' to West Bank Amid Invasion") contrasts sharply with NCPR's headline ("Stefanik's hearing focuses on UN impact, Chinese influence, and antisemitism"). Whereas the latter is purely descriptive (and also, importantly, selective), the former makes a clear effort to offer context as a way of shining light on the material implications of Stefanik's words: Endorsing the idea of "biblical rights" functioned as a green light to Israel at precisely the moment that it was ramping up its violent attacks in the West Bank.

For its part, the independent outlet *Middle East Monitor* also zeroed in on how Stefanik's support for Israel's supposed "biblical rights" put her in direct contradiction with international law. The article situates this contradiction within the context of the first Trump administration's record, noting that Trump had already taken steps to solidify and extend US support for Israel's control of Jerusalem, the Golan Heights, and the West Bank (all of which are considered occupied territory under international law).[28]

Of course, independent outlets have their loyal audiences who may be predisposed to take a critical view of a figure such as Stefanik. Yet one does not need to be a partisan journalist catering to a partisan audience to report accurately and critically on the positions taken by a major public figure. On the contrary, we saw with the Stefanik hearing coverage that independent outlets were doing what establishment outlets claim to do consistently: holding the powerful to account.

We see a similar pattern when we compare establishment and independent coverage of Stefanik's testimony on antisemitism. In the *Truthout* article, Zhang did not flinch when informing readers that there may be good reason for skepticism when accusations of antisemitism are made in response to expressions of support for Palestinian freedom and human rights. Similarly, Zhang contextualized the significance of Stefanik's refusal to condemn Musk's obviously neo-Nazi salute:

> Elsewhere in the hearing, Stefanik indicated that she would have a hostile relationship toward the UN, with her and many senators repeatedly claiming, without evidence, that the international body has had a bias against Israel amid the genocide.
>
> "How would you describe the attitude of the United Nations as a whole toward Israel?" one senator asked later in the hearing. "I would say it's antisemitic," Stefanik said, levying an accusation often used by Zionists against people who criticize Israel's actions—even as, at one point, Stefanik denied that Elon Musk had performed a Nazi salute that has been widely celebrated by neo-Nazis.

By contrast, the NCPR report makes no mention of Zionism at all, suggesting that the widespread use of antisemitism accusations to deflect and punish criticism of Zionism is somehow not relevant to a story about Stefanik's testimony, despite the fact that Stefanik herself was clearly referencing her own efforts to tar university students with the brush of antisemitism. Similarly, NCPR's article only mentions Israel once—in reference to Hamas's Oct. 7 attack, but not in reference to Israel's occupation of Palestine, bombing of Gaza, or other actions.

What this brief comparison between the NCPR report and the coverage provided by independent media demonstrates is that, despite the establishment media's tendency to tread cautiously and avoid contextual information that might unmask Israel's violations of international law, it is entirely possible for news organizations to do more than simply take Elise Stefanik at her word.

THE DEEPER COSTS OF DECONTEXTUALIZATION

For all the reasons explored above, the shallow, decontextualized, and sometimes misleading establishment media coverage of the Stefanik hearing fits the category of news abuse. But unmasking news abuse within the coverage itself is not sufficient. It is also essential to recognize and explore the serious consequences of news abuse by asking questions such as: At the end of the day, what is the cost of *not* providing the public with critical contextual information? What is the cost of allowing the dominant ideology to frame coverage? And, perhaps most provocatively, how does news abuse contribute to the rising tide of authoritarianism we see all around us today?

Addressing these questions in the context of the Stefanik case requires tracing the roots of the wave of anti-democratic measures that marked the initial months of the second Trump administration. Stefanik's role as a faithful MAGA surrogate and a leading figure in the repressive response to the anti-genocide protests on US campuses reminds us that these authoritarian trends have been building for some time. Throughout this period, advocates for Palestinian liberation—including those targeted by Stefanik herself—have been pointing out that Israel's intensifying policies of annexation and elimination on the ground in Palestine, combined with its promotion of aggressive actions against its critics around the world, reflect and reinforce a wider project of global repression. In this sense, as has so often been the case throughout the past century, Palestine alerts us to what is coming.[29]

Stefanik went before the Senate committee on January 21, 2025. By the second week of March, daily headlines were full of the name Mahmoud Khalil, a Columbia University graduate and pro-Palestinian organizer who had served as a mediator between student activists and the university administration at Columbia during protests against the genocide in Gaza. Khalil was detained in New York by Immigrations and Customs Enforcement (ICE) agents on March 8, 2025, and transferred to a holding facility in Louisiana. The government stripped him of his permanent residency status, an action that suddenly rendered him a "deportable alien." Secretary of State Marco Rubio openly admitted that Khalil had committed no crime but was being targeted for removal from the country purely because of his beliefs.[30] Stating that fighting antisemitism and protecting the safety of Jewish students was a top policy priority for the Trump administration, Rubio argued that allowing Khalil to stay in the US would "severely undermine" that objective.

Too much of the subsequent coverage from US establishment media outlets represented a slow, much-overdue attempt to catch up to the reality that organized targeting of Palestine activists in the United States actually dated back to at least the 1970s. Groups involved in coordinating this harassment have included Betar, the Jewish Defense League, and the website Canary Mission, which in 2014 began doxxing and otherwise seeking to undermine the reputations and careers of undergraduate, graduate students, and faculty involved in Palestine-related research and advocacy. Both Khalil and Rümeysa Öztürk, a Tufts University graduate student abducted on the streets of Somerville, Massachusetts, by masked federal agents in late March, had been profiled by Canary Mission, and Betar directly targeted Khalil as part of a "deportation list" shared with the Trump administration.

As the Khalil case continued to reverberate as a symbol of the administration's crackdown on dissent and wider assault on constitutionally protected speech, the *New York Times* finally published a lengthy article about Canary Mission on April

1, 2025.³¹ Yet the article's characterization of the website as "mysterious" and "shadowy" ironically drew attention to the consequences of establishment media failures; after all, the *Times* could have investigated the story at any point during the previous decade, when those targeted by Canary Mission were anxious to sound the alarm and tell their stories.³²

The repression of pro-Palestinian activists is a key tip of the MAGA spear. Yet despite increasing attention from establishment media outlets, the framing of their episodic coverage of this point typically leaves the public with either a jumble of explanations premised on dominant ideologies or explanatory vacuums. In this case, however, the dominant ideology has an interest in pinning the problem entirely on Trump, even though the Democratic Party (which infamously chose to distance itself from anti-genocide protesters during the 2024 campaign) actively participated in the repression even before Trump was elected. Reckoning with this would require acknowledging that support for Zionism—a repressive, expansionist, colonial project—has been a bipartisan effort in which "liberal" US institutions, such as major universities, have been complicit.

Finally, as we have seen with the coverage of the Stefanik case, establishment media's long-term failure to distinguish between anti-Zionism and antisemitism has helped lay the foundation for the resurgence of the far right by normalizing a fundamental element of its entire political project of transnational authoritarian governance.³³ This element puts Palestinians at risk by leaving them vulnerable to genocidal Israeli violence. It puts anti-Zionists, both Jewish and non-Jewish, at risk by falsely claiming they are antisemitic and by encouraging police, courts, and institutions to crack down on them. And it puts all Jews at risk by empowering openly racist groups whose vicious antisemitism—recall the chilling "Jews will not replace us" chants at the 2017 "Unite the Right" rally in Charlottesville—magically disappears when media outlets indulge disingenuous debates about the UN and student protesters.

This is the price of stubbornly ignoring what advocates for human rights in Palestine have been warning for decades. Corporate media failures in the early stages of the second Trump administration reflected long-standing ideological patterns that paved the way for ongoing assaults on Palestinian lives, international students, immigrants, academic freedom, the rule of law, and democracy itself. With this much at stake, establishment media outlets should have the courage to speak the truth before it's too late. When they fail to do so on their own, critical analyses of news abuse can play an important role in informing and inspiring efforts to pressure those outlets to fulfill their responsibilities to the public.

JOHN COLLINS is the editorial director at *Weave News* and Emeritus Professor of Global Studies at St. Lawrence University. He is the author of *Global Palestine* (Hurst, 2011) and *Occupied By Memory* (NYU Press, 2004), the co-author of *Social and Cultural Foundations in Global Studies* (Routledge, 2017), and the co-editor of *Collateral Language: A User's Guide to America's New War* (NYU Press, 2002) and *Globalizing Collateral Language: From 9/11 to Endless War* (University of Georgia Press, 2021).

NOTES

[1] Quoted in Will Kaufman, *Woody Guthrie, American Radical* (University of Illinois Press, 2011), 31.
[2] Daniel Falcone, "Ivy League Presidents at Congress Hearing Threw Student Protesters Under the Bus," *Truthout*, December 22, 2023.
[3] John Collins, Nicole Eigbrett, Jana Morgan, and Steve Peraza, "The Magic Trick of Establishment Media: News Abuse in 2017–2018," in *Censored 2019*, ed. Mickey Huff and Andy Lee Roth with Project Censored (Seven Stories Press, 2018).
[4] It should be noted that NCPR's news mission is primarily regional; while it carries national NPR news programming, the station addresses national and international issues in its own coverage when they have a local or regional angle, such as a connection with Stefanik. See Zach Hirsch, "In 2016, Stefanik Promised to Push Back Against Trump. Today, She Is 'Ultra MAGA'," North Country Public Radio, June 8, 2022; and Emily Russell, "Stefanik Speaks at CPAC, Makes False Claims About the FBI," North Country Public Radio, March 7, 2023.
[5] Emily Russell, "Stefanik's Hearing Focuses on UN Impact, Chinese Influence, and Antisemitism," North Country Public Radio, January 21, 2025.

6. Shealeigh Voitl, Andy Lee Roth, and Project Censored, *Beyond Fact-Checking: A Teaching Guide to the Power of News Frames* (The Censored Press, 2025), 5.
7. "U.N. Chief Warns Israeli Leaders Seeking to Fully Annex West Bank," *Democracy Now!*, January 23, 2025.
8. Sharon Zhang, "Trump Reportedly Resuming Shipments of 2,000-Pound Bombs to Israel," *Truthout*, January 21, 2025.
9. See Michele Kelemen, "Trump's Pick for U.N. Ambassador Is Elise Stefanik. Here's What to Know," NPR, January 21, 2025; Farnoush Amiri and Edith M. Lederer, "Stefanik Pledges an 'America First' Agenda at the UN and a Review of US Funding," Associated Press, January 21, 2025; Karoun Demirjian, "Elise Stefanik Pledges to Back Trump's Vision of a 'Reformed' U.N.," *New York Times*, January 21, 2025; and Cybele Mayes-Osterman, "Elise Stefanik Pledges Support for Trump, Israel at UN Ambassador Confirmation Hearing," *USA Today*, January 21, 2025.
10. See Mjriam Abu Samra and Sara Troian, "Palestine Beyond the Colonial Logic of International Law," *Mondoweiss*, April 2, 2025.
11. "Elise Stefanik Confirmation Hearing," *Rev*, accessed April 29, 2025.
12. "UNRWA: Claims Versus Facts," United Nations Relief and Works Agency for Palestine Refugees in the Near East, March 4, 2024.
13. Guardian staff and agencies, "Israel Minister Condemned for Saying Starvation of Millions in Gaza Might Be 'Justified and Moral'," *The Guardian*, August 7, 2024.
14. "Israeli Minister Reiterates Calls for Palestinians to Leave Gaza," *Al Jazeera*, December 31, 2023.
15. Reuters Fact Check, "Fact Check: US UNRWA Funding Already Halted in 2024, Not by Trump 2025 Order," Reuters, January 28, 2025.
16. "Which Countries Have Cut Funding to UNRWA, and Why?" *Al Jazeera*, January 28, 2024.
17. "Israel's New Laws Banning UNRWA Already Taking Effect," United Nations, January 29, 2025.
18. Isabel Debre, "Israel's Ban on UN's Palestinian Aid Agency Has Come Into Effect. Here's What That Looks Like," Associated Press, January 30, 2025.
19. Peter Beinart, "The Campaign to Abolish UNRWA," *Jewish Currents*, February 13, 2024.
20. Edward Said, "Permission to Narrate," Journal of Palestine Studies 13, no. 3 (1984): 34.
21. John Collins, "The Deepest Fake News: Establishment Media and the Erasure of the Colonial Present," *Weave News*, July 19, 2022.
22. Sari Bashi, "Gaza: Two Rights of Return," *New York Review of Books*, January 27, 2024.
23. In a powerful Facebook post on January 25, 2025, Ramzy Baroud hailed the return of Palestinians from Southern Gaza, to which they had been forced to flee during Israel's intensive bombing campaign, back toward their homes in Northern Gaza. For Baroud, this collective action needed to be seen, optimistically, in the context of an ongoing struggle against settler colonial dispossession. "Never before have our people truly 'returned.' Never before have Palestinian refugees from Gaza ever moved north. From the Palestinian Nakba of 1948 to this historic moment on January 25, 2025, we have only drifted deeper into the diaspora. Yet, throughout it all, we

have clung to the dream of one day realizing our right to return…The right of return is not just a dream; it is no longer a distant hope. It is a reality. And it begins today—thanks to Gaza, and the immense sacrifices of Gaza's people." Ramzy Baroud, "Never before have our people truly 'returned.' Never before have Palestinian refugees from Gaza ever moved north. From the Palestinian Nakba of 1948 to this historic moment," Facebook, January 26, 2025.

24. Russell, "Stefanik's Hearing."
25. Jewish Voice for Peace, "On Antisemitism, Anti-Zionism, and Dangerous Conflations," Jewish Voice for Peace, November 9, 2023.
26. See North Country Public Radio, "If All Else Fails (Podcast)," North Country Public Radio, January 2024.
27. Sharon Zhang, "Trump's UN Pick Says Israel Has 'Biblical Right' to West Bank Amid Invasion," *Truthout*, January 21, 2025.
28. "The Bible Grants Israel Rights to Occupied West Bank Says Trump's UN Envoy Pick," *Middle East Monitor*, January 23, 2025.
29. See John Collins, *Global Palestine* (Hurst and Company, 2011).
30. Chloe Atkins and Matt Lavietes, "Marco Rubio Memo Cites Mahmoud Khalil's Beliefs in Justifying His Deportation," NBC News, April 10, 2025, updated April 11, 2025.
31. Stephanie Saul, "A Mysterious Group Says Its Mission Is to Expose Antisemitic Students," *New York Times*, April 1, 2025.
32. Prior to this, the *New York Times*, along with other prominent national news outlets had all but ignored Canary Mission, despite substantive reporting from independent news outlets, including *The Intercept* and *The Nation*. See Miranda Morgan and Allison Ford, "Canary Mission Blacklists Pro-Palestinian Activists, Chilling Free Speech Rights," in *State of the Free Press 2022*, ed. Andy Lee Roth and Mickey Huff with Project Censored (The Censored Press and Seven Stories Press); also available online.
33. See Stephen Prager, "The Right Doesn't Actually Care About Antisemitism," *Current Affairs*, March 21, 2025.

— CHAPTER 5 —

MEDIA DEMOCRACY IN ACTION:
A COUNTERVAILING FORCE AGAINST AUTOCRACY

Contributions by RYAN GRIM (*Drop Site News*), MAYA SCHENWAR and LARA WITT (Movement Media Alliance), Joe Lauria (*Consortium News*), LAUREN HARPER (Freedom of the Press Foundation), and JODI RAVE SPOTTED BEAR (Indigenous Media Freedom Alliance); compiled and introduced by MISCHA GERACOULIS

INTRODUCTION

MISCHA GERACOULIS

With open contempt for the separation of powers, due process, rule of law, and the free press—democracy itself—Trump 2.0 has unleashed the threats outlined in Project 2025. Through the endorsement or acquiescence of citizens, public institutions, and even private law firms, the past year witnessed a full-scale Trump-Musk seizure of the White House, federal agencies, Congress, and the courts.[1] Although Trump and Musk's fixation on each other has predictably unraveled, the administration's unconstitutional retribution campaigns and sweeping claims to unchecked power have put dictatorial-style rule on glaring exhibit. Largely unchallenged by a deferential corporate press and those voters who either want authoritarian "technogarchic" rule, or have become accepting of, or apathetic toward, it, signals a renewed demand for First Amendment rights.[2]

In a March 2025 letter to the American people, the Lemkin Institute for Genocide Prevention and Human Security warned that "public cynicism and demoralization constrain the ability of a population to resist."³ The letter reminded Americans of the 2024 presidential election results. Trump did not win a majority—32.41 percent of the votes went to Trump, 31.35 percent went to Harris, and the rest abstained. The Institute, thus, urged US citizens to seize on their agency and the power of collective action. If a mere 3.5 percent of the population—approximately twelve million people—engaged in civic discourse and nonviolent civil disobedience, the letter pointed out, a resistance would emerge strong enough to shift the nation's trajectory.

INCLUSIVE, COLLABORATIVE ACTION LEADS THE CHARGE

The essays in this chapter by Jodi Rave Spotted Bear of the Indigenous Media Freedom Alliance and Maya Schenwar and Lara Witt of the Movement Media Alliance display similar foresight. They highlight the proactive, cross-sector collaborations that are reorienting journalism to its core mission to serve the public. While both essays acknowledge ongoing challenges to the First Amendment, not the least of which are censored and erased facts, expanding news deserts, and inadequate protections for journalists, they champion community-driven media and grassroots engagement as guidestars in the effort to restore democratic values and practices.

In May 2025, A.G. Sulzberger, publisher of the *New York Times*, pontificated on how press subservience facilitates the keeping of secrets and the rewriting of reality by those with power.[4] Duly noting that a democratic society cannot survive without a free press, Sulzberger described the anti-press playbook crafted to degrade the press' watchdog role to that of an obedient lapdog. The irony of Sulzberger's remarks was hard to miss—leaks revealed in 2024 by Ryan Grim and Jeremy Scahill at *The Intercept* showed that top editors at Sulzberger's own paper had instructed reporters on which terms to use or avoid when covering Gaza, downplaying facts inconvenient to governments and omitting necessary context.[5]

Recognizing that stenographic reporting undermines both the field of journalism and the public's best interest, Grim and Scahill launched *Drop Site News* to counter the corporate media's drift toward passive, uncritical coverage. Grim's essay in this chapter offers a compelling glimpse into how community-centered, fact-based, investigative journalism strengthens democracy by encouraging discourse and exposing information that the public deserves to know.

The public in a democratic society is also served by critical media literacy education, a cornerstone of Project Censored's fifty-year mission. Underscoring the urgent need for improved media literacy, 2024 studies published in the *American Economic Review* and in Harvard's *Misinformation Review* found that almost half of the Americans surveyed could not distinguish fact from opinion.[6] That statistic becomes even more alarming in light of Jeff Bezos's 2025 announcement that the *Washington Post*'s opinion pages would be restructured to only featuring the defense and promotion of free markets.[7]

Corporate and partisan ideologies already dominate the daily news cycle. As Joe Lauria emphasizes in his essay, ideologies and journalism are incompatible, but much of what passes for "news" is commercialized persuasion. For more than three decades, Lauria's *Consortium News* has remained steadfast in its mission to hold the powerful to account, no matter who occupies the White House. Unlike corporate media executives who pay lip service to journalistic integrity, Lauria—and all the contributors to this chapter—consistently practice the values they profess.

PRESS FREEDOM CORRELATES TO SOCIETAL TRUST

Explaining the United States's further decline in the 2025 World Press Freedom Index (from fifty-fith position in 2024 to fifty-seventh), Reporters Without Borders (RSF) cited the concentration of media ownership, crisis-level news deserts, and a hyper-partisan environment that perpetuates the Trumpian falsehood that journalists are the "enemy of the people."[8] According to RSF, the intended result is a surge in hostility toward the press, incited not only by the administration but by a distrustful and poorly informed populace—a reality that *Consortium News* and *Drop Site News* know all too well.

Addressing this climate of manufactured societal suspicion, Lauren Harper, the inaugural Daniel Ellsberg Chair on Government Secrecy at Freedom of the Press Foundation, explains in her essay how DOGE-induced information silos and government secrecy obscure the public's right to know.[9] Instead of relying on the press to hold leaders accountable, many Americans, conditioned by Trump-Musk messaging, blame the media wholesale for their government's failings.

The United States also saw a decline in its ranking in the 2025 World Happiness Index. Among the factors contributing to this drop was a pronounced erosion of social trust, reflected in the rise of extremist ideologies, nationalistic and religious fervor, and growing disdain for social institutions.[10] Harper describes various ways that government secrecy undermines civil society—no sector is left untouched, including communications and the media. Just as an insulated executive branch deepens public suspicion and cynicism, it fuels a broader culture of distrust and discontent.

By contrast, the Netherlands and the Scandinavian nations rank high in both the press freedom and happiness indexes. This suggests a correlation. Where there is confidence in government transparency, strong social protections, and basic trust among citizens, an accessible and unfettered press is also trusted to serve the public good.

PRESS FREEDOM, INVESTIGATIVE REPORTING, AND CRITICAL MEDIA LITERACY TO ENSURE THE FUTURE

It's often said that journalists write the first draft of history. Now fifty years strong, Project Censored continues to shine a light on those who take up that task with courage, reporting the truth despite powerful forces that seek to censor, manipulate, and mislead. The contributors to this chapter are exemplary counteragents to this era's cynicism, distrust, and secrecy. Commemorating Project Censored's fiftieth anniversary alongside these leading voices in media freedom is both an honor and a testament to the Project's enduring mission to educate on the necessity of a free and ethical press and an informed public for democracy to succeed.

Alliance-building, resilience in the face of despotism, and other themes recurrent in this chapter offer a plausible vision of cooperative action in defense of an open and just society. In the spirit of collaboration, lifting up journalistic principles and constitutional rights, we celebrate this milestone and look forward to many years to come.

DROP SITE NEWS: ADVERSARIAL JOURNALISM IN AN AUTHORITARIAN AGE

RYAN GRIM

Drop Site News is a non-aligned, nonprofit investigative news organization dedicated to combating the rise of authoritarianism worldwide and exposing the crimes of the powerful, particularly in overt and secret conflicts where the US government plays a key role. At a time when the world desperately needs hard-hitting journalism, establishment and corporate media outlets are failing the public and democracy itself. Now more than ever, uncompromising, independent reporting is essential to preserving democratic values and rebuilding public trust. We launched *Drop Site* to fill that gap—to operate free from corporate and government influence, report difficult and risky stories no one else will, build community, foster discourse, and fulfill our duty to hold the powerful accountable.

Our vision is to create an outlet that actively cultivates a community of engaged readers who seek to understand and challenge the world around them. In contrast to traditional media, which often present the news as a one-way broadcast, *Drop Site* attempts to foster meaningful discourse and collaboration. We seek to create spaces where readers can critically engage with the news and contribute their own insights. On our recently launched Discord server, we invite dedicated readers to help shape our coverage by sharing video clips, translating international reports, and offering valuable perspectives. This community-driven approach not only strengthens independent journalism but also empowers active participation in identifying and shaping stories.

Traditional media outlets are increasingly constrained in their ability to challenge the status quo. Conflicts of interest, reliance on advertising revenue, and the need to maintain access to powerful sources lead to self-censorship and diluted reporting. We reject these compromises by operating a newsroom funded entirely by readers and independent donors. Because we do not sell corporate ads or collect ad revenue, we are able to make editorial decisions free from financial pressures that might otherwise compromise our integrity. Our refusal to place our reporting behind a paywall ensures that crucial investigative journalism remains accessible to everyone, not just those who can afford it. We maintain a small team with a lean and focused approach that allows us to maximize our resources, cut through the official narratives, and deliver the most impact.

Investigative journalism is inherently dangerous, but it is the first, and often only, means of exposing corruption and systemic abuses of power. *Drop Site* embraces this challenge and the implicit consequences, prioritizing difficult, high-risk stories that others shy away from. We measure our effectiveness by the support and growth of our readership and by the reactions of those abusing power across the globe. Barely two months into *Drop Site*'s existence, we made enemies of at least three governments, were banned in Pakistan, and saw our ongoing coverage of the genocide in Gaza censored across Meta's platforms. We interpreted these ferocious, authoritarian responses from centers of power as clear validation of our effort to build a newsroom that always strives to challenge the status quo.

Much of our work centers around conflicts in the Middle East, particularly where the US government is involved. We launched in July 2024, in large part motivated by Israel's genocidal war on Gaza and the profound inadequacy of the establishment media's reporting on the atrocities. The Committee to Protect Journalists' annual report called 2024 the deadliest year on record for journalists;[11] more than two-thirds of those deaths were our Palestinian colleagues, including *Drop Site* contributor Hossam Shabat, who was directly targeted and killed by the Israeli military on March 24, 2025. Hossam was a tremendous young journalist who exhibited remarkable courage and tenacity as he documented the US-facilitated genocide against the Palestinians of Gaza. One of the few journalists who didn't leave the northern Gaza Strip, Hossam was murdered in Beit Lahia, the site of some of the most intense Israeli bombing and mass killing operations.[12]

As the existing media landscape in the MENA region is dominated by state narratives, subject to government censorship, and extremely dangerous for local reporters, *Drop Site* is ideally positioned to fill the vacuum. Our reporting is founded on strong networks of local reporters and sources across the region, expertise in legal and security risks, and significant experience publishing ambitious journalism. *Drop Site* is a platform for local, independent journalists who face real dangers and a daily threat of being silenced. We amplify their important work on the ground to reach a wider, global audience. With authoritarianism on the rise and institutional failures running rampant, independent journalism stands as one of the last lines of defense for democracy. *Drop Site* wholeheartedly embraces the adversarial role of the press, exposing corruption, policy failures, and abuses of power by publishing rigorous, fact-based investigations free from undue influence.

While traditional media outlets have softened their stance toward authority, celebrating neoliberalism and Big Tech oligarchy, *Drop Site News* provides a model of what journalism must become in the fight to preserve democratic values. By bridging the gap between journalists and the public, we strive to create a global body that challenges the legacy media's myopic, top-down paradigm.

In an era when misinformation, disinformation, and media consolidation threaten the very fabric of free society, we aim to exemplify what a free and fearless press should be—uncompromising, community-driven, and dedicated to the truth.

RYAN GRIM is the co-founder of *Drop Site News* and previously led the Washington bureaus for *The Intercept* and *HuffPost*. At *HuffPost*, his team was twice a finalist for the Pulitzer Prize and won once. Grim has spent years chronicling the rise of progressives in Congress, and his most recent book is *The Squad: AOC and the Hope of a Political Revolution*, which followed his best-selling *We've Got People*. He's also the author of the 2009 book *This Is Your Country on Drugs*.

MOVEMENT MEDIA ALLIANCE: AN ESSENTIAL ANTIDOTE TO ESTABLISHMENT MEDIA'S CAPITALIST PRIORITIES

MAYA SCHENWAR and LARA WITT

There is no power for the people without journalism by and for the people.[13]

In November 2023, twenty-five media-makers from independent US-based organizations gathered around a long table at Chicago's Haymarket House to discuss the future of media and how we might build it together.

Although our organizations differed in focus, audience, size, and perspective, we all believed in the power of media to inform and fuel social movements that transform the world. Many of us embraced the concept of movement journalism, defined by Project South as "the practice of journalism in the service of ... social, political, and economic transformation."[14] We gathered to explore a pressing question: How can we work collaboratively to sharpen and grow the practice of movement journalism?

We convened amid cataclysmic changes in media (and more have transpired since). We'd seen a flood of shutdowns, layoffs, and bankruptcies.[15] Some publications had come close to shutting down, and others had been acquired by larger, syndicated outlets, accelerating the decline in access to a plurality of media.[16] A Medill analysis found "the loss of local newspapers accelerated in 2023 to an average of 2.5 per week."[17]

Meanwhile, events since October 2023—including Israel's genocide in Gaza, its escalation of attacks in the West Bank, the suppression of protest in the United States, and an overtly fascist and White supremacist Trump administration—have exposed how establishment media often fuel grave political harm by platforming the perpetrators of these injustices and showing deference to them. When the United States's most prominent media outlets acquiesce to a single established narrative, they help manufacture consent for imperialist wars, while distracting readers from capitalist class warfare against the poor and working classes. Movement journalism is an essential antidote.

When our organizations met, we originally planned to focus on covering the 2024 election. Instead, we pivoted because an emergency was at hand: the US government's support of Israel's genocide in Gaza combined with the corporate media's role in bolstering genocidal rhetoric and minimizing the extent of the atrocities required a strong, immediate response.

Over two days, we built the collaboration that became

Media Against Apartheid and Displacement (MAAD), a curated media hub that aggregated articles from trustworthy, independent sources on the ongoing genocide and occupation of Palestine, the international complicity that supports occupation and genocide (including the arming of Israel by the United States and European countries and widespread disinformation campaigns that bolster Zionism), and the rising movements for Palestinian liberation.[18] MAAD represented an unprecedented coalition of twenty-one media platforms. Together, we united to say, "We refuse to participate in the journalistic status quo. We choose truth."

Throughout the winter and spring, our organizations worked together in stops and starts, and we recognized an essential and oft-forgotten truth through our work together: We can't make long-term change alone.

MAAD was just one example of what we can do when we come together. We can meet emergencies with real strength. Our individual outlets may be small relative to the largest corporate media, but together, we're formidable.

In June 2024, our movement media organizations convened again. Together, we began work on Communities Beyond Elections, a project that looked at the impact of electoral politics on a range of oppressed groups and delved into how these communities are building liberatory futures inside and beyond those political realms. We also embarked on a groundbreaking discussion of how our organizations could collaborate to support each other financially, with the knowledge that a vibrant, varied, sustainable movement journalism ecosystem benefits us all.

We made a big decision to launch the Movement Media Alliance (MMA), a coalition of grassroots-aligned, social justice-driven journalism organizations committed to accurate, transparent, accountable, principled, and just media.[19] Our members include *Truthout, Prism, In These Times, Convergence Magazine,* Project Censored, *Waging Nonviolence, Scalawag,* Inquest, The Real News Network, *Baltimore Beat,* Palestine Square, *Mondoweiss, TransLash, Hammer & Hope,* The Dig,

Respair Production & Media, *The Forge*, and Haymarket Books.

We're building power together based on shared principles and a vision of accountable, transparent, accurate journalism that fuels justice and liberation for all oppressed communities.

We share a vision that eschews White supremacist notions of "objectivity"—because the myths of objectivity, impartiality, and "balance" create false equivalencies between justice and injustice, equity and inequity, and right and wrong. We refuse to be stenographers for the maintenance of the status quo. As movement media organizations, we proudly hold ourselves to rigorous, evidence-based reporting, interviews, and fact-checking standards.

Fascist movements are growing.[20] In these treacherous times, movement media help connect communities to share organizing strategies; they inform readers and listeners how to lead divestment efforts and build solidarity to protect one another from harm; and they can inspire worker efforts to form unions.

But movement media can't survive on values alone, and most of our organizations consistently struggle for adequate resources. We are building the MMA in part to create a future in which member organizations are economically secure enough to avoid dead-end choices between closure or corporate takeover, a future in which we can provide our staff members with more abundance, expansive solidarity, and safety, while creating new movement journalism jobs in marginalized communities. In short, we want to make this work sustainable for the long term. Movement media-makers should have pensions, support for families of all structures, comprehensive health care, and the space and time to think creatively and without the fear of scarcity or layoffs. We believe pursuing this future is best done together, pooling our ideas for resource-sharing, community-building, and collaboration.

Our individual outlets can't afford to compete under capitalist frameworks or survive by conforming to the establishment media's compromised priorities to produce revenues. We also can't afford to abandon democracy and oppressed communities by letting our publications die.

Fascist movements are well funded, as are right-wing, White supremacist media outlets.[21] By allowing the proliferation of mis- and disinformation, we move even further away from the possibility of a society where everyone is safe and autonomous. The Movement Media Alliance is just one solution among many, but it's a powerful step forward. Our dream of a media future that is collaborative and abundant is within reach—if we commit to it.

LARA WITT is an award-winning editor and journalist, the editor-in-chief of *Prism*, and co-founder of the Movement Media Alliance (MMA) and Media Against Apartheid & Displacement (MAAD). Their goal is to provide platforms for marginalized voices and to reshape the landscape of media altogether as a tool for liberation.

MAYA SCHENWAR is director of the Truthout Center for Grassroots Journalism. She is also *Truthout*'s editor-at-large and board president. She is the co-author of *Prison by Any Other Name: The Harmful Consequences of Popular Reforms* and author of *Locked Down, Locked Out: Why Prison Doesn't Work and How We Can Do Better*. Maya is a cofounder of the Movement Media Alliance and Media Against Apartheid and Displacement. She lives in Chicago.

CONSORTIUM NEWS: 30 YEARS OF DEFIANCE IN JOURNALISM

JOE LAURIA

As Project Censored celebrates its fiftieth anniversary, 2025 has been a special year for *Consortium News*, marking thirty years as the oldest, independent online news publication in the United States.

In 1995, Robert Parry, one of the country's leading investigative reporters at the time, started a website that was unlike any. Thirty years later, it is still going.

Bob uncovered major stories for the Associated Press and *Newsweek*. He blew the cover on Iran-Contra, one of the greatest scandals in US history. He helped reveal that the Reagan administration unconstitutionally evaded Congress's decision to stop funding the Nicaraguan Contras by secretly selling arms to Iran and using the proceeds to fund the guerrilla group.

Parry had first reported on the CIA's relationship with the Contras and their narcotic shipments into the United States. He then put the spotlight on the first October Surprise in the 1980 US presidential election—the Reagan campaign team's deal with Iran to delay release of the US hostages until after the election in exchange for arms shipped via Israel.[22]

But revealing crimes and corruption by the US government did not sit well with his establishment editors. They tried spiking his stories. They set up absurd demands—like asking Lieutenant Colonel Oliver North, who played a key role in the Iran-Contra operation, to confess—and at one point told Parry to stop asking too many questions "for the good of the country."

After working on an October Surprise documentary for PBS's *Frontline*, Bob left establishment journalism so he could at last do his job unhindered.

Parry began *Consortium News* (*CN*) on November 15, 1995, to provide a publication for a consortium of independent journalists whose work, often critical of the United States, was similarly suppressed by their editors.

It went online five days before *Salon.com* and weeks before established outlets like the *New York Times,* the *Washington Post*, and the *Wall Street Journal* launched their internet editions.

Parry's mission was to provide coverage of whole stories or angles omitted or suppressed by the establishment media. To this day, *CN* does not receive or accept a penny from any government, corporation, or advertiser, but is strictly funded by readers.

The new publication continued to break stories about the Reagan era into the 1990s, including the existence of a secret "perception management" program run by the CIA from within the White House.[23]

Consortium News was at the forefront of skepticism about the rationale for the 2003 invasion of Iraq and became the home of the Veteran Intelligence Professionals for Sanity, a consortium of former intel officers who exposed the faulty intelligence leading to the war. Like honest reporters just trying to do their jobs, Parry said there were also honest intelligence officers trying to do theirs.

For this work and for opposing the US invasion, Parry and other *CN* writers were hit with a torrent of smears, labelling them "Saddam Hussein apologists."

Parry and a host of writers then produced groundbreaking stories critical of the Obama administration's regime change wars in Syria and Libya, and especially on the 2014 US-backed coup in Ukraine and its provocation of Russia.

Consortium News was also at the forefront of skepticism of the now thoroughly debunked Russiagate story, peddled by unnamed intelligence sources. For its coverage of Ukraine and Russiagate, *Consortium News* has been maliciously accused of being Putin puppets or pro-Trump. Parry was especially fierce about Democrats who lost their skepticism and embraced the intelligence agencies during this period. He wrote:

> Ironically, many 'liberals' who cut their teeth on skepticism about the Cold War and the bogus justifications for the Vietnam War now insist that we must all accept whatever the US intelligence community feeds us, even if we're told to accept the assertions on faith.

Parry defended Julian Assange as early as 2010 against government designs to arrest and imprison him, which did not please many Democrats, especially after the 2016 election.[24] The Assange case became the signature story for *Consortium News*, including reporting from the London courtroom. Following Bob's untimely death in January 2018, I took over as editor-in-chief on April 1, 2018.

Consortium News routinely upsets both Republican and Democratic partisans by taking an independent stand based on where the facts lead, and on international conflicts, providing historical context as well as both sides of the story.[25]

That's because we practice strict, non-partisan journalism, the only kind worthy of the name. Ideology and journalism do not mix, leading to personal and institutional attacks on *Consortium News* from Republicans and Democrats, each equally oblivious to the fact that *CN* is critiquing their political enemies, too.

In an age of growing censorship and suppression of news, *Consortium News* is not exaggerating when it says it has abundant evidence of efforts to marginalize or silence us.

From 2016 until now, *CN* has been targeted eight times:[26] blacklisted by PropOrNot; falsely accused by a Canadian intelligence agency and major TV network of being in the forefront of a Russian cyber-attack against Canadian politicians;[27] flagged by NewsGuard, which warns its subscribers to take "extreme caution" because *CN* "severely violates" journalistic standards; permanently banned by PayPal for what could only be *CN*'s reporting;[28] and, for three days in October 2024, hacked and shut down.

It is a perilous environment for a free press, but there is no way forward but to continue in dissent against repression.

JOE LAURIA is editor-in-chief of *Consortium News* and a former UN correspondent for the *Wall Street Journal, Boston Globe,* and other newspapers, including the *Montreal Gazette,* the London *Daily Mail* and *The Star* of Johannesburg. He was an investigative reporter for the *Sunday Times* of London, a financial reporter for *Bloomberg News* and began his professional work as a 19-year-old stringer for the *New York Times*. He is the author of two books, *A Political Odyssey,* with Senator Mike Gravel and a foreword by Daniel Ellsberg; and *How I Lost by Hillary Clinton,* with a foreword by Julian Assange.

HOW GOVERNMENT SECRECY ERODES DEMOCRATIC PARTICIPATION

LAUREN HARPER

At Freedom of the Press Foundation, we take the threat posed by excessive government secrecy and the legacy of our co-founder and board member Daniel Ellsberg seriously. We regularly question the government's classification claims and practices, and advocate for reforms to the secrecy system.

This task begs some important questions, namely: What is government secrecy, what forms does it take, and how can we demonstrate the harm it causes?

Government secrecy, at its core, is a control mechanism. It can take many forms, including federal agencies deleting information from their websites, needlessly classifying information that could embarrass the government or reveal misdeeds, not responding to public records requests, or refusing to share information with Congress.

One of the most effective ways to counter the government's knee-jerk, self-perpetuating need for secrecy is by highlighting reporting that shows how overclassification hurts everyday Americans and how forcing transparency has improved people's lives.

Often, when we think about government secrecy, we think about intelligence agencies and national security issues—as we should. We know too little about even the most basic elements of how the intelligence community operates; for example, we still don't know individual intelligence agencies' staffing levels and budgets.

The difficulty in understanding the implications of the Trump administration's directive to the CIA to allocate more resources to the fight against Mexican drug cartels is a case in point.

We need to know what resources will be pulled from other concerns in other areas of the world.[29] The lack of public details makes it impossible for the public and for Congress to debate the wisdom of such a pivot effectively.

Secrecy doesn't just stifle debates around spies and intelligence agencies. It permeates nearly every policy area imaginable—from domestic debates about water safety and the economic impacts of climate change, to foreign policy discussions about security agreements and international aid.[30]

Following Daniel Patrick Moynihan's foreword to the 1997 report on government secrecy, I always think of secrecy as a form of government regulation. Excessive government secrecy prevents full participation in the democratic process at all levels and leaves the public ill-prepared to rein in the government when its actions are not in the public interest. We cannot hold the government accountable if we don't know what it's doing.

This systemic power imbalance, which has existed to varying degrees under Democratic and Republican administrations alike, is made exponentially more dangerous now that the Supreme Court has granted the president broad immunity for "official acts."[31] This will make it easier for the chief executive to, if they are so inclined, weaponize all levers of the secrecy system for their political and personal goals.

Weaponization could take many forms, including mass firing of public records officials, threatening to retaliate against agencies if they release information, or by ruthlessly persecuting whistleblowers for leaking information about the government to the press.

Transparency is essential to restoring equilibrium between the public and the government because it can, among other things, counter the narrative that the government tells about itself.

The leak of the Pentagon Papers in 1971 and the publication of the Afghanistan Papers in 2019 both demonstrate, nearly fifty years apart, that the government consistently lies to the public about the costs of war and the likelihood of success.[32] Releasing information that contradicts the government's official line, whether through leaks or FOIA releases, doesn't guarantee that the United States won't continue to wage and prolong ill-advised wars, but it can force officials to reconsider war plans and justify the Defense Department's ballooning military budget.

Transparency also shows how well or poorly the government has planned to respond to public health issues, such as the COVID-19 pandemic, the Flint water crisis, and the health implications of the East Palestine, Ohio, train derailment. It can also inform citizens if government agencies are prepared for and respond to national disasters, including the effects of climate change.

Importantly, transparency should also make it more difficult for the government to break the law. It's not an accident that the executive order governing the handling of classified national security information, EO 13526, says material may not be classified with the specific intent of hiding wrongdoing. This language means that agencies can still classify records showing they broke the law so long as they are, allegedly, not classifying information specifically to hide that fact. Agencies exploit this loophole and will continue to do so as long as it exists.

As of writing this, America finds itself in the midst of a turbulent political environment, the outcome of which is anybody's guess. What is clear, however, is that the extent to which we can fight against pernicious secrecy in the short term will have an outsized impact on the degree to which we can participate in our democratic process in the years to come.

LAUREN HARPER is the first Daniel Ellsberg Chair on Government Secrecy with Freedom of the Press Foundation, a position established to honor and continue the legendary whistleblower's fight for secrecy reform.

TRIBAL CITIZENS RECOGNIZE NEED FOR LOCAL MEDIA SHIFT: MOVEMENT AFOOT TO REDEFINE JOURNALISM WITHIN NATIVE NATIONS

JODI RAVE SPOTTED BEAR

Federal Indian law scholar Felix S. Cohen said lawmakers should weigh how their decisions affect society. In 1934, a Congressional act moved many Native nations to create their own constitutions. But Congress made no clear call to include First Amendment protections to safeguard rights critical to Native nations' new governance models.

As a result, the rights to freedom of speech, press, and assembly show up inconsistently in tribal constitutions, most notably through inclusion in the 1968 Indian Civil Rights Act. Enforcement is often unclear, leaving Native communities with legal gaps and no consistent way to protect civil liberties.

What happens to a society when it can't speak freely or tell its own stories?

At the Indigenous Media Freedom Alliance and through our news site, *Buffalo's Fire*, we respond to underreporting, misinformation, and disinformation. We are building a collaborative, Indigenous-led media network that protects data sovereignty, reclaims the narrative, and redefines journalism from within Native communities.

As journalists, we uphold the third pillar of tribal sovereignty that holds leaders to account. We amplify the voices of the people so they can be heard by tribal leaders who are good at exercising the other two sovereignty pillars, including protecting sacred places and advancing self-determination.[33]

Data Sovereignty

Just as Native nations are reclaiming data to reflect their own values and realities, Indigenous media are working to restore narrative power to their communities. The push for accurate, community-informed journalism is part of the broader data sovereignty movement. Both aim to correct structural imbalances in how Native people are seen, heard, and understood.

When Indigenous journalists are restricted, censored, or denied independent press systems, public narratives become distorted—just like when tribes are left out of datasets. In both cases, invisibility disempowers communities.

We're keenly aware that Native communities are often left out of reliable media research, and know our people want better.

Reclaim the Narrative

To change that, the Indigenous Media Freedom Alliance has been holding listening sessions and gathering insights from Native news consumers. Our research and listening sessions show a clear need to rethink "local" news. For Native communities, local means more than geography—it's a shared experience across tribal nations. What happens to one often echoes in another.

This movement is bigger than the media. It's about reclaiming narrative power and shaping our future—on our terms.

Participants voiced strong support for Native-led journalism. They want reporting rooted in the community but free from political interference. Press freedom, they said, isn't just a value, it's a necessity. Without it, people don't know what decisions are being made or how to speak up.

Many participants were surprised to learn how few Native news outlets operate independently. That realization drove home a deeper point: Media institutions matter. Moreover, these institutions deserve protection and room to grow.

Across conversations, one theme rose again and again: News about Native communities should come from Native journalists. That connection shapes how stories are told and whose voices are lifted. People want reporting that's accurate, culturally-grounded, and trauma-informed. How a story is told can build trust—or break it.

Surveys echoed these insights. Over 80 percent said tribal meeting minutes should be accessible. Most community members did not know who owns their local news outlet. When asked if they would support greater independence for tribal media, the affirmative response was 8.4 out of ten. People want government accountability. They also want reporting that asks the hard questions and reflects who they are.

Redefine Journalism

For generations, Native communities have lived without consistent access to reliable, independent journalism. In that absence, misinformation and disinformation have taken root. Outside voices shape the narrative, largely misrepresenting Indigenous people or ignoring them altogether.

At the heart of the problem is access. Most tribal news outlets operate under political pressure. Independent Native newsrooms are rare. Tribal leader decision-making often happens behind closed doors, typically in executive sessions. Tribal citizens are aware they're being left in the dark.

Without Indigenous-centered journalism, Native people are cut off from critical information and from each other. The result is isolation, distortion, and a lack of tribal government accountability. For too long, Native voices have been silenced—by so-called mainstream media and our own governments. But we are storytellers, and our stories must live. The Indigenous Media Freedom Alliance is breaking that silence by building an Indigenous-led media network rooted in independent media, truth-telling, cultural integrity, trust and sovereignty.

IMFA's collaborative idea is bold yet grounded in creating an alliance of Native newsrooms that share resources, support one another, and tell stories that reflect our people and homelands. This isn't about copying Western models. It's about building something new, starting with an infrastructure that respects tribal sovereignty and follows Indigenous values.

This is more than an idea, it's a movement. IMFA is helping to create an Indigenous-led media system that informs, empowers, and returns the power of storytelling to Native communities.

JODI RAVE SPOTTED BEAR is the founder and executive director of the Indigenous Media Freedom Alliance, the publisher of *Buffalo's Fire*, a digital news site. The IMFA also leads the Bismarck Documenters, the first Indigenous-led and first rural program in the national Documenters Network. The nonprofit news organization is based in Bismarck, North Dakota. Jodi, who is enrolled with the Mandan, Hidatsa and Arikara Nation, lives on her ancestral homelands. As an advocate for tribal citizens' civil liberties, the Indigenous Journalists Association awarded Jodi the Tim Giago Free Press Award in 2023.

Notes

1. Rachel Beatty Riedl, et al., "Pathways of Democratic Backsliding, Resistance, and (Partial) Recoveries," *Annals of the American Academy of Political and Social Science* 712, no. 1 (2025); Michael S. Schmidt, et al., "Why Trump Is Punishing Law Firms," *New York Times*, April 7, 2025.
2. Mischa Geracoulis and Mickey Huff, "Technogarchy Goes to Washington," Project Censored, February 20, 2025.
3. Lemkin Institute Team, "Letter to the American People," Lemkin Institute, March 27, 2025.
4. A.G. Sulzberger, "A Free People Need a Free Press," *New York Times*, May 13, 1025.
5. Jeremy Scahill and Ryan Grim, "Leaked NYT Gaza Memo Tells Journalists to Avoid Words 'Genocide,' 'Ethnic Cleansing,' and 'Occupied Territory'," *The Intercept*, April 15, 2024.
6. See Charles Angelucci and Andrea Prat, "Is Journalistic Truth Dead? Measuring How Informed Voters Are About Political News," *American Economic Review*, April 2024; and Matthew Mettler and Jeffery J. Mondak, "Fact-Opinion Differentiation," *Misinformation Review*, March 7, 2024.
7. Jeff Bezos, "X Post," X, February 26, 2025.
8. Mickey Huff and Andy Lee Roth, "The Free Press as 'Enemy of the People,'" Project Censored, August 2, 2017.
9. Lauren Harper, "The Signalgate Problem Nobody Is Talking About," Freedom of the Press Foundation, March 30, 2025.
10. World Happiness Report, 2025.
11. "2024 Is Deadliest Year for Journalists in CPJ History; Almost 70% Killed by Israel," Committee to Protect Journalists, February 12, 2025.
12. "Statement from Drop Site News on Israel's Murder of Our Colleague Hossam Shabat: We Hold Both Israel and the U.S. Government Responsible," *Drop Site News*, March 24, 2025.
13. This is a revised version of an article we originally published on August 28, 2024 at *Truthout* and *Prism*.
14. Anna Simonton, "Out of Struggle," Project South, August, 2017.
15. See, e.g., David Bauder, "Think the News Industry Was Struggling Already? The Dawn of 2024 Is Offering a Few Good Tidings," Associated Press,

February 2, 2024; "Journalism Layoffs," Institute for Independent Journalists, accessed April 8, 2025; Associated Press, "Vice Media Files for Bankruptcy, the Latest in a String of Digital Media Setbacks," *Los Angeles Times*, May 15, 2023.

16 Peter Kafka, "RIP Sports Illustrated. And RIP, Magazines," *Business Insider*, January 19, 2024.

17 "Medill Report Shows Local News Deserts Expanding," Northwestern Medill, October 23, 2024.

18 "Media Against Apartheid & Displacement (MAAD)," Movement Media Alliance, accessed March 8, 2025.

19 "Grassroots-Aligned, Social Justice-Driven Journalism," Movement Media Alliance, 2024.

20 Amy Goodman, interview with Jason Stanley, "'Erasing History': Prof. Jason Stanley on Why Fascists Attack Education and Critical Inquiry," *Democracy Now!*, September 17, 2024.

21 See, for example, Parker Molloy, "Media Matters Report on Conservative Media Dominance Reveals What Progressive Donors Don't Want to Hear," *The Present Age*, March 17, 2025; Peter Stone, "Powerful Conservative Funds Hand Out Millions to Pro-Trump Far-Right Groups," *The Guardian*, April 16, 2024.

22 *Consortium News*, "October Surprise Series," *Consortium News*, April 21, 2025.

23 Robert Parry, "The Victory of 'Perception Management'," *Consortium News*, December 28, 2014.

24 Robert Parry, "All Investigative Journalists Do What Julian Assange Did," *Consortium News*, April 18, 2019 (originally published December 16, 2010).

25 Joe Lauria, "Ukraine Timeline Tells the Tale," *Consortium News*, February 25, 2025; Amy Goodman, interview with Joe Lauria, "As U.S. Funnels Money & Arms to Ukraine, Independent Media Faces Pressure to Parrot Official Narrative," *Democracy Now!*, July 12, 2022.

26 Joe Lauria, "The War on Consortium News," *Consortium News*, December 4, 2024.

27 Joe Lauria, "Consortium News Sues Canadian TV Network for Defamation over Report CN Was Part of 'Attack' 'Directed' by Russia," *Consortium News*, October 13, 2020.

28 Joe Lauria, "'Mistaken' PayPal Email Means CN is Permanently Banned," *Consortium News*, May 6, 2022.

29 Warren P. Strobel and Isaac Stanley-Becker, "Under Trump, CIA Plots Bigger Role in Drug Cartel Fight," *Washington Post*, February 17, 2025.

30 See, e.g., Rachel Santarsiero, "The Climate Intelligence Assessment the Government Doesn't Want You to See," National Security Archive, February 28, 2025; Svetlana Savranskaya and Tom Blanton, "NATO Expansion: What Yeltsin Heard," National Security Archive, March 16, 2018; Lauren Harper, "USAID's Future Is in Doubt. The Status of Its Records Shouldn't Be," Freedom of the Press Foundation, February 4, 2025.

31 Samuel Breidbart, "The Supreme Court's Presidential Immunity Ruling Undermines Democracy," Brennan Center, October 1, 2024.

32 Lauren Harper, "The Pentagon Papers," Freedom of the Press Foundation, March 13, 2025; Craig Whitlock, Leslie Shapiro, and Armand Emamdjomeh, "The Afghanistan Papers," *Washington Post*, December 9, 2019.

33 On the pillars of tribal sovereignty, see David E. Wilkins, *Red Prophet: The Punishing Intellectualism of Vine Deloria Jr.* (Fulcrum Publishing, 2018).

— CHAPTER 6 —

Understanding the Digital Public Square

A Critical Media Literacy Guide to Infographics

ILLUSTRATED BY
REAGAN HAYNIE &
KATE HORGAN

WRITTEN BY
SHEALEIGH VOITL
& REAGAN HAYNIE

How Activism Becomes Visual

In recent years, social media platforms have become a primary gateway into activism. For many, a post is their first act of resistance—a signal of awareness, an expression of solidarity, or a call to action. Apps like Instagram, X, and TikTok now serve as both digital organizing spaces and virtual public squares, where hashtags can spark movements, stories go viral, and a single graphic can evoke outrage, empathy, or, in the best cases, mobilization. However, while they may seem to operate like public forums, it's important to remember that these platforms are run by private companies. As such, the speech posted there is not protected in the same way it would be in a government-controlled public space, and the companies are free to set and enforce their own content rules.

Visual media has long played a central role in political movements...

From ***The Black Panther newspaper***, established in 1967, which featured illustrated health guides, community announcements, and bold artwork that both empowered and informed readers in the fight for racial justice—

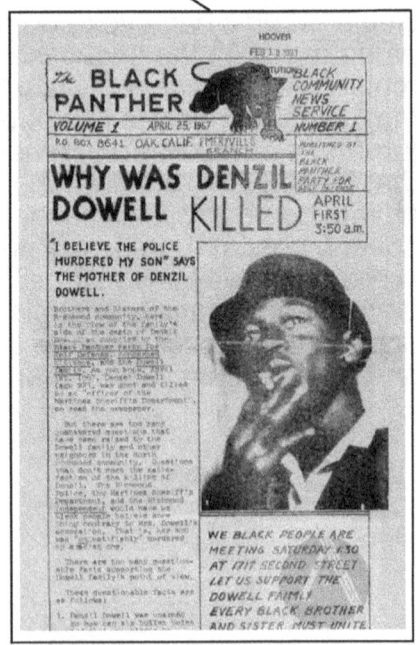

to the **Gay Liberation Front (GLF)** which used newspapers and bulletins for community-building, political education, and mobilization.

Today's digital infographics are optimized for online viewing and social media, featuring scrollable content that is easy to digest and share. Despite these advantages, producers and consumers of today's digital infographics must be aware that the online attention economy often prioritizes simplicity over nuance and clarity over accuracy.

As media theorist **Marshall McLuhan** famously stated, "The medium is the message," meaning that the form through which users deliver messages can shape their impact as much or more than the content itself.[1]

Infographics don't just communicate a cause—they shape how we relate to the cause itself. By design, infographics turn complex issues into quick and visually appealing messages.

This practice makes them powerful tools, but it also risks oversimplifying complex issues and reducing important matters to performative actions.

As social media activism becomes increasingly visual, questions arise about the power of infographics to effect real, tangible, and enduring change.

A Pew Research study found that "nearly **half of social media users [had] been politically active on social media**" between 2022 and 2023.[2]

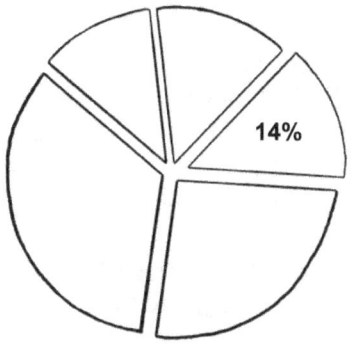

However, **only 14 percent** of those users had "looked up info on protests or rallies happening in their area." But that doesn't mean that all online engagement is futile.

According to Katherine White, a professor and researcher at the University of British Columbia's Sauder School of Business,

> **"Small acts of slacktivism (digital activism without any real-world action) can, under certain conditions, actually lead to meaningful support, such as when people privately commit to a cause and when their values are highly aligned with that cause."**[3]

"I've found that women can be condemned for posting advocacy-related content, while men are praised for the same action,"

said Julia Kyi, co-author of *Better Connected: How Girls Are Using Social Media*.

"Ideally we would critique performative activism while encouraging more activism in real life, and using social media as a tool to facilitate concrete, real-life movements."[4]

Nowadays, initial interest in supporting a movement often takes the form of sharing a graphic on an Instagram story or signing an online petition. Although these actions seem small, they can be important first steps toward broader engagement, and dismissing them outright or actively discouraging them is shortsighted.

However, navigating these digital spaces without strong critical media literacy tools leaves us vulnerable to spreading misinformation, slanted narratives, and content that reinforces harmful ideologies.

So, how can you tell the difference between a post meant to *inform* and one designed to *chase* engagement metrics?

And how can you avoid these pitfalls when creating infographics yourself?

infographics should be strategic, *not superficial*

Digital infographics have evolved quickly to take several different forms. For our purposes, we define *infographics* as visual representations of information designed to communicate a message quickly and clearly, often combining text, images, data, and design to educate, persuade, or mobilize an audience.

> While traditional infographics may include charts, graphs, and statistics, our definition extends to include more symbolic visual communication, such as the use of a single **black square** posted across social media platforms during the **#BlackoutTuesday** collective action.

In that context, the image itself was meant to signal solidarity with the **Black Lives Matter movement**, raise awareness about systemic racism and police violence, and act as a time, particularly for White people, to "reflect and acknowledge their privilege and educate themselves on systemic racism in America."[5]

Unfortunately, the black squares were literally *and* figuratively saying nothing, and therefore, were unhelpful in educating those who came across these posts on their feeds. In fact, channels of communication within the **#BlackLivesMatter** hashtag, which previously included important information about protests, mutual aid resources, and police activity, were suddenly flooded with irrelevant content.

The "Black Square" infographic type is less effective, as on its own, it lacks meaningful steps for users to engage beyond simply posting online, leading users to dismiss the graphic as "**slacktivism**" or "**virtue signaling**."

Infographics can be exceptionally powerful tools in activist spaces, capable of mobilizing both attention *and* action. While skepticism toward performative posting, such as black squares, may be warranted, it's crucial not to let that cynicism discourage meaningful digital engagement. As Noor Noman wrote for NBC News, "Posting a black square on Tuesday doesn't inherently make you a bad ally — but it doesn't inherently make you a good one, either."[6]

Instead, our goal is to equip audiences with critical media literacy tools that support responsible, impactful online activism and media creation.

The infographics you share or create should include three components:

1. Clear and accurate information

2. Context and purpose

3. Call to action or next steps

Without these, users may scroll away confused, disengaged, or worse, misinformed. Now, you can adapt the specifics of these components to fit your message and movement. For example, clear and accurate information might include verified statistics, quotes from reputable sources, or other key updates in an ongoing issue.

Context and purpose should help answer the questions: **Why this now? And why does this matter?** Perhaps you could provide a brief historical background, a connection to current events, or comparative data.

The page **@StopCopCity** dedicates its content to informing the public about the controversial plan to build a $90 million police training facility in the Weelaunee Forest near Atlanta, a project widely criticized for environmental destruction, militarized policing, and the silencing of repression and broader dissent.

Drawing connections between police expansion and protester struggles against racial and environmental injustice, the page situates the fight against "Cop City" within a long history of community resistance to state violence—and in the wake of mass protests following the 2020 murder of George Floyd, it raised urgent questions about whose safety is prioritized, at what cost, and who gets to decide.

Finally, the call to action doesn't always have to be a protest event or a donation opportunity. It could be as simple as providing further reading or asking users to contact their representatives about a specific issue, even offering a rough script to give first-time callers a clear expectation.

Political participation can take many forms

On February 28, 2025, the **People's Union USA** movement called for a nationwide "economic blackout" by launching an infographic. The goal of the economic blackout was simple: Refrain from spending for 24 hours to protest corporate power and economic inequality.[7]

The message, spread largely through infographics and carousel posts by various artists, was quickly amplified across Instagram and X. The boycott briefly appeared to gain traction.

In the days that followed, critics raised concerns about the boycott's lack of clarity and direction. Participation levels were difficult to track, and no major corporation reported a noticeable impact on its operations.

Scholars cited in *The Intercept* noted that without the backing of organized labor or any attempt to disrupt supply chains or shareholder value, the protest remained purely symbolic.[8]

Others online questioned the logic of "boycotting capitalism" for a **single day**, only to return to their routine consumption afterward.

Boycotts can be an effective, legitimate form of protest, but many people who saw the post, and perhaps even shared it, neglected to examine who coordinated the effort.

The People's Union USA was also simultaneously fundraising for "legal fees, organization development, web development, outreach, marketing, event organization, and more."[9] At one point, its website had a tab breaking down how more than $100,000 worth of crowdsourced funds was being spent. As of June 26, 2025, that page no longer exists.

A post or an organization's ability to go viral **doesn't ensure their trustworthiness.**

It is up to us to determine what constitutes good-faith engagement in movement-building, and what might be opportunistic clout-chasing, by applying **critical media literacy** tools to what we see in our feeds.

- Engage in **lateral reading** by taking information from posts online and conducting independent searches to assess their accuracy and credibility. Even with their emphasis on grabbing your attention, the strongest infographics still provide transparent sourcing to validate the claims they make.

- **Analyze** *the* framing *of the post.* How does the post formulate a problem that requires action? Who or what does it blame for the problem? How does it propose to address the issue? Are the visuals misleading? For example, are the featured charts distorted? Is the design manipulating emotion by overusing the color red, alarming images, or exaggerated symbols that provoke rather than inform? Is the data current, or does the post use outdated information to encourage users to draw incorrect conclusions? Finally, does the visual match the claim, or is it implying causation where only correlation exists?

- *Identify* **missing** or **silenced voices.** Is the post speaking *for* the community it's working to advocate for, or does the movement *include* that community within its organizing work?

In May 2024, an AI-generated graphic with the words **"All Eyes on Rafah"** exploded across social media, appearing in millions of posts within days. It featured a hauntingly symmetrical tent camp nestled in a desert landscape. Despite the flood of images emerging about Rafah, this was, by far, the most widely circulated.

The image aligns with the algorithmic formula that promotes **visually striking**, **emotionally resonant**, and **shareable content optimized for platforms with brief text, centered composition,** and **high contrast.**

The image quickly eclipsed the countless real photographs and videos emerging from Rafah, many of which were taken down or buried by content moderation policies. In contrast, the "All Eyes on Rafah" graphic offered a sanitized version of solidarity, one that was visually symbolic but ultimately stripped of context. Many posts that shared the graphic lacked links to reporting, calls to action, or background on the humanitarian crisis unfolding.

To be clear, the "All Eyes on Rafah" graphic was not originally designed to deceive. Malaysian artist Zila AbKa said she wanted to make something that would inspire people to "do whatever they could to show solidarity with Gazans."[10] Initially, users even overlooked the post's use of AI, as it spread rapidly across the internet.

And then, in a roundabout way, the delayed backlash to the graphic's use of AI seemed to overshadow the core message of Palestinian liberation. It became a sort of cautionary tale for creators using political imagery on social media platforms.

How do you create a graphic that achieves algorithmic success *without* compromising your mission, while still conveying the topic's complexity and inspiring collective action?

Still, the overwhelming number of shares was encouraging. With the huge wave of support the "All Eyes on Rafah" graphic sparked online, the question isn't really **"Why aren't you doing more?"** Instead, we need to ask, **How do we turn this moment into something real and lasting?** How do we move from symbolic gestures, devoid of real-world engagement, to sustained action—action that supports, for example, Palestinian voices on the ground, that challenges systems enabling violence and censorship, and that refuses to let this moment fade into the next news cycle?

Again, sharing something online is a low-barrier entry point. But it's essential to move beyond social media participation and start engaging with real news from independent media sources about the topic you're posting about. Durable **solidarity** starts with informed **understanding.**

Follow and amplify the voices of grassroots organizations and activists. Use social media to boost their offline campaigns, messages, protest events, and fundraisers.

Challenge misinformation and censorship. Use these critical media literacy tools to identify biased coverage or algorithmic suppression, and use your platform to speak out against this erasure.

Evaluate the call to action

Calls to action are crucial in an infographic. Done well, they transform a passive viewer into an *active* participant. But that's a high bar to clear. Posts that aim only to raise awareness may not be enough to mobilize offline engagement or sustain long-term interest. **Awareness is just the beginning, not the end.**

Ideally, calls to action should **encourage users to participate in collective efforts, particularly within their own communities**. This fosters a sense of shared responsibility and localized change.

The call to action should be:

1. **Specific -** "Get involved" is vague and uninspiring, but "Attend next Monday's city council meeting" or "Volunteer your time by organizing and sorting donated items for asylum seekers in the area" gives users something to *do*

2. **Accessible -** Provide links to actions people can attend or donate to, or clear instructions on where to find more information

3. **Relevant -** Whatever you're asking of users should be tied directly to the infographic's topic or data

4. **Ongoing -** Give users information about how to participate in the long-term, not just at one-off events

More questions to consider:

1. Is there a **clear demand** embedded within the infographic?

2. Is there a concrete **outcome** or **accountability** plan?

3. Are there real-world (offline) networks involved, such as a **union**, **advocacy group**, or **mutual aid organization**?

Amplifying Reliable Sources

For every online account that botches an infographic by spreading misinformation, oversimplifying issues, or prioritizing aesthetics over accuracy and context, there are numerous online outlets that carefully craft posts to inform and empower audiences to effect change.

For example, **Slow Factory** (@slowfactory), an environmental and social justice nonprofit, creates thoughtfully researched, visually compelling graphics that break down complex topics, such as colonialism, climate justice, and systemic inequality, while providing users with additional resources to learn more.

So Informed (@so.informed), a page created by organizer Jess Natale, dissects social issues through infographics and short videos, with a special emphasis on current events. Natale's purpose is to unpack heavier topics, "to inform people of all ages, educational backgrounds, and learning capabilities in cogent and concise slideshows."

Other campaigns and organizations, including **No Tech for Apartheid** (@notechforapartheid) and **More Perfect Union** (@perfectunion), harness the collective power of working people, informing users about the rise of tech militarism and their rights in their workplace.

Be *Intentional* With Your Activism

As **Project Censored** celebrates its fiftieth anniversary, its continued presence on social media is more than just a reflection of changing times. It's a strategic extension of the organization's core mission: to promote critical media literacy, challenge corporate narratives, and uplift independent, underreported news.

In this digital era, infographics and short-form content, like clips from **The Project Censored Show**, hosted by Mickey Huff and Eleanor Goldfield, have become vital tools in this work, offering accessible entry points into deeper stories and urgent issues often overlooked by corporate news media.

But with this expanded reach comes responsibility. Consuming infographics responsibly means going beyond surface-level visuals. It requires asking: Who made this and why? What's being emphasized, marginalized, or omitted?

Responsible media users are not **passive** scrollers; they are **active** investigators. Media literacy provides the resources for critical investigation.

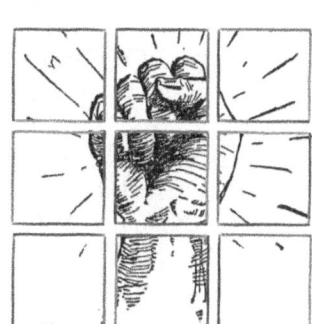

Likewise, producing infographics responsibly means treating visual storytelling not just as content creation, but as a form of communication based on ethical principles. Designers and activists alike must prioritize accuracy, clarity, transparency, and inclusivity, avoiding sensationalism and distortion. Ideally, infographics encourage not only solidarity but also reflection.

Project Censored's work has historically equipped people with tools to think critically about the media they consume and to demand that it serve democracy, not corporate power. **Now, in the digital age, we're reclaiming infographics as tools for education and transformation.**

Project Censored continues to engage a new generation of media-literate citizens, who are eager not only to stay informed but also to **critically analyze** the media they consume, ask **deeper questions**, and take part in conversations that shape a more just and **inclusive** media landscape.

As we look ahead, the call is clear: Whether we're scrolling or sharing, designing or decoding, we must engage with infographics not as ends in themselves, but as gateways to deeper understanding, meaningful dialogue, and collective action.

About the authors:

Shealeigh Voitl is the associate director of Project Censored. This is her second time co-editing *State of the Free Press*. In addition to her involvement with the Project's Campus Affiliates Program and the yearbook series, Shealeigh also helped develop and write Project Censored's *Beyond Fact-Checking: A Teaching Guide to the Power of News Frames*, alongside Andy Lee Roth, and co-hosts Project Censored's YouTube series, "Frame-Check."

Reagan Haynie is Project Censored's social media manager. She also co-authored this year's Junk Food News chapter and co-hosts Project Censored's YouTube series, "Frame-Check."

NOTES

1. Marshall McLuhan, "The Medium Is the Message," in *Understanding Media: The Extensions of Man* (McGraw-Hill Book Company, 1964); online version accessible at https://web.mit.edu/allanmc/www/mcluhan.mediummessage.pdf.
2. Samuel Bestvater, et al., "2. Americans' Views of and Experiences With Activism on Social Media," Pew Research Center, June 29, 2023.
3. Carolyn Ali, "Online Activism Isn't Just Slacktivism," University of British Columbia, February 22, 2023.
4. Quoted in Ali, "Online Activism."Noor Noman, on Instagram Was a Teachable Moment for Allies Like Me," NBC News, June 6, 2020.
5. Nuha Hassan, "Black Lives Matter and the Problem of Performative Activism," Medium, May 9, 2021.
6. Noor Noman, "'Blackout Tuesday' on Instagram Was a Teachable Moment for Allies Like Me," NBC News, June 6, 2020.
7. For news coverage of the People's Union blackout, see, for example, Anne D'Innocenzio and Haleluya Hadero, "Economic Blackout: Will a 24-Hour Boycott Make a Difference?" AP News, February 28, 2025.
8. Jonah Valdez, "How to Turn an 'Economic Blackout' Into an All-Out War on Corporate Power," *The Intercept*, February 28, 2025.
9. Rebecca Schneid, "Meet the People's Union USA, the Movement Behind the Feb. 28 'Economic Blackout'," *Time*, March 1, 2025.
10. Bobby Allyn, "'All Eyes on Rafah' Is the Internet's Most Viral AI Image. Two Artists Are Claiming Credit," NPR, June 3, 2024.

IMAGE CREDITS

Page 173: Cut-out figures inside squares, created by Reagan Haynie for Project Censored.

Page 174: Eyes: Image from *With the Children on Sundays, Through Eye-Gate, and Ear-Gate into the City of Child-Soul* (1911). Digitized by the Library of Congress. Uploaded by Internet Archive Book Images on Flickr (Aug. 10, 2014). Public domain.

Page 176: Black Panther newspaper clipping: From *The Black Panther* 1, no. 1 (Oakland/San Francisco, April 25, 1967). Digitized and available on the Marxist Internet Archive.

Page 177: Gay Workshops London flyer: *Gay Workshops London 1981 programme*. Uploaded June 29, 2022, by LSE Library. No known copyright restrictions.

Page 178: Drawing of Marshall McLuhan, created by Reagan Haynie for Project Censored.

Page 179: Pie chart, created by Reagan Haynie for Project Censored.

Page 185: Stop Cop City poster, created by Reagan Haynie using landscape element from Canva user @cgterminal.

Page 186: 24 Hour Boycott poster, created by Reagan Haynie for Project Censored.

Page 190: Stage, from Canva user @Vectortradition.

Page 191: All Eyes on Rafah graphic, created by Reagan Haynie for Project Censored.

Page 192: Pointing finger and exclamation mark, *Canadian Forest Industries* (July–December 1923), pg. 785. Via Internet Archive Book Images / University of Toronto. Public domain.

Page 193: Boot stepping out of phone graphic, created by Kate Horgan for Project Censored.
Page 194: Call to Action graphic, created by Reagan Haynie for Project Censored using paperboy element from Canva user, @Pixabay.
Page 195: Speech bubbles with questions, from Canva user @ZdenekSasek.
Page 197: Fist inside boxes, created by Reagan Haynie for Project Censored, with fist element from *My Flag and My Boy, and Other War Poems* (1918), page 38. Via Internet Archive Book Images / Library of Congress. Public domain.
Page 199: Cutout people, from Canva user @Nounproject.

FURTHER READING

"About the So.Informed Page," SoInformed, accessed May 27, 2025.

For more information about framing, see Shealeigh Voitl, Andy Lee Roth, and Project Censored, "Beyond Fact-Checking: A Teaching Guide to the Power of News Frames," Project Censored, 2025.

"Infographics: Simplified Media Guides from Project Censored," Resources, Project Censored, accessed July 9, 2025.

Jolynna Sinanan, "Blackout Tuesday: The Black Square Is a Symbol of Online Activism for Non-Activists," *The Conversation*, June 4, 2020.

Omar Zahzah, "AI on Rafah," in *Terms of Servitude: Zionism, Silicon Valley, and Digital Settler Colonialism in the Palestinian Liberation Struggle* (Seven Stories and The Censored Press, 2025).

ACKNOWLEDGEMENTS

This book represents the commitment, coordination, and contributions of many people. We welcome the opportunity to thank many of them here.

Nora Barrows-Friedman, Mischa Geracoulis, Veronica Santiago Liu, T.M. Scruggs, and Dan Simon serve with us on the editorial board of the Censored Press. Now entering its fifth year of operation under this group's wise guidance, the Censored Press publishes books that promote political engagement informed by independent journalism and critical media literacy.

Anson Stevens-Bollen created original artwork for *State of the Free Press 2026*. We're energized by our ongoing partnership with Anson, who also created the story icons that add visual vim to Chapter 1.

We are grateful for the extraordinary generosity of our donors, many of whom have supported us for years, including James Coleman, Alma DeBisschop, Jan De Deka, Charles A. Eldridge, Larry Gassan, Michael Hansen, Susan Krebser, Sheldon Levy, Tony Litwinko, James March, Harry Mersmann, Kyra Pearson, John and Lyn Roth, T.M. Scruggs, David Stanek, Lana Touchstone, Michelle Westover, and Montgomery Zukowski.

We also thank Integrity Media NFP, Isabel's Charitable Gift Fund, The Free Press, Northern Trust Charitable Giving Program at the Chicago Community Foundation, the Reynolds Journalism Institute, the Silicon Valley Community Foundation, Janet M. Strothman Estate, Tarbell Family Foundation, and the Unitarian Universalist Congregation of Santa Rosa for their essential support.

The Media Freedom Foundation's (MFF) board of directors, identified below, provides key counsel and support for our ongoing operations. We are grateful to them and our emeritus director/president, Peter Phillips, for his many years of service to the Project and its mission.

Project Censored's staff is small but mighty; we are able to do a lot with a little because each of our staff members, noted below, is extraordinary.

Warm thanks to our 2024–2025 student interns for their great work and good cheer: Da'Taeveyon Daniels, Jayden Henry, Lamees Hijazi, Elizabeth Insuasti, Leo Koulish, Jayden Lawrence, Nicole Mendez-Villarubia, Ella Mrofka, Vivian Rose, Olivia Rosenberg, Caitlin Suda, and Jackie Vickery.

The credibility of the Project hinges on the factual accuracy of its work. *State of the Free Press 2026* has benefited from careful fact-checking and proofreading by Jayden Lawrence, Alefiya Presswala, Vivian Rose, and Jackie Vickery.

The Project Censored Show on Pacifica Radio, which originates from the historic studios of KPFA in Berkeley, California, continues to broadcast on more than fifty stations across the United States, from low-power FM stations to major urban areas. Special thanks to co-host and associate producer Eleanor Goldfield; our senior producer and man behind the curtain for fifteen years, Anthony Fest (we wish him all the best as he retires from the show this year); and the great team at KPFA.

We are fortunate to work with wonderful people who not only share our mission to promote press freedom but also help to spread the word about the Project's work, including Heidi Boghosian and Steve Rohde, *Law and Disorder Radio*; Bob Buzzanco and Scott Parkin, cohosts of the *Green and Red* podcast; Jill Cody of *Be Bold America!* on KSQD; Matt Crawford with *The Curious Man* podcast; Davey D at *Hard Knock Radio*; Kat Duncan at the Reynolds Journalism Institute; R.J. Eskow, host of *The Zero Hour*; Annie Esposito and Steve Scalmanini, hosts of the Alliance for Democracy's *Corporations and Democracy* radio show; Stephanie Flores-Koulish; John Fugelsang, host of the *Tell Me Everything* podcast; Greg Godels and Pat Cummings, hosts of the *Coming From Left Field* podcast; Aaron Good, host of the *American Exception* podcast; Kevin Gosztola of *The Dissenter*; Steve Grumbine of *Macro N Cheese*; Lucas Hagin and the team at Swissnex in San Francisco; Lauren Harper, the Daniel Ellsberg Chair on Government Secrecy at the Freedom of the Press Foundation; Bob Hennelley and Keziah Glow at WBAI; Nolan Higdon and Sydney Sullivan of *The Disinfo Detox*; Mitch Jesserich of *Letters and Politics*; Dorothy Kidd; Michael Koretzky; J.G. Michael of *Parallax Views*; Jason Myles of *This is Revolution* podcast; Danbert Nobacon; Primo Radical; Mitch Ratcliffe, host of *Earth 911*; Mark Ray and the members of the Media Literacy Communities of Practice group; Francesca Rheannon of *The Writer's Voice* podcast; Cynthia Sandler; Robert Scheer, host of *Scheer Intelligence*; Cyndy Scheibe and Chris Sperry of Project Look Sharp; Maya Schenwar, Lara Witt and the Movement Media Alliance; Celine Schreiber and John Collins of *Weave News*; Adam Sennott, Society of Professional Journalists; Linda Shaw at Solutions Journalism Network; Sandy Sohcot with Human Rights Educators, USA; Ryan Sorrell of the *Kansas City Defender*; Seth Stern of the Freedom of the Press Foundation; Norman Stockwell of *The Progressive*; Jim Tarbell, Nancy Price, and David Delk of the Alliance for Democracy and *Justice Rising*; Clayton Weimers of Reporters Without Borders; and Zara Zimbardo.

Mickey thanks his longtime colleagues and supporters at Diablo Valley College where he has been a faculty member since 2000, including departing President Susan Lamb, Dean Lisa Ratchford, Lisa Martin, Michael Levitin, Adam Bessie, Carmina Quiarte, John Corbally, Matthew Powell, Jason Mayfield, Jacob Van Vleet, Katie Graham, Albert Ponce, and Sangha Niyogi. He also thanks his new colleagues at Ithaca College and the Park Center for Independent Media for their warm welcome, including Dean Amy Falkner, Associate Deans Rob Gearhart and Melodye MacAlpine, along with Brandy Hawley, Mickie Quinn, April Johanns, Ben Basem, Erin Schiefelbein, Staci Hall, Devan Accardo, Ari Kissiloff, Devan Rosen, John Scott, Cathy Michael, James Rada and the Journalism Department, as well as Marcy Sutherland, Todd Schack, Jeremy Lovelett, Jeff Cohen, Raza Rumi, Maura Stephens, Hannah Brooks, Rachel Leon, and Adelaide Park Gomer.

Shealeigh is deeply thankful for her family, her friends, her extremely supportive colleagues and mentors at Project

Censored, and her perfect dog Elizabeth Francine. Mickey is grateful for the ongoing support from his loving family, brilliant colleagues, and especially the amazing students he's had the privilege to teach and learn from the past 25 years. He also gives a heartfelt heavy metal salute to his late father-in-law, "Sheffield" (1943–2024), with whom he'd talk about the Project, media, and music. Andy dearly misses John Douglass (1968–2024) and Marian Boyd (1924–2025), and he's grateful beyond words for the love and joy Elizabeth Boyd shares with him: "Tell me, what did the blackbird say to the crow?"

And, finally, thanks to you, our readers, for the continuous support and encouragement, which inspire and enhance the Project's work to promote press freedom, media literacy, and informed civic engagement.

MEDIA FREEDOM FOUNDATION BOARD OF DIRECTORS

Adam Armstrong (treasurer), Ben Boyington, Kenn Burrows, Allison Butler (vice president), Eleanor Goldfield, Doug Hecker, Mickey Huff (president), Veronica Santiago Liu, Christopher Oscar, Andy Lee Roth (secretary), and T.M. Scruggs.

PROJECT CENSORED STAFF

Adam Armstrong (chief financial officer), Lorna Garano (publicist), Mischa Geracoulis (managing editor), Eleanor Goldfield (producer and co-host, *The Project Censored Show*), Reagan Haynie (social media manager), Kate Horgan (website design and media assistant), Meg Huff (administrative assistant), Mickey Huff (director) Andy Lee Roth (editor-at-large), Lyssa Schmidt (grant development, Presence & Company), and Shealeigh Voitl (associate director).

PROJECT CENSORED 2024–2025 JUDGES

*Indicates having been a Project Censored judge since our founding in 1976.

ROBIN ANDERSEN. Writer, commentator, and award-winning author. Professor Emerita of Communication and Media Studies at Fordham University. She edits the Routledge Focus Book Series on Media and Humanitarian Action. Her latest books include *Media, Central American Refugees, and the U.S. Border Crisis*, and *Censorship, Digital Media, and the Global Crackdown on Freedom of Expression*. Her upcoming book is *The Complicit Lens: US Media Coverage of Israel's Genocide in Gaza*. She writes for Fairness & Accuracy in Reporting (FAIR).

AVRAM ANDERSON. Collection Management Librarian, California State University, Northridge. Member and advocate of the LGBTQI+ community researching LGBTQ bias and censorship. Co-author of *The Media and Me: A Guide to Critical Media Literacy for Young People* (2022), and "Censorship by Proxy and Moral Panics in the Digital Era" in *Censorship, Digital Media, and the Global Crackdown on Freedom of Expression* (2024). They also contribute to the *Index on Censorship*, *In These Times*, and *Truthout*.

KENN BURROWS. Teacher of Holistic Health Studies at San Francisco State University since 1991. Founder and Director of SFSU's Holistic Health Learning Center, an award-winning interdisciplinary library and community center. Since 2001, under his direction, the Center has hosted a biennial conference, "The Future of Healthcare," and annual educational events, including Food Awareness Month and the Gandhi-King Season for Nonviolence, an eighty-day educational campaign demonstrating how nonviolence empowers our personal and collective lives.

BRIAN COVERT. Journalist, author, and educator based in Japan. Worked as a staff reporter and editor for English-language daily newspapers in Japan and as a contributing writer to Japanese and overseas newspapers and magazines. Contributing author to past editions of the *Censored* yearbook series. He is currently a lecturer in the Department of Media, Journalism, and Communications at Doshisha University in Kyoto.

GEOFF DAVIDIAN. Investigative reporter, publisher, editor, war correspondent, and educator. He has taught journalism in the US, UK, and India and reported on international terrorism, Middle Eastern affairs, Congress, local government corruption, and breaches of legal and judicial ethics, for which he twice received the Gavel Award from the State Bar of Texas. Founding publisher and editor of the *Putnam Pit*.

MISCHA GERACOULIS. Managing Editor at Project Censored and The Censored Press, contributor to Project Censored's *State of the Free Press* yearbook series, Project Judge, and author of *Media Framing and the Destruction of Cultural Heritage* (2025). Her work focuses on human rights and civil liberties, journalistic ethics and standards, and accuracy in reporting.

ROBERT HACKETT. Professor Emeritus of Communication, Simon Fraser University, Vancouver. Co-founder of NewsWatch Canada (1993), Media Democracy Days (2001), and OpenMedia.ca (2007). His eight books on media and politics include *Journalism and Climate Crisis: Public Engagement, Media Alternatives* (with S. Forde, S. Gunster, and K. Foxwell-Norton, 2017) and *Remaking Media: The Struggle to Democratize Public Communication* (with W.K. Carroll, 2006). Winner of the 2018 SFU Award for community impact. He writes for thetyee.ca, nationalobserver.com, rabble.ca, and other media.

NOLAN HIGDON. Founding member of the Critical Media Literacy Conference of the Americas, author, and lecturer at Merrill College and the Education Department at the University of California, Santa Cruz. Author of *The Anatomy of Fake News* (2020); coauthor of *Let's Agree to Disagree* (2022), *The Media And Me* (2022), and *Surveillance Education: Navigating the Conspicuous Absence of Privacy in Schools* (2024).

KEVIN HOWLEY (PhD, Indiana University, 1998). Writer and educator. His work has appeared in *Journalism: Theory, Practice and Criticism*; *Social Movement Studies*; *Literature/Film Quarterly*; and *Interactions: Studies in Communication and Culture*. His most recent book is *Drones: Media Discourse and the Public Imagination*.

NICHOLAS JOHNSON.* Author, *How to Talk Back to Your Television Set* (1970) and nine more books, including *Columns of Democracy* (2018) and *What Do You Mean and How Do You Know?* (2009). Commissioner, Federal Communications Commission (1966–1973); Professor, University of Iowa College of Law (1981–2014, media law and cyber law). More at nicholasjohnson.org.

CHARLES L. KLOTZER. Founder, editor, and publisher emeritus of *St. Louis Journalism Review* and *FOCUS/Midwest*. The *St. Louis Journalism Review* has been transferred to Southern Illinois University, Carbondale, and is now the *Gateway Journalism Review*. Klotzer remains active at the *Review*.

NANCY KRANICH. Teaching Professor, School of Communication and Information, Rutgers University. Past president of the American Library Association (ALA) and member of ALA's Freedom to Read Foundation Roll of Honor. Author of hundreds of publications, including *Libraries and Democracy: The Cornerstones of Liberty* (2001), "Civic Literacy: Reimagining a Role for Libraries" (2024), "Free People Read Freely" (2024), and "Libraries: Guardians of Democracy" (2025).

PETER LUDES. Former Professor of Culture and Media Science at the University of Siegen (Germany) and of Mass Communication, Jacobs University, Bremen. Visiting Positions at the Universities of Newfoundland, Amsterdam, Harvard, Constance, and Cologne; Founder of the German Initiative on News Enlightenment (1997). Recent publications on brutalization and banalization (2018), collective myths and decivilizing processes (with Stefan Kramer, 2020) and tacit knowing (2025).

DANIEL MÜLLER. Head of the Postgraduate Academy at the University of Siegen, in Germany. Researcher and educator in journalism, mass communication studies, and history at public universities for many years. Has published extensively on media history, media-minority relations in Germany, and nationality policies and ethnic relations of the Soviet Union and the post-Soviet successor states, particularly in the Caucasus. Jury member of the German Initiative on News Enlightenment.

JACK L. NELSON.* Distinguished Professor Emeritus, Graduate School of Education, Rutgers University. Former member, Committee on Academic Freedom and Tenure, American Association of University Professors. Recipient, Academic Freedom Award, National Council for Social Studies. Author of seventeen books, including *Critical Issues in Education: Dialogues and Dialectics*, 9th ed. (with S. Palonsky and M.R. McCarthy, 2021) and *Human Impact of Natural Disasters* (with V.O. Pang and W.R. Fernekes, 2010), and about two hundred articles.

PETER PHILLIPS. Professor Emeritus of Political Sociology, Sonoma State University. Director, Project Censored, 1996–2010. President, Media Freedom Foundation, 2010–2016. Editor or co-editor of fourteen editions of the *Censored* yearbook series. Author of *Giants: The Global Power Elite* (2018) and *Titans of Capital* (2024). Co-editor (with Dennis Loo) of *Impeach the President: The Case Against Bush and Cheney* (2006).

MICHAEL RAVNITZKY. Attorney, writer, editor, engineer, and Freedom of Information Act expert who has developed tools to broaden access to public records in the public interest.

T.M. SCRUGGS. Professor Emeritus (token ethnomusicologist), University of Iowa. Various publications on media in Central America and Venezuela. Involvement with community radio in Nicaragua, Venezuela, and the United States, including the KPFA (Berkeley, CA) Local Station Board and Pacifica National

Board. Executive producer at The Real News Network (Baltimore), and of several documentaries.

SHEILA RABB WEIDENFELD.* Emmy Award-winning television producer. Former press secretary to Betty Ford and special assistant to the President; author, *First Lady's Lady*. President of DC Productions Ltd. Director of community relations of Phyto Management LLC and Maryland Cultivation and Processing LLC.

HOW TO SUPPORT PROJECT CENSORED

NOMINATE A STORY

To nominate a *Censored* story, forward the URL to shealeigh@projectcensored.org. The deadline to nominate stories for the next yearbook is March 31, 2026.

Criteria for Story Nominations

1. A censored news story reports information that the public has a right and a need to know but to which the public has had limited access.
2. The news story is recent, having been first reported no later than one year ago. Stories submitted for the 2025–26 news cycle should be no older than April 2025.
3. The story is fact-based, with clearly defined concepts and verifiable documentation. The story's claims should be supported by evidence—the more controversial the claims, the stronger the evidence necessary.
4. The news story has been published, either electronically or in print, in a publicly circulated newspaper, journal, magazine, newsletter, or similar publication from a journalistic source.

MAKE A TAX-DEDUCTIBLE DONATION

We depend on tax-deductible donations to continue our work. Project Censored is supported by the Media Freedom Foundation, a 501(c)(3) nonprofit organization. To support our efforts on behalf of independent journalism and freedom of information, send checks to the address below or donate online at projectcensored.org. Your generous donations help us oppose news censorship and promote media literacy.

Media Freedom Foundation
PO Box 9
Ithaca, NY 14851

ABOUT THE EDITORS

SHEALEIGH VOITL is the associate director of Project Censored. She first began her research with the Project at North Central College alongside Steve Macek, co-authoring the "Déjà Vu News" chapter in the *State of the Free Press 2022* and *2023* as well as the Top 25 chapter in *SFP 2023*. In addition to her editorial contributions to the yearbook series and work with the Campus Affiliates Program, Shealeigh helped develop the *State of the Free Press 2024* teaching guide, *Beyond Fact-Checking: A Teaching Guide to the Power of News Frames*, and the Project's YouTube series "Frame-Check." Her writing has also been featured in *Truthout*, *The Progressive*, and *Ms. Magazine*. Shealeigh lives in Chicago, Illinois.

ANDY LEE ROTH is editor-at-large at Project Censored. In 2024–2025, a Reynolds Journalism Institute fellowship supported his work on *Algorithmic Literacy for Journalists*, a free, online toolset to promote AI journalism that better informs the public. Roth is the co-author of *Beyond Fact Checking*, a teaching guide to the power of news frames and "frame-checking," and *The Media and Me*, Project Censored's guide to critical media literacy for young people. Roth began working with Project Censored in 2006, serving as its associate director from 2012–2024. He has published research and articles in many outlets, including the *Index on Censorship*; *The Progressive*; *In These Times*; *YES! Magazine*; *Truthout*; *Media, Culture & Society*; and the *International Journal of Press/Politics*. Roth earned a PhD in sociology at the University of California, Los Angeles, and a BA in sociology and anthropology at Haverford College. He lives in Winthrop, Washington, with his sweetheart.

MICKEY HUFF is the director of Project Censored and president of the nonprofit Media Freedom Foundation. To date, he has coedited seventeen editions of the Project's yearbook. He is also co-author, with Nolan Higdon, of *Let's Agree to Disagree* (Routledge, 2022), a practical handbook on critical thinking and civil discourse, and *United States of Distraction* (City Lights Books, 2019); and a co-author of *The Media and Me: A Guide to Critical Media Literacy for Young People*. A professor of social science, history, and journalism at Diablo Valley College since 2000, Huff joined Ithaca College in fall 2024, where he now serves as the Distinguished Director of the Park Center for Independent Media and Professor of Journalism at the Roy H. Park School of Communications. He is the founding co-host and executive producer of *The Project Censored Show*, the Project's syndicated public affairs radio program. A longtime musician, he lives with his amazing wife, two awesome offspring, and heavy metal pets Lemmy the dog and Ozzy the cat in Ithaca, New York.

INDEX

A
Aaron, Craig, 10
ABC, 9, 78, 79
ABC News, 86, 105
AbKa, Zila, 191
Abu Al Qumsan, Faisal, 13
ACLU. *See* American Civil Liberties Union
Afghanistan Papers, 165
Aguirre, Gabriella, 49
Ahtone, Tristan, 38
AI. *See* artificial intelligence
Alaska Natives, 52
ALFA Institute, 44–45
"All Eyes on Rafah" (graphic), 190–92
alliance-building, 153
Al-Udaini, Wafa, 13
Amazon, 46–48
American Chemistry Council, 66
American Civil Liberties Union (ACLU), 9, 31, 42, 53
American Economic Review (journal), 151
American Indian Higher Education Consortium, 36
American Privacy Rights Act, 45
The American Prospect (magazine), 47
Ananny, Mike, 7
Andersen, Robin, 114
Annenberg School for Communication and Journalism, at University of Southern California, 7
Antarctic ice sheets, 54–56
anti-BDS "gag law," 14, 89–92
Anti-Defamation League, 97
anti-intellectualism, 11
antisemitism, 115, 128–29, 137, 140, 142
    anti-Zionism equated with, 15, 68, 138–39, 145
    on college campuses, 90
    at UNRWA, 132
"anti-woke" legislation, 11
anti-Zionism, 15, 68, 137–40, 145
AP. *See* Associated Press

Applegate, David, 32
Arkansas, 57, 92
Arkansas Times (newspaper), 91–92
artificial intelligence (AI), 5, 44, 97, 109, 190
Assange, Julian, 8, 162
Assembly Bill 800 (California), 70
Associated Press (AP), 79, 90–91, 99, 131, 135, 161
Atlanta Journal-Constitution (newspaper), 91
"At Work and Under Watch" (Oxfam America), 46, 48
authoritarianism, xviii, 77, 97, 118, 155
Axios (news website), 45

B
Bagdikian, Ben, xii
Baldoni, Justin, 98
Barbaricum, 30
Baron, Ethan, 34
Baroud, Ramzy, 147n23
Barrera, Melissa, 115
Barth, Brian, 48, 50, 51
Bayer, 86, 87
BDS. *See* Boycott, Divestment and Sanctions
Bearing Witness (documentary), 113
Beinart, Peter, 135
Bendib, Khalil, 16
Ben-Gvir, Itamar, 130
Benjamin, Walter, 77, 79, 80
Betar, 144
Better Connected (Kyi), 180
Bezos, Jeff, 52, 151
"biblical law," 131
"biblical rights," 129–32, 141
Biddle, Sam, 29, 30
Biden, Joe, 8, 11, 31, 83–84
Big Tech, 4, 8, 42–45, 110, 119, 156
Big Tobacco, 43, 45
billionaires, 59
Bill of Rights, 24, 104

Birnbaum, Linda, 64
#BlackLivesMatter, 183
The Black Panther (newspaper), 176
Black people, police violence against, 52
Bolts (magazine), 53, 54
Bondi, Pam, 84
Boorstin, Daniel, 98, 106, 107
Bouie, Jamelle, 59
Boycott, Divestment and Sanctions (BDS), 14, 89–92
boycotts, 92, 186–87
Bradley, Alexander T., 55, 56
brain rot, xxn13
The Brass Check (Sinclair), xvi
"breaking news," 12
Brennan Center for Justice, 31, 84
British Antarctic Survey, 55
Brody, David, 44
Buffalo's Fire (news website), 167
Bush, George W., xiii
Business Insider (news website), 48
Buxbaum, Amy Grim, 14
Buzzfeed, 25

C
CAIR. *See* Council on American-Islamic Relations
Calhoun, Melissa, 104
California, 7, 47, 48–51, 69–70
call to action, 193–95
CalMatters, 5
Campaign Zero, 52
Campus Affiliates Program, 14
Canada, 163
Canary Mission, 144–45, 148n32
cancer, 85–86
Cantwell, Maria, 45
capitalism
  boycotting, 187
  surveillance, 6, 43
Carnes, Nicholas, 57, 58, 59
The Carolina Journal, 58
Carr, Brendan, 78
Carter, Jimmy, x
CBS, 9, 78

celebrity news, 118
Censored 2020, 79
censorship, 5, 7, 62, 192
  by proxy, 2
  on social media, 41
Center for American Progress, 103
Center for Working-Class Politics, 59
Charity & Security Network, 67
Charlottesville, "Unite the Right" rally in (2017), 145
Chicago Police Department (CPD), 53
Chicago Tribune (newspaper), 25, 66
China, 62
Chomsky, Noam, xii, 3
Church & Dwight, 64
City of Grants Pass v. Johnson, 49, 50
civil courage, xviii
civil rights, 44–45
Civil Rights Act (1964), 68–69
Clarke, Yvette D., 45
climate change, ix, 33, 54–56
Clinton, Bill, 59
CN. See Consortium News
CNIL. *See* French Data Protection Authority
CNN, 6, 25, 56, 78, 83, 101, 106
  on ICE, 9–10
  24-hour news cycle and, 4
Cohen, Etan, 11
Cohen, Felix S., 167
Cohen, Ilona, 62
Cohen, Mark H., 90–91
Cold War, xvii, 162
collaborative action, 150–51
collective punishment, 134
Collins, John, 15
colonialism, settler, 113, 128, 136, 147n23
Colorado, 103
Columbia University, 81, 116, 144
Combs, Sean "Diddy," 98, 99
Comcast, 78
Commission on Civil Rights, US, 37
Committee to Protect Journalists (CPJ), 41, 155

Common Dreams (news website), 29, 34, 56, 66, 112
Communities Beyond Elections, 158
Compton Unified School District, 102
condoms, 63–66
conglomeration, media, 17
Congo, 67
Conservative Political Action Conference (CPAC), 106
Consortium News (*CN*), 151, 152, 160–63
Constitution, US, 24
    Eighth Amendment, 49
    First Amendment, xvii, 7–8, 30, 45, 91–92, 149–50, 167
    Fourth Amendment, 53
Consumer Financial Protection Bureau, 110
Corbett, Jessica, 56
Coristine, Edward, 109
corporate media, xi, xii, 38, 51, 105–7, 112. *See also specific outlets*
    on ICE, 31
    major issues with, xiv
    McChesney on, 25
    Trump and, 9
    Tucker on, xiii
Corporation for Public Broadcasting, 10, 78
Council on American-Islamic Relations (CAIR), 41, 90
CounterPunch (magazine), 55, 56, 90
COVID-19 pandemic, 50
Cox, Joseph, 31
CPAC. *See* Conservative Political Action Conference
CPD. *See* Chicago Police Department
CPJ. *See* Committee to Protect Journalists
critical analysis, 198
critical media literacy, xv, 6, 16, 18, 151–53, 188
Cronkite, Walter, xi
Currier, Cora, 81
Cushing, Tim, 30
cybercrime, 60–62
"Cybersecurity 202" series (*Washington Post*), 62
Cybertruck, 108–9

D

Al Dahdouh, Hamza, 13
The Daily Yonder (news website), 39
Daniels, Ugochi, 67
data privacy protections, 42–45
data sovereignty, 167–68
The Death and Life of American Journalism (McChesney), 23
DEI. *See* Diversity, Equity, and Inclusion
democracy, 7, 23–26, 149
    collaborative action and, 150–51
    Consortium News and, 160–63
    Drop Site News and, 153–56
    government secrecy and, 164–66
    investigative reporting and, 152–53
    MMA and, 156–60
    for Native nations, 167–70
    societal trust and, 151–52
Department of Agriculture, 36, 88
Department of Education, 12, 99, 102–3
Department of Government Efficiency (DOGE), 15, 38–39, 99–100, 106, 108–10, 113
Department of Health and Human Services, 110
Department of Homeland Security, 117
Department of Justice (DOJ), 10, 14, 78, 79, 81–84
Department of Transportation, 53
Des Moines Register (newspaper), 79
Diakun, Anna, 83
DiamondCDN, 109
"Digital Democracy" initiative, 5
The Digital Disconnect (McChesney), 24
disinformation, 133
Disney, 9, 78, 114
displacement, internal, 66–67
distortion, 7, 78
Diversity, Equity, and Inclusion (DEI), 10, 78, 99

DOGE. *See* Department of Government Efficiency
DOJ. *See* Department of Justice
Donahue, Phil, 13
Doomsday Glacier, 56
Downs, Hugh, xi
Drake (rapper), 15, 99, 101–3
Drop Site News (news website), 16, 40–41, 151–56
drought, 32–34
dual criminality, 61
Duke University, 57, 58

E
Earth.com, 56
economic blackout, 185
education, 101–5
    Department of Education, 12, 99, 102–3
    higher, 36, 68–69
    special, 99
Egeland, Jan, 67
Egypt, 40
Eighth Amendment, 49
Electronic Frontier Foundation, 61
Elez, Marko, 109
Ellsberg, Daniel, xviii, 164
"enemies of the American people," press as, xiv
engagement metrics, 181
Environmental Protection Agency, 64
Eos (magazine), 56
establishment press, xvii
European Union, 88

F
Facebook, 4, 14, 31, 39–42, 47
fact-checkers, xii
Fairness Doctrine, x
"fake news," xii, xiii, 7
fascism, 15, 80, 97, 159–60
FBI. *See* Federal Bureau of Investigation
FCCs. *See* food contact chemicals
Fear, David, 115–16

Federal Bureau of Investigation (FBI), 83, 84
Federal Communications Commission, 27
Federal Reserve, 107
Fefferman, Nicolle, 70
FEMA, 12
First Amendment, xvii, 7–8, 30, 45, 91–92, 149–50, 167
FISA. *See* Foreign Intelligence Surveillance Act
Flatwater Free Press (news website), 38
FleishmanHillard, 86–88
Florida, 11, 33, 51, 103–5, 117
Floyd, George, 53, 185
FOIA. *See* Freedom of Information Act
food contact chemicals (FCCs), 63, 65
Food Packaging Forum Foundation, 65
Forbes (media company), 31, 105
Foreign Intelligence Surveillance Act (FISA), 14, 79, 80–84
Foreign Intelligence Surveillance Court, 82
forever chemicals, 33, 63–66
for-profit model of journalism, xv
fossil fuel pollution, ix
404 Media (media company), 31
Fourth Amendment, 53
Fourth Estate, x, xii, xvi
Fowler, Jonathan, 134
FOX 32 (TV program), 66
Fox News, 12, 62
framing, 189
Freedom House, 60–62
freedom of information, 2, 42
Freedom of Information Act (FOIA), 9, 31, 81
Freedom of the Press Foundation, 9, 16, 68, 81, 83, 164
Free Press, 10, 24
Free Press Action, 10
free speech, 8, 10
    anti-BDS law and, 91–92
    Israel and, 41, 118

of Martin, 90–91
Musk and, 6
NetChoice and, 45
French Data Protection Authority
    (CNIL), 88
Frontline (PBS), 161

G
Gadot, Gal, 15, 113–16
Gannett, 79
Gardena High School, 69
Gay Liberation Front (GLF), 177
Gaza, xix, 13, 41, 99, 115, 128, 155
    internal displacement in, 67
    UNRWA in, 133–34
Gedeon, Joseph, 130, 131
genitalia, PFAS and, 64
Georgia, 80, 89–92
Georgia Southern University (GSU), 89
German Informatics Society, 112
Geueke, Birgit, 65
Giant Oak Search Technology
    (GOST), 31
GIJN. *See* Global Investigative
    Journalism Network
Gillam, Carey, 32, 35, 85
GLF. *See* Gay Liberation Front
Global Citizen, 102
Global Investigative Journalism
    Network (GIJN), 38
"Global Report on Internal
    Displacement" (Internal
    Displacement Monitoring
    Center), 66
Global Voices, 61
glyphosate, 85, 88
Golan Heights, 141
Goldfield, Eleanor, 197
Goodman, Matthew, 64
Google, 4, 83
GOST. *See* Giant Oak Search
    Technology
Governing (publication), 58
government secrecy, 8, 164–66
Grants Pass, Oregon, 49

grassroots organizations, 193
The Great March of Return (2018), 136
"Great Replacement," 140
Grim, Ryan, 16, 150, 151
Grist (media organization), 33, 37–39,
    100
GSU. *See* Georgia Southern University
The Guardian (newspaper), 51, 84–86,
    115, 130
    on homelessness, 49–50
    on ICE, 31
    on PFAS, 33, 63, 64
    on water usage, 34
    on working class, 59
Guastella, Dustin, 58, 59
Gulf of Mexico, 79, 99
Guthrie, Woody, 127

H
habeas corpus, 11–12
HackerOne, 62
Hamas, 133
Hansen, Eric, 57, 59
happiness indexes, 152
Harper, Lauren, 9, 152
Harris, Kamala, 79, 150
Harvard Crimson (newspaper), 117
Harvard University, 151
Haymarket House, 157
Hechinger Report (news outlet), 39
Hegseth, Pete, 12, 100
Heritage Foundation, 97, 100
Herman, Edward, xii, 3
Hewitt, Ian J., 55, 56
High Country News (magazine), 37, 38, 39
higher education, 36, 68–69
The Hill (political website), 44
The History of the Standard Oil Company
    (Tarbell), xvi
Hofstadter, Richard, 11
Holder, Eric, 80, 82
homeless camps, 48–51
homogenization, media, 17
hostile surveillance technology, 46–48
HR 6408, 67

Huff, Mickey, 2, 197
human rights, 60–62, 146
Hunziker, Robert, 55, 56

I

ICE. *See* Immigration and Customs Enforcement
ICEBlock, 10
ice sheets, Antarctic, 54–56
Ide, Wendy, 115
IDF. *See* Israel Defense Forces
Idiocracy (film), 11, 106
I.F. Stone's Weekly (Stone), xvi, xvii
IGF. *See* Internet Government Forum
The Image (Boorstin), 98, 107
IMFA. *See* Indigenous Media Freedom Alliance
Immigration and Customs Enforcement (ICE), 14, 25, 29–31, 104, 116–17, 144
The Independent (newspaper), 31
Independent Florida Alligator (newspaper), 117
independent journalism, xiii–xvi
Indian Civil Rights Act (1968), 167
Indigenous Media Freedom Alliance (IMFA), 150, 167, 168, 169
Indigenous people, 35–39, 52. *See also* Native Americans
In Fact (Seldes), xvi
information-action ratio, 112
Inge, Regis, 102
Injustice Watch (news outlet), 53, 54
In Search of Light (Murrow), xvi
Inside Paradeplatz (news outlet), 69
Instagram, 14, 39–42, 115, 175, 186
The Intercept (news outlet), 6, 29–30, 68, 81, 114, 150, 187
internal displacement, 66–67
Internal Displacement Monitoring Center, 66
International Critical Media Literacy Conference, 89
International Organization for Migration, 67

Internet Government Forum (IGF), 62
investigative journalism, 16, 35, 88, 151–54
Iran, 11
Iran-Contra, 161
Iraq, 162
Ireland, 134
The Irish Star (news outlet), 48
Israel, 11, 13, 15, 39–42, 68–69, 89–91, 127. *See also* Zionism
  anti-Zionism and, 137–40
  "biblical rights" and, 129–32, 141
  decontextualization and, 143–46
  dominant ideologies and, 135–37
  missing context for, 140–43
  NCPR and, 128–29
  October 7 attacks, 39–40, 113, 133–34, 142
  UNRWA and, 132–35
Israel Defense Forces (IDF), 113

J

Jacobin (magazine), 46
Al Jazeera (media company), 91
Jensen, Carl, x–xi, xii, xiv, 3, 27, 98
Jerusalem, 141
Jewish Currents (magazine), 68
Jewish Defense League, 144
Jewish Voice for Labour, 42
Jewish Voice for Peace, 139
Johnson, Nicholas, 26
Jordan, 40
Journal of Exposure Science & Environmental Epidemiology, 63, 65
Judaism, 90. *See also* antisemitism; Israel; Zionism
Judge, Mike, 11, 106
The Jungle (Sinclair), xvi
Junk Food News, xi, 2, 15, 98, 101, 118–19
Just Security, 61

K

Kane, Alex, 68
Khalil, Mahmoud, 116, 117, 144
King, Arieh, 135

King, Martin Luther, Jr., 18
Knight First Amendment Institute, 81, 83
Knight Institute, 81, 83
Komisar, Lucy, 69
Kootenai Tribe, 38
Krishnan, Ramya, 81
Krupnick, Matt, 36, 37
Kurtz, Josh, 58
Kyi, Julia, 180
K-Y Jelly, 64

L

Lamar, Kendrick, 15, 99, 101–3
lateral reading, 189
The Latin Times (newspaper), 31
Latinx rights, 30
Lauria, Joe, 16, 151
Lawrence, Jayden, 14, 15
Lebanon, 13
Lee, Micah, 6
Lemkin Institute for Genocide Prevention and Human Security, 149–50
Leveritt, Alan, 92
Levin, Sam, 85
Libya, 162
Lively, Blake, 98, 99
Los Angeles, California, 49–50, 69–70
Los Angeles Times (newspaper), 4, 25
Louisiana, 57
Loyola University Chicago, 57
lubricants, 63–66
Lumbee Tribe, 38

M

MAAD. *See* Media Against Apartheid and Displacement
Macek, Steve, 14, 15
Madison, James, 24
MAGA movement, 11, 15, 127–29, 143
mainstream media, xi
malinformation, xii
Mamavation, 63, 64, 66

Mangione, Luigi, 98
Manufacturing Consent (Herman and Chomsky), 3
Mapping Police Violence, 51–54
March on Washington for Jobs and Freedom (1963), 18
Marinship, 50
Martin, Abby, 14, 80, 89–92
Marx, Karl, 12
Maryland Matters (news website), 58
McCarthy, Kevin, 44
McCarthyism, xvii
McChesney, Robert "Bob," xii, 13, 23–25
McDonald, Laquan, 53
McLuhan, Marshall, 178
McMahon, Linda, 12, 103
Media Against Apartheid and Displacement (MAAD), 158
Media Democracy in Action, 15
media guidelines, 82
media literacy, critical, xv, 6, 16, 18, 151–53, 188
Megan Thee Stallion, 101
Merchants of Poison (US Right to Know), 88, 89
Meta, 14, 39–42, 155
Middle East Monitor (news outlet), 141
Mijente (Latinx rights group), 30
Milei, Javier, 106
Milley, Mark, 97
Minaj, Nicki, 101
MintPress News, 90
misinformation, 6, 133, 193
Misinformation Review (news outlet), 151
Mississippi, 57
MMA. *See* Movement Media Alliance
Moms for Liberty, 11, 105
Le Monde (newspaper), 88
Mongabay (news outlet), 65
Monsanto, 14, 80, 85–89
The Monsanto Years (Young), 86
Montana, 38
More Perfect Unions, 195
Morning Edition (NPR), 62
movement journalism, 157

Movement Media Alliance (MMA), 150, 156–60
Moyers, Bill, 13
Mrofka, Ella, 14
Mrs. Warren's Profession (Shaw), 5
MSNBC, 78
Murdoch, Rupert, xviii
Murphy, Chris, 106, 137, 138, 139
Murrow, Edward R., xvi
Musk, Elon, 15, 104, 106, 139
   DOGE and, 99–100, 109–10
   Nazi salute of, 97, 137, 142
   Neuralink and, 100, 108, 110–11
   New York Times on, 107, 111–12
   Trump and, 78, 97, 105, 113, 149
   "wokeness" and, 10
   X and, 6, 105

N

Nader, Ralph, xi
Nakba (1948), 147n23
Natale, Jess, 195
National Archives and Records Administration, 9
National Homelessness Law Center, 50
National Labor Relations Board (NLRB), 69–70
National Park Service, 11
National Press Club, xvii
National Public Radio (NPR), 62, 65, 78, 131, 135
national security letters (NSLs), 82
Native Americans, 35–39, 52
   data sovereignty for, 167–68
   journalism redefined by, 169–70
   narrative reclaimed by, 168–69
Native Hawaiians, 52
Nature Geoscience (journal), 54, 55, 56
Nazism, 138
NBC News, 25, 78, 106, 184
NCPR. *See* North Country Public Radio
Nebraska, 38, 59
Nelson, Jack L., 26
Netanyahu, Benjamin, 130
NetChoice, 45
the Netherlands, 152
Networked Press Freedom (Ananny), 7
Neuralink, 100, 108, 110–11
New Deal, x, 106
The New Lede (news outlet), 32, 33, 35
news abuse, xii, 15, 128
NewsGuard, 163
news inflation, 3–4
Newsweek (magazine), 33, 35, 66, 105, 161
New York, 114
The New Yorker (magazine), 100
New York Post (newspaper), 105
New York Times (newspaper), 38–39, 59, 99, 131, 144, 150, 161
   on anti-BDS laws, 92
   on DOJ, 83
   on drought, 34
   on ICE, 31
   on Israel, 114
   libel lawsuits against, 78
   on Musk, 107, 111–12
   on NetChoice, 45
   on PFAS, 66
   on police violence, 52, 54
   on Zegler, 116
New York University, 117
Nexis Uni, 28
9/11 terrorist attacks, xiii
nitrogen, 33
Nixon, Richard, ix, xvii
NLRB. *See* National Labor Relations Board
Noem, Kristi, 10, 11–12
Noman, Noor, 183
non-Hodgkin lymphoma, 86
nonprofit organizations, tax-exempt status of, 67–68
North, Oliver, 161
North Carolina, 38, 47, 57, 58
North Carolina State University, 58
North Country Public Radio (NCPR), 128–35, 137–43, 146n4
Norway, 134

Norwegian Refugee Council, 67
No Straight Road Takes You There (Solnit), 1
No Tech for Apartheid, 196
NPR. *See* National Public Radio
NSLs. *See* national security letters

O
Obama, Barack, 8, 81, 162
objectivity, 5, 159
Occupied Palestinian Territory, 13
OCR. *See* Office for Civil Rights
October 7 attacks, in Israel, 39–40, 113, 133–34, 142
Office for Civil Rights (OCR), 68
Office of Personnel Management, 9
"official acts," 165
116th Congress, 59
One Big Beautiful Bill Act (2025), 44, 68
OpenSecrets, 58
Oregon, 49, 57
Oregon Public Broadcasting, 39
Osborn, Dan, 59
O'Sullivan, Donie, 6
Oxfam America, 46–48
Oxford Dictionary, xxn13, xiii
Öztürk, Rümeysa, 116–17, 144

P
Pacific Islanders, 52
Page, Carter, 82
Pakistan, 155
Palestine, 14, 89, 99, 114–16, 118, 128–29. *See also* Gaza
  "All Eyes on Rafah," 190–92
  Drop Site News on, 40
  Golan Heights, 141
  internal displacement in, 67
  journalists killed in, 13
  Nakba in, 147n23
  pro-Palestine language, 68–69
  refugees, 132–35
  UNRWA and, 132–35
  West Bank, 134, 141
Paramount, 9

Parry, Robert, 160–61, 162
Patrick Moynihan, Daniel Patrick, 165
PayPal, 163
PBS. *See* Public Broadcasting Service
Pentagon Papers, xviii, 165
People's Union USA, 186–87
per- and polyfluoroalkyl substances (PFAS), 33–34, 63–66
"perception management" program, 162
performative activism, 180, 189
Perkins, Tom, 33, 63, 64, 66
Pew Research, 179
PFAS. *See* per- and polyfluoroalkyl substances
Phillips, Peter, xii, xvi, xviii, 2
phosphorus, 33
Platt, Marc, 114–15
PNAS (journal), 56
police violence, 51–54
Politico (news outlet), 45, 88, 106
Pollan, Michael, 88
Poor Things (film), 116
Postman, Neil, xii, 112
"post-truth," xxn13, xiii, xiv
"Power to the People," xviii
Poynter (news outlet), 10
Prager, Stephen, 34
preemption, 43
Press, Alex N., 46
Project 2025, 97, 100, 149
Project Censored. *See specific topics*
Project South, 157
pro-Palestine language, 68–69
PropOrNot, 163
ProPublica, 36, 37, 39
ProQuest, 28
Public Broadcasting Service (PBS), 78, 161
Public Citizen, 110, 111
public knowledge, 7–12
public trust, xiii–xvi, 4, 5
Putin, Vladimir, 162

Q
Qudah, Sara, 41

R
radical muckraking journalism, xviii
Rafah, 190–92
Reagan, Ronald, x, 161
Reed, Dexter, 53
refugees, Palestinian, 132–35
reliable sources, 196
Reporters Without Borders (RSF), xvii, 9, 151–52
Reuters, 64, 66, 85, 87
Richardson, David, 12
Rich Media, Poor Democracy (McChesney), 23
Riebe, Kathleen, 58
rights
  "biblical," 129–32, 141
  civil, 44–45
  human, 60–62, 146
  Latinx, 30
  workplace, 69–70
Rodgers, Cathy McMorris, 45
Rodriguez, Cinthya, 30
Rodriguez, Katitza, 61
Rogan, Joe, 98
Rolling Stone (magazine), 115
Rosane, Olivia, 66
Rose, Maria Parazo, 37, 38
Roth, Andy Lee, 14, 129
Roundup, 80, 85, 87
Rozsa, Matthew, 55, 56
RSF. *See* Reporters Without Borders
Rubio, Marco, 41, 144
Ruffalo, Mark, 116
"runaway melting," 54
Russell, Emily, 129
Russia, 11, 62, 81, 83, 162, 163
Rustin, Bayard, 18

S
Sabino, Pascal, 53, 54
Sadowsky, Justin, 91
SAG-AFTRA. *See* Screen Actors Guild-American Federation of Television and Radio Artists
Said, Edward, 135
Salish Tribe, 38
Salon (media outlet), 55, 56
San Francisco, California, 49
San Francisco Standard (news website), 49
San Jose, California, 49–50
Santee Sioux Tribe, 38
Sauder School of Business, at University of British Columbia, 179
Saudi Arabia, 62
Scahill, Jeremy, 150, 151
Schenwar, Maya, 16, 150
Scientific American (magazine), 61
Scream (film series), 115
Screen Actors Guild-American Federation of Television and Radio Artists (SAG-AFTRA), 116
sea level rise, 54–56
secrecy, government, 164–66
Securities and Exchange Commission, US, 69
Seife, Charles, 117
Seldes, George, xv, xvi
Sequeira, Robbie, 50, 57
settler colonialism, 113, 128, 136, 147n23
SEVIS. *See* Student and Exchange Visitor Information System
Shabat, Hossam, 155
The Shame of the Cities (Steffans), xvi
Shaw, George Bernard, 5, 13
Sidley Austin (law firm), 87–88
SiliconValley.com, 34
Sinclair, Upton, xvi
Sinyangwe, Samuel, 52
60 Minutes (TV program), 78, 79
slacktivism, 179, 183
Slow Factory, 196
Smith, Anna V., 37–39
Smotrich, Bezalel, 130, 134
Snelling, Larry, 54
Snow, Jake, 42–43, 44
Snow White (film), 99, 113, 114
Snyder, Timothy, xvii
social media, xi, xii, 25, 29–31, 39–42, 47, 175–79. *See also specific platforms*

societal trust, 151–52
So Informed, 196
solidarity, 193
Solnit, Rebecca, 1, 4, 5, 13
Sonoma State University, x
Soon-Shiong, Patrick, 4
Soros, George, 140
South Carolina, 57
SpaceX, 100, 112
Spain, 134
special education, 99
Spotify, 101
Spotted Bear, Jodi Rave, 16, 150
Sprague, Lori, 33
Spyglass, 115
Starbucks Workers United, 69–70
Starr, Barbara, 83
Stateline (news outlet), 50, 57, 58
State of the Free Press 2021, 14, 17, 80
State of the Free Press 2025, 114
State of the Free Press 2026, 10, 13, 14–16
Stefanik, Elise, 15, 127
   antisemitism and, 137–40
   "biblical rights" and, 129–32, 141
   decontextualization and, 143–46
   dominant ideologies and, 135–37
   missing context for, 140–43
   NCPR and, 128–29
   UNRWA and, 132–35
Steffens, Lincoln, xvi
Stephanopoulos, George, 79
Stern, Seth, 68
Stevens-Bollen, Anson, 16
Stone, I.F. "Izzy," xi, xiv, xvi, xvii, xviii
Stonewall National Monument, 11
"stop-and-frisk," 53
@StopCopCity, 185
Stop WOKE Act, 11
Stories That Changed America (Jensen), xvi
Student and Exchange Visitor Information System (SEVIS), 117
Suda, Caitlin, 14
Sudan, 67
Sulzberger, A.G., 150

Sunkara, Bhaskar, 58, 59
Super Bowl halftime show, 101
surveillance capitalism, 6, 43
surveillance technology, hostile, 46–48
Svoboda, Mark, 34
Syria, 162

T
Tarbell, Ida, xvi
Taylor, Andrew, 58
Techdirt (blog), 30, 31
technocracy, 105–13
Tech Policy Press (media outlet), 42, 44
Telecommunications Act (1996), x
Tennessee, 57
Terms of Servitude (Zahzah), 201
Tesla, 106, 109, 112
Texas, 12, 32–33, 57
"Theses on the Philosophy of History" (Benjamin), 77
Thiel, Peter, 108, 109
Thwaites Glacier (Doomsday Glacier), 56
TikTok, 175
Time (magazine), 45
Timm, Trevor, 81, 83
Title VI, of Civil Rights Act, 68–69
Tomorrow, Tom, 16
Top Censored Stories list, 98
transparency, 165–66
tribal colleges, 36
Trojan condoms, 64–65
Trump, Donald, xxn13, 79, 81–84, 90, 116–17, 141, 150
   billionaires appointed by, 59
   corporate media and, 9
   Corporation for Public Broadcasting and, 10
   DOGE and, 38–39
   education and, 103
   First Amendment and, 7, 8
   Gulf of Mexico and, 99
   ICE and, 31
   MAGA movement, 11, 15, 127–29, 143

Musk and, 78, 97, 105, 113, 149
One Big Beautiful Bill Act of, 44, 68
on press as "enemies of the American people," xiv
second administration of, xvii, 3, 6–9, 78
tribal colleges defunded by, 37
UNRWA and, 134
water usage and, 34
X and, 6
trust lands, 36, 37, 39
"truth emergency," xiii, xiv
Truthout (media company), 31, 35, 41, 52, 141–42
Tucker (construction company), 49, 50
Tucker, Emma, xii, xiii
Tufts University, 116, 144
24-hour news cycle, 4
Twitter. *See* X
Type Investigations (news outlet), 49, 51

U

UBS Bahamas, 69
Ukraine, 11, 162
UN. *See* United Nations
"Understanding the Digital Public Square," 16
United Nations (UN), 15, 60–62, 127, 139
United Nations Convention against Cybercrime, 60
"Unite the Right" rally, in Charlottesville (2017), 145
Universal Music Group, 101
University of Arizona, 38
University of British Columbia, Sauder School of Business at, 179
University of Central Florida, 117
University of Florida, 117
University of Oxford, 55
University of Southern California, Annenberg School for Communication and Journalism at, 7
University of South Florida, 117

UNRWA, 15, 132–35
US Agency for International Development (USAID), 88, 110
USA Today (newspaper), 52, 131
US Geological Survey (USGS), 32–35
US National Health and Nutrition Examination Survey, 65
US Right to Know, 85, 88, 89
Utah, 34, 57, 58
Utah News Dispatch (news outlet), 58

V

Validated Independent News stories (VINs), 14, 27
Vance, JD, 99, 109
Vance, Usha, 109
Van Hollen, Chris, 130, 131
Vanity Fair (magazine), 115
Variety (magazine), 113, 114
Veteran Intelligence Professionals for Sanity, 162
v-Fluence, 88
Vietnam War, ix, xiii
VINs. *See* Validated Independent News stories
violence
  against journalists, 9, 13, 155
  toward Native Americans, 36
  police, 51–54
Virginia, 33, 57, 145
virtue signaling, 183
visual media, 176
Voitl, Shealeigh, 129

W

Wall Street Journal (newspaper), xii, 31, 105, 161
Walmart, 46–48
Ward, Harvey, 51
Washington Post (newspaper), 62, 66, 78, 83, 151, 161
  on American Privacy Rights Act, 45
  on DOGE, 39
  on drought, 34
  on police violence, 52

on working class, 59
Watergate scandal, ix, xiii
water scarcity, 25, 32–35
Weave News (news outlet), 15
WEF. *See* World Economic Forum
Weidenfeld, Sheila Rabb, 26
Weiner, Anna, 100
West, Kanye, 98, 99, 102
West Bank, 134, 141
White, Katherine, 179
White supremacy, 157, 159, 160
Whitewash (Gillam), 85
WHO. *See* World Health Organization
WikiLeaks, 8
Wilkins, Brett, 29, 30
Williams, Rob, 38
Witt, Lara, 16, 150
"wokeness," 10–11, 100
working class, as underrepresented, 57–59
Working Class Heroes Fund, 59
workplace harassment, 98
Workplace Readiness Week, 70
workplace rights, 69–70
workplace surveillance technology, 46–48
World Economic Forum (WEF), xii, xiv
World Happiness Index (2025), 152
World Health Organization (WHO), 129
World Press Freedom Index, 151

Zhang, Sharon, 41, 52, 141, 142
Zionism, 113–18, 145, 158
    anti-Zionism and, 137–40
    protection of, 132
ZNetwork (news outlet), 42
Zuckerberg, Mark, 98

X

X (Twitter), 4, 85, 99, 109, 114, 175, 186
    Martin on, 90
    Musk and, 6, 105

Y

Yarvin, Curtis, 108
yellow journalism, xi
Young, Neil, 85, 86
Youssef, Ramy, 116
YouTube, 102

Zamora, Alexa, 61
Zegler, Rachel, 15, 99, 114–16, 118

⌐CP⌐ THE CENSORED PRESS

The Censored Press is the publishing imprint of Project Censored and its nonprofit sponsor, the Media Freedom Foundation. Building on the Project's yearbook series, website, weekly radio show, and other educational programs, the Censored Press advances the Project's mission to promote independent investigative journalism, media literacy, and critical thinking.

To date, the Censored Press has published a number of award-winning titles, in partnership with Seven Stories Press. These books include Omar Zahzah's *Terms of Servitude: Zionism, Silicon Valley, and Digital Settler Colonialism in the Palestinian Liberation Struggle* (2025); Peter Phillips's *Titans of Capital: How Concentrated Wealth Threatens Humanity* (2024); Kevin Gosztola's *Guilty of Journalism: The Political Case Against Julian Assange* (2023); Adam Bessie and Peter Glanting's *Going Remote: A Teacher's Journey* (2023); and *The Media and Me: A Guide to Critical Media Literacy for Young People*, by Project Censored and the Media Revolution Collective (2022); and the 2022–2025 editions of Project Censored's *State of the Free Press* yearbook series.

In 2025, The Censored Press published *Beyond Fact Checking: A Teaching Guide to the Power of News Frames*, by Shealeigh Voitl, Andy Lee Roth, and Project Censored. Future Censored Press titles include Allison Butler's *The Judgment of Gender: Pop Culture Conversations that Center and Silence Women* and Cynthia Sandler's *Savvy: A Critical Media Literacy Roadmap for Educators*.

The generosity of several founding donors ensures the sustainability of The Censored Press, but support from new donors expands our capacity to produce additional titles and provide new opportunities for reporting, teaching, and thinking critically.

https://censoredpress.org/

www.ingramcontent.com/pod-product-compliance
Lightning Source LLC
Chambersburg PA
CBHW020536030426
42337CB00013B/871